Angels

Angels

Ancient Whispers of Another World

Andy Angel

CASCADE *Books* · Eugene, Oregon

ANGELS
Ancient Whispers of Another World

Cascade Books
A Division of Wipf and Stock Publishers
199 W. 8th Ave., Suite 3
Eugene, OR 97401

www.wipfandstock.com

ISBN 13: 978-1-4982-1457-5

Cataloging-in-Publication data:

Angel, Andrew R.

    Angels : ancient whispers of another world / Andy Angel.

    xiv + 198 p. ; 23 cm. Includes bibliographical references and index.

    ISBN 13: 978-1-4982-1457-5

    1. Angels—Biblical teaching. 2. Angels—Judaism—History of doctrines. Angels—History of doctrines. 4. Angels. I. Title.
      3.
BT966.2 A58 2012

Manufactured in the U.S.A.

To Marcus and Will:
You may not be angels
but thanks for your timely help.

Contents

Preface

I was waiting in the atrium of the British Library. I had never been taken out to lunch by a publisher before. He had written to ask for the names of possible authors for a book on angels. I gave him three—none of them my own. He rejected them and asked for more. I wrote back that I had given him my best names already. He asked me out to lunch. And so I stood there in the Library awaiting his arrival. Within half an hour of his arrival, and over a very pleasant lunch in what was then Leith's restaurant, I found myself agreeing to consider writing a book on angels.

He was charming and very persuasive. He thought me a reliable sort of person to write the kind of book he had in mind. There was a gap in the market. There did not seem to be anything written on angels in the second temple period as background to the stories about and allusions to angels that we find in the New Testament (NT). We needed a book that would introduce undergraduates and interested Christians to the texts, stories, and ideas of angels that we find in what scholars sometimes call the second temple literature. Although this way of referring to the literature is not perfect (after all, some of it was written after the destruction of the second temple in Jerusalem in AD 70), it designates those texts we find in the Apocrypha and Old Testament Pseudepigrapha that were written roughly between 500 BC and AD 200. They also include the Dead Sea Scrolls, the writings of the Jewish philosopher Philo (20 BC to AD 50), and the Jewish historian Josephus (AD 37–100). (Brief introductions to this literature and where to find it in English translations are given in the Appendix). The book needed to draw on this literature as many students at universities and theological colleges are unaware of it (or only vaguely aware of it) when embarking on their theological studies. Moreover most Christians rarely get access to it in the regular teaching programs of their churches. This literature casts light on the ideas of angels that are found in the NT and generally on the cultural world in which the NT was written. I found myself agreeing to consider the project.

The conversation moved on at one point to the question of modern beliefs in angels. There was a growing belief in angels both inside and outside Christian churches. There now exists a reasonably large body of literature in the field of contemporary spirituality that draws in part on this ancient literature in describing the world of the angels. Within certain streams of the Christian churches, there are increasing numbers of books on angel encounters—and these books are being written for the secular market also. Rarely do the worlds of academic research, popular theology, and contemporary spirituality on angels meet. Perhaps they ought to. I wondered if this part of the conversation ought to be part of the brief for the book—after all, I had just been offered a free hand in its design.

As the researching and writing of the book has developed, I have made this increasingly a part of the brief. The contemporary interest in angels (as those with whom I have discussed the book project have constantly reminded me) is aroused by the possibility that angelic encounters might be real. As these friends and colleagues have also reminded me on a fairly regular basis, very few people are interested in the second temple Jewish and early Christian literature for its own sake. So I have interspersed stories of modern religious experience amongst the studies of the ancient texts and what they say about angelic encounters and the world of angels. I have compared and sometimes contrasted the two sets of experience and often noted some basic similarities between these sets of experience. This method of studying the data is admittedly pretty basic but I am not quite sure what other method to use. How do you use ancient literature to demonstrate or prove the existence of something spiritual? Even amongst people who accept the texts of the Old Testament (OT) and NT as authoritative for their religious faith, there are a variety of views on the existence of angels and the reality of angel encounters. How much more difficult then to demonstrate anything at all from texts in the Pseudepigrapha, the Dead Sea scrolls, and Josephus (which nobody regards as authoritative religious texts, so far as I am aware) about the existence and nature of angels! Nonetheless for those who draw on ancient literature to explore the world of angels, I hope that what I have written is informative. So as not to leave the study too open-ended, I do draw on what we find in this literature to make a few comments about and speculate a little on angels from my own perspective in the final chapter of the book.

Any book on angels runs the risk of saying more about the perspective of the author than it does about the reality and nature (or otherwise) of the subject matter. Like any other author I come to the project with my own perspective, which has informed the writing of the work, at least at points. I am a Christian from the evangelical and charismatic traditions who enjoys critical theology but whose focus is increasingly on growth in the spiritual life. (I happen to believe that the two can work together very fruitfully but am aware that this is not the experience or desire of everybody.) I write from a Western background (white, English, with a little Welsh and Sicilian blood) and I am a man. I do talk to other people and I live with a Chilean woman (my wife), so I am very likely influenced by other perspectives too. I try to be open to learning and I hope that my perspectives contribute to the enjoyment of reading what I have written and engaging with the material rather than detracting from it.

Writing a book is not a solitary exercise, and many people have contributed to writing this one in different ways. Thanks are due to various people who have given generously of their time and have been a great encouragement to me in the writing of this book. I would like to thank Robin Parry who first invited me to look into this fascinating area and encouraged me to take on the writing of the book.

The greater part of this book was researched and written during study leave granted by the South East Institute for Theological Education and St. John's College, Nottingham. I moved from one to the other during the period of researching and writing. Rarely does a newly appointed lecturer begin his duties with study leave and so particular thanks are due to Christina Baxter, Principal of St. John's, for her generosity in granting me this privilege.

Many thanks are due to friends who have supported me during the writing of this book. Particular thanks are due to Marcus Throup and William Rogers—there are some conversations one will never forget. Dave and Jane Martin have been a great encouragement both in this project and in ministry generally. Carolyn Lucas and Rachel Wilson deserve special thanks for reading and commenting on the draft. Thanks also go to Tim and Margaret Cave and Barbara and Winston Thomas for drawing attention to books I had not come across. Thanks are also due to Miriam Barker,

Barry Evans, Graham Fairbairn, and Jill Wright whose encouragement over the book and, indeed, the last few years generally is much appreciated.

So far as I can tell to date, no one working for an academic institution finds the time to read and write without the help of good administrative staff and librarians. Such help has been provided for me during the course of writing this book and many thanks are to go to Linda LeGrys, Joanne Keane, and Becky Young. For their work now (and during a former research project) many thanks also go to Evelyn Pawley, and particularly to Christine Ainsley, who is surely a treasure amongst librarians.

Thanks again to my family for putting up with another book. Particular thanks are due to my gorgeous wife Fabiola, not least for living with my somewhat esoteric research subjects: first dragons and now angels—her patience is exemplary. Thanks also to my wonderful sons, Sebastian and Jason, who have put up with Daddy being in his study, the library, and going down to London when he really ought to be playing football. Thanks to my siblings Charis, Jon, Ryland, and Tim for their love and support—particularly Ryland for his constant nagging that I write and Jon for many timely conversations during the writing of this book. Thanks again to my parents, Gervais and Evelyn Angel who have shared the faith journey and have encouraged me in their different ways to keep my theology alive, fresh, and of some use to Christ and his church. Particular thanks are due to my father Gervais for proofreading the whole text and greatly improving its style.

Since I accepted the invitation to write something on angels, friends have begun to share their own angel experiences. I was rather hoping for some angel encounters of my own whilst writing this book but none, discernibly, have appeared. However if speaking with the tongues of angels comes a poor second to love, then maybe so do angel encounters—and I shall be grateful for the love shown me by all those I mention above and others who have helped me in many different ways.

Abbreviations of Ancient Texts

Abr.	Philo, *On Abraham*
Alleg. Interp.	Philo, *Allegorical Interpretation*
Ant.	Josephus, *Antiquities*
Apoc. Ab.	*Apocalypse of Abraham*
Apoc. Zeph.	*Apocalypse of Zephaniah*
b. B. Bat.	Babylonian Talmud, *Baba Batra*
b. Yoma	Babylonian Talmud, *Yoma*
2 Bar.	*2 Baruch*
3 Bar.	*3 Baruch*
Dial.	Justin Martyr, *Dialogue with Trypho*
Dreams	Philo, *On Dreams*
1 En.	*1 Enoch*
2 En.	*2 Enoch*
Ezek. Trag.	Ezekiel the Tragedian
Gen. Rab.	*Genesis Rabbah*
Giants	Philo, *On the Giants*
Herm. *Mand.*	Shepherd of Hermas, *Mandate*
Jos. Asen.	*Joseph and Aseneth*
Jub.	*Jubilees*
Lad. Jac.	*Ladder of Jacob*
L.A.B.	*Liber Antiquitatum Biblicarum*
LXX	Septuagint
1 Macc	1 Maccabees
2 Macc	2 Maccabees

Abbreviations of Ancient Texts

3 Macc	3 Maccabees
4 Macc	4 Maccabees
m.Ber	Mishnah, *Berakhot*
Pr. Jos.	*Prayer of Joseph*
Sacr.	Philo, *On Sacrifice*
Sir	Sirach
Sg Three	Song of the Three
T. Ab.	*Testament of Abraham*
T. Dan	*Testament of Daniel*
T. Jac.	*Testament of Jacob*
T. Job	*Testament of Job*
T. Jud.	*Testament of Judah*
T. Levi	*Testament of Levi*
T. Naph.	*Testament of Naphtali*
T. Reu.	*Testament of Reuben*
T. Sol.	*Testament of Solomon*
Tob	Tobit
War	Josephus, *Jewish War*
Wis	Wisdom of Solomon

1

Are Angels Real?

Raising the subject of angels often leads to the raising of eyebrows. Researching and writing a book on angels has involved me in many conversations about them both with friends and with complete strangers. Reactions to the subject matter have surprised me. Most have been interested and engaged. Many have been amused. Only one person has shown complete, but polite, lack of interest. The vast majority of people have been intrigued and seemed keen to talk about the subject for quite some while. However, the most interesting feature of these conversations has been how people have begun with a wry smile and only shown genuine personal interest when sufficient trust has been established within the conversation to ask the embarrassing question without fear of appearing somehow naïve or unintelligent.

The embarrassing question is, of course, *are angels real?* Belief in God is generally socially acceptable. Even people who view religious faith as something of a vice tend to acknowledge that intelligent people can (for whatever reason!) believe in God. However, this grace does not extend as far as angels. Even among religious people there can be something of an embarrassment surrounding the subject of angels.

This may partly be accounted for by culture and history. Some of the Protestant Reformers have left us a legacy of mocking belief in angels. The infamous question of how many angels can dance on the head of a pin was never asked by any medieval Roman Catholic theologian. It was most likely made up by Protestants to discredit medieval Roman Catholic theology.[1]

1. Kreeft, *Angels*, 70–71.

1

Angels

From there it has passed into the history books or at least the kind of history teaching where many of us first heard it. The threat of being on the receiving end of such mockery can render us disinclined to ask whether angels are real.

Difficulty in speaking about religious matters is nothing new to those who research religion. In the summer of 1986 the psychologist of religion David Hay conducted a survey of religious experience in the UK with Gordon Heald, director of Gallup Poll London. In answer to the question "Have you told anyone else about this experience?" an average of 40 percent of respondents replied that they had never told anyone else of their religious experiences.[2] In another project Hay recounts how he changed research method from survey to interview. Whereas surveys in the UK and USA suggested that 30 percent of people have had a religious experience, in research from interviews this figure rose to 60 percent. Interviews afforded the time, space, and sense of trust necessary for people to share their (often highly personal) religious experiences.[3] Hay records the reasons people gave for not disclosing their religious experiences: fear of ridicule and fear of being thought foolish or insane.[4] Many people are simply too embarrassed to talk about their religious experience. If talking about religious experiences is difficult, how much more so openly conversing about the reality of angels?

I suspect that there is another reason that many people are nervous of asking the question. Interest in angels has grown in the last few decades. Angels have taken the lead roles in some films and television programs. Increasing numbers of books are being written about angels. There are many "spiritual advisors" who offer to help people to get in touch with "their angel." Angels are in the public domain. This makes for increased interest in them and goes some way to making them an acceptable topic of conversation or artwork. However, it does not make belief in them either easy or comfortable. If I may put it this strongly, there is a certain snobbery around actual belief in angels. There seems to be a cultural assumption that only certain sorts of people believe in angels—those branded religious nuts and flaky new-agers—and we are not those sorts of people, so we do not believe. This sort of attitude seems as prevalent in religious circles as outside

2. Hay, *Exploring*, 163.
3. Ibid., 123–24; Hay, *Religious Experience*, 57–59.
4. Hay, *Exploring*, 163–64; Hay, *Religious Experience*, 58.

2

of them.[5] Hence the lowering of tone of voice I so often encountered as my conversation partners turned to the topic of the reality of angels.

ARGUMENTS FOR ANGELS

So, are angels real? Are those branded religious nuts and flaky new-agers deserving of the general disapproval they receive for their credulity? Or do they see more clearly what those who bow the knee to social acceptability will never enjoy? Currently, the balance might be beginning to tip towards favoring those who assume that angels exist. Probably the last time that angels were generally assumed to exist was the Middle Ages but one of the surprises awaiting those who start the study of angelology is that angels are beginning to make tentative inroads into serious philosophical enquiry once again.[6]

Those who are enquiring into angels are interested in establishing the existence of angels and describing their nature and functions. However, demonstrating that angels exist is no easy task. People tend to assume that the existence of something must be proven if they are to believe in it, and proof of angels that satisfies the skepticism of the average punter is hard to find.

For many the only acceptable proof is personal experience or the experience of others whose testimony they trust. If we can see, hear, smell, touch, or taste something, then we have evidence of its existence. We can sense it. Our senses enable us to observe and measure it, and this enables us to describe it. Once we have described it we assume we have knowledge of it. The physical sciences work a little like this and there is a great advantage to this kind of knowledge as it is public knowledge.[7] Most people are able to

5. Heathcote-James, *After-Death*, 26–30, 178.

6. For a review of the development of beliefs about angels down the ages, see Adler, *Angels and Us*, 33–95; and the superbly readable review in Macy, *Shadow*, 26–47. For philosophical defences of angels, see Adler, *Angels and Us*; Kreeft, *Angels*; Williams, *Case for Angels*.

7. I am aware that this is simplifying matters and that philosophers of science might find the assumption of basic empiricism here anything from naïve to insulting. However, the fact remains that many people do work with a practical empiricism in everyday life and empirical evidence is fundamental to the physical sciences. For key texts in the twentieth-century debates about the way the physical sciences function, see Ayer, *Language, Truth and Logic*; Popper, *Scientific Discovery*; Kuhn, *Scientific Revolutions*. For an older but very readable introduction to the subject, see Barbour, *Issues*, 137–74.

share it because they can use their senses in the same way to establish the same set of facts about the same object. The shared nature of the knowledge makes the knowledge more secure—there is safety in numbers.

However, this way of arriving at knowledge is not practical for some forms of knowledge. The classic example would be that of history. Leaving aside for the moment the idea of time travel, we have no firsthand access to past events. To obtain any knowledge of historical events we rely entirely on what people from the past have told us—most often, although not always, in written documents. Although anyone can gain access to these documents in order to establish the truth about what they say concerning past events, no one can gain firsthand access to the events themselves. Therefore we have to trust the testimony of the documents we have and what they say about the past. If we have good reason not to trust them then this avenue to the past becomes closed to us. The fewer the documents we deem trustworthy, the smaller our database for understanding the past. To gain any knowledge of past events we have to trust the testimony of at least some of the documents we possess. Trustworthy testimony is foundational to establishing knowledge in some areas.

In fact, trustworthy testimony is far more fundamental to the gaining and sharing of knowledge than we tend to recognize. It lies right at the heart of our educational system. Basically we cannot afford to do otherwise. We cannot send all school and university students studying geography to Brazil in order to check for themselves that what the textbooks say about the favelas (shanty towns) is true. We are unable to take all students studying the Old Testament or the ancient Near East on archaeological tours of Turkey, Iraq, Israel, and Egypt. We cannot provide all physics students with a particle accelerator as we do not have the money. Although they are introduced to the theory of using and assessing data, students have to take on trust the evidence that is provided by teachers and textbooks for the greater part of their education. This seems reasonable given the advantages of receiving an education. We trust our teachers to tell the truth and to provide access to the evidence necessary to gain understanding of any particular topic. So the truth is that most of our knowledge comes from trustworthy testimony rather than firsthand experience.

On the whole the average person generally accepts that there are certain things that can be known about the physical universe which experts in the physical sciences teach us. Moreover, said person has knowledge of other aspects of the material universe on the basis of their experience, which experience is shared with others and so considered to provide reliable knowledge. However, there remain other sorts of things about which people claim to have knowledge. In his *An Essay Concerning Human Understanding* John Locke describes them thus: "There remains that other sort [of thing], concerning which men entertain opinions with varieties of assent, though *the things be such, that falling not under the reach of our senses, they are not capable of testimony.* Such are (1) The existence, nature, and operations of finite immaterial beings without us; as spirits, angels, devils, etc."[8] Locke claims that nobody can sense angels with any of the five senses. If this is true then nobody is capable of giving or receiving reliable testimony about angels and it is here, with this argument for the unattainability of reliable knowledge of angels that the arguments for the reality of angels begin.

Arguments from Experience

One argument challenges the assumption that there is no trustworthy testimony of angels. There are many books of angel stories on the market at the moment that offer testimonies of experiences of angels. Some simply offer such testimonies with a few comments of spiritual encouragement.[9] Others offer their testimonies within a doctrinal framework that enables the reader to understand how these stories fit into the lived experience of the religious faith or spirituality of the author.[10] All these books relate a substantial number of stories about angelic activity—particularly of deliverance from danger, healing, or comfort in a time of great need—in order to challenge the reader to accept the reality of angels or encourage the reader with the reality of a God who sends angels to help in crises.

The argument does not only take this form. Perhaps the more powerful form of the argument is that of personal testimony. In the course of writing this book people have shared some of their own angel encounters with me. One such took place in Carroty Wood, Kent (UK) in the early 1970s. The man who reports the encounter was helping to lead a youth camp. At

8. Locke, *Essay*, Book IV, chapter XVI, section 12, 324.

9. E.g., Anderson, *Where Angels Walk*.

10. Classically, Graham, *Angels*. For more recent examples, Hickey, *Angels All Around*; Law, *Truth about Angels*.

the time he was suffering from myalgic encephalomyelitis (chronic fatigue syndrome) and had agreed to help out, against the advice of his wife (a qualified nurse). He was up early and, while drinking his morning tea outside, felt prompted to pray over the camp. While praying he heard a voice telling him to walk and pray around the perimeter of the camp. This he did, and as he did so he was aware of the presence of two huge beings—one either side of him. With one hand they were holding him up as he walked and in the other they held flaming swords. As he walked he felt a deep spiritual awakening and physical empowering inside himself. Other camp leaders were struck not only that he was walking but that his energy remained throughout the time of the camp—only leaving him as he left it. The story is remarkable and will be easy for the cautious or skeptical reader to dismiss as they (or perhaps you) are only encountering it on paper—which gives them (or you) the advantage of distance. The further away we are from strange events the easier they are to disbelieve. However, I have no such advantage. I know the man who recounted this experience. I know him not only to be perfectly sane but also to be a very down to earth sort of man. The fact that I know the witness tells the truth makes me listen. When the testimony comes from someone we trust it is a good deal more persuasive.

Nevertheless, personal testimony has its limits. Only those who know the witness have access to the relationship of trust that makes the witness credible. Therefore the majority of people who do not have this relationship of trust with the witness are less likely to accept their reliability or the truth of their testimony. When the trusted testimony of a friend becomes the extraordinary account of an unknown person, then many people find themselves unable to accept the account without further evidence.

Intrigued by stories of angels, Emma Heathcote-James set out to examine accounts of angel experiences using social-scientific methods in order to assess further the nature and reliability of such accounts. Rather than dismiss angel encounters or accept reports of them uncritically, she hoped that the more rigorous examination of these reports would provide a social-scientific assessment of them that was sociologically and psychologically informed and free from religious partisanship.[11]

Her study reveals that people encountered angels in different ways. Sometimes the angel appeared as a stereotypical angelic figure dressed in

11. Heathcote-James, *Seeing Angels.*

white (31.1 percent of respondents) and others reported angels appearing as human beings (16.9 percent). Fewer but still significant numbers of respondents report the angel manifesting itself in the form of a scent (9.7 percent), of light (12.6 percent), or as sound (4.9 percent). Some encountered the angel through some sort of physical sensation (9.4 percent) or internal sensation (4.9 percent). The remainder experienced the angelic presence in some other manner (10.5 percent).[12]

Heathcote-James catalogued a variety of angel experiences. Some people described their encounter in terms of having been touched by an angel. This touch came in various forms. Some experienced the brief physical touch, or what was sometimes described as the "smile," of an angel that gave strength in the moment of an emotional crisis. Others experienced being enveloped in light or in the wings of an angel that provided protection from harm. Others report having been confronted by a force that physically prevented them from danger or certain death.[13]

There are many reports of angels appearing to avert trouble or rescue both individuals and groups of people from danger.[14] A particular group of rescue experiences shared the pattern of encountering someone who appeared to come from nowhere at a time of crisis in which instant action was necessary, but was unavailable through ordinary means or by the best efforts of those in trouble, and this someone solved the problem before disappearing as suddenly and inexplicably as they appeared.[15]

Other people saw nobody or were only dimly aware of a physical presence or a light but they heard words spoken, which words were comforting to them in their time of crisis.[16] Many people experienced a sudden or inexplicable scent of flowers, which appeared, more often than not, at the time of the death of a loved one or on the anniversary of their death. Sometimes the scent lasted an extraordinarily long time, and nowhere were flowers present.[17]

People tended to report encountering angels in time of crisis. Angels appeared when there was need of deliverance from pain or medical difficulty.

12. Ibid., 31–44.
13. Ibid., 45–60.
14. Ibid., 61–78.
15. Ibid., 79–91.
16. Ibid., 113–25.
17. Ibid., 127–40.

Angels

They were present at birth (particularly difficult births) and at the end of life. Angels appeared both to patients and the dying, and to their friends and relatives.[18] Some people encountered angels whilst asleep or nearly asleep.[19] Others reported encounters of angels that were quite unexpected.[20]

Heathcote-James examines alternative explanations of these experiences in order to assess which make better sense of them. So, for example, altered states of consciousness resulting from changes in brain activity might account, or partially account, for visions of angels while the subject is asleep or almost asleep.[21] However, evidence from three blind people who reported having seen angels seemed difficult to explain away and she suggests that this throws into disarray notions that angel encounters are culturally determined. How can someone blind from birth describe the appearance of an angel unless they have had some kind of experience? Heathcote-James acknowledges that someone might learn from a sighted person how to describe the physical features of angels. However, the vividness of the account of Stephanie (who was blind from birth) suggests to Heathcote-James that her account stems from real experience rather than being concocted from the descriptions of others.[22] Similarly she suggests that grief cannot account for all angel encounters around the time of death because many of these encounters took place before death (i.e., before the starting point of grief).[23] The counterargument might be put that grief often begins before death where death is expected and this might account for angels appearing before death. Heathcote-James suggests that sometimes angels appeared shortly before unexpected deaths.[24] However, her published catalogue of extraordinary appearances before unexpected deaths contains no accounts in which people claim to have experienced angels shortly before unexpected deaths.[25] This fact counts against her argument.

18. Ibid., 141–66.

19. Ibid., 193–215.

20. Ibid., 216–28.

21. Ibid., 190–93, 215.

22. Ibid., 94–112.

23. Ibid., 169–71.

24. Private communication.

25. In a private communication Heathcote-James suggests that she catalogues such experiences of angels in her *After-Death Communication*. However, the evidence (Heathcote-James, *After-Death*, 38–42) she presents does not include one instance

Angel encounters were reported as having happened throughout life with no particular age group being more susceptible to such encounters. If there was a slight preponderance among any age group it was those in midlife (thirty-one to fifty years of age). Although more women responded to the survey than men, there were no types of angel encounter to which one gender was significantly more susceptible than the other. Angel experiences were reported by those of all faiths and none. Almost as many atheists (4 percent) and lapsed Christians (4.3 percent) reported angelic encounters as new-agers (4.6 percent). The only group to have significantly more angel encounters were Protestant Christians (39.1 percent)—the largest group after this was "unknown religion" (28.9 percent) and then Roman Catholic (6.3 percent). The places where angel encounters happened were fairly evenly spread—almost as many took place in hospital or on some form of transport as in places of worship—except for the preponderance of angel encounters that took place in the home, particularly the bedroom. The study concludes that no sociological, physiological, or psychological explanations of angel encounters can account for all the evidence—although its author declines to comment on the reality of angels.[26]

Heathcote-James does not set out to prove the existence of angels nor does she wish to comment on this. Her study does not prove the existence of angels. It simply demonstrates that many people have had what they report to be experiences of angels. However, its results may help those who might wish to argue that belief in angels is not irrational. Heathcote-James suggests that no sociological, physiological, or psychological explanation of angel encounters explains all the evidence. Belief in angels can account for the facts but requires trust in the testimony of extraordinary experiences. This may be asking too much of those who have no experience of angels nor access to accounts of angelic encounters by those whom they trust, but Heathcote-James suggests that there are no other viable explanations of all the data. However, this study does help remove an obstacle to belief in angels from those who believe they have trustworthy testimony of angels.

---

of an angelic appearance. The reported experiences can only be accepted as angelic if one makes the assumption that angels, ghosts, spirits, energies and apparitions are all the same phenomenon framed differently by different people, as Heathcote-James does (ibid., 14–15). Given the fact that many religious traditions have for centuries distinguished carefully between such entities, this is quite an assumption to make.

26. Heathcote-James, *Seeing Angels*, 229–57.

Angels

If alternative explanations are questionable, then they may not discredit the testimony of angel encounters that someone is inclined to accept on the basis of the reliability of the witness.

Arguments from Reason

Another line of argument for the plausibility of the existence of angels attempts to prove that our experience of reality does not necessarily support the view that angels do not exist but might support the view that angels do exist. This line of argument attempts to undercut the idea that our experience of reality suggests that the existence of angels is impossible.

The argument that our experience suggests that the existence of angels is impossible begins with the definition of angels. Angels are incorporeal; they have no bodies. They are spirits—they possess intelligence, emotion, and will, or at least this is how they are depicted. However, our experience tells us that there are no such things as incorporeal minds. We only ever experience minds as being within bodies. Whether we attribute minds or intelligence to animals or only to humans, our experience teaches that minds only exist within the body of a living physical being. From our experience we conclude that incorporeal minds do not exist. If incorporeal minds or spirits do not exist, then angels do not exist.

Certain philosophers of religion have put forward counterarguments.[27] At the outset it is worth noting that the argument above does not prove that angels do not exist. It merely demonstrates that we have no experience in everyday life of bodiless beings with minds, like angels, and so find belief in them difficult—but this is not the same thing as disproving the existence of angels. Somebody else may have such experience and so argue the opposite case, as people who claim angelic encounters do. Moreover, the fact that we do not experience something does not mean that it does not exist. Atoms and subatomic particles existed before human beings discovered their existence—and it may be of interest to note that John Locke would have put them in much the same category as angels. Note the above quotation from *An Essay Concerning Human Understanding* continues: "*the*

---

27. What follows draws largely on these works: Adler, *Angels and Us*, 104–13; Kreeft, *Angels*, 25–43; Williams, *Case for Angels*, 16–73. I simply summarise some of their points. Their arguments are worth reading by anyone interested in this question of the existence of angels.

things be such, that falling not under the reach of our senses, they are not capable of testimony. Such are (1) The existence, nature, and operations of finite immaterial beings without us; as spirits, angels, devils, etc." It continues, "Or the existence of material beings which, either for their smallness in themselves or remoteness from us, our senses cannot take notice of."[28] Atoms and subatomic particles were certainly too small for observation and so would have been deemed incapable of testimony but they existed nonetheless.

Our lack of knowledge of a thing does not demonstrate that it does not exist. Disproof of angelic existence must be made on stronger grounds than this. A bodiless mind, or incorporeal spirit, may not be a regular part of everyday experience but it is conceivable. The existence of angels may not be written off just because they are not a common part of human experience, but the question whether there is any good reason to believe that incorporeal spirits or bodiless minds might exist needs asking.

Minds are commonly identified with brains and brains are physical objects. Common sense might dictate, therefore, that minds are not separate from brains. Indeed minds seem dependent on them. If this is so, is there any reason to believe that a mind could ever be independent of a body? For if a mind cannot be independent of a body, there is no reason to believe that bodiless minds or incorporeal spirits exist.[29]

While common sense (and medical knowledge) dictates that minds are not separate from bodies, it surely equally suggests that minds are not identical with brains either. What goes on in the brain is *electrical activity*. What goes on in the mind is *thought*. As yet it is difficult to reduce thoughts, concepts, emotions, and ideas to varieties of electrical impulse. Even where we can trace the way in which certain electrical impulses in

28. Locke, *Essay*, Book IV, chapter XVI, section 12, 324.

29. In what follows, I avoid the question of Cartesian dualism—which asserts that the only undoubtable truth is that *I am thinking* ("I think, therefore I am") and thus all knowledge starts with the reality of the mind (and all physical things may be doubted as false perceptions—e.g., the laptop on which I am typing this nonsense may not really exist but be a figment of my imagination). For those who wish to follow it up, two classic works on either side of the debate are, Descartes, *Discourse*; Ryle, *Concept of Mind*. For my part, I am happy that Descartes used language to express his doubts, which language he acquired from others (as we all do), which proves a reality beyond his mind (the others from whom he acquired language), without which reality he would never have been able to express his doubts. However, those persuaded otherwise will have little, or at least less, difficulty in accepting that minds may exist independently of bodies.

the brain are related to certain forms of mental activity, the nature of the electrical impulse is not the same as the thought, concept, or picture inside the mind. Surely there must be some degree of independence between the mind and the brain.[30]

If there is some degree of independence between the mind and the brain, how far can it go? Their interdependence seems clear enough to common sense. The whole argument starts with the observation that, in everyday reality, minds do not exist (or do not generally appear to us to exist) outside of bodies. There is one case, however, in which some claim they do. This is the case of the out of body experience (OBE). Consider the following testimony:[31]

> About six months after the death [of his father], while staying over one night with a group of lads at his friend's house, Tom experienced an OBE. He felt himself lift out of his body until he was looking down on himself. Panicking, he shouted down to his friends, who were all asleep on the floor, but they were all asleep and could not hear him. The main thing that concerned Tom was what would happen in the morning, when the others woke up to find him dead. His body would be carried away and burnt, leaving him all alone hovering above it! He continues: After the initial panic, I felt a presence by my side guiding me along a long tunnel until I came to a fork and had to decide which way to go—I looked to my right and saw a huge and very beautiful staircase ascending upwards. On it, stood at every six or so steps, were pairs of angels, dressed in long white gowns, with wings clasped behind them. I really believe had I have gone up that staircase I would have been in "heaven," with my dad, but I felt there was so much more to do on earth, that I wasn't ready to go there yet. Suddenly, with a jerk I landed back inside my body. I awoke and burst into tears, waking my other friends up, [and explained] hysterically what I'd just gone though.

Tom recounts an experience of being dead and his mind or soul leaving his body. Regardless of whether he was clinically dead or not, Tom experiences his mind or spirit looking down on his body in the room where the sleepover was taking place. He describes an experience of his mind being outside of his body. From this one might conclude that his mind and his body were separate at this time—he expresses concern that his mind or spirit would be left hovering after his body had been cremated.

---

30. See further Williams, *Case for Angels*, 22–39.

31. Heathcote-James, *Seeing Angels*, 176.

This point suggests that he did not experience his mind as dependent upon his body at this time in order to function. He is clearly seeing in his mind (he looks at his friends asleep on the floor). He experiences emotion (he panics about the situation, is concerned for his friends' reactions and worries about his mind being left outside his body after the funeral). He uses his volition, or will, in making the decision not to go up the staircase. He is thinking throughout the experience. There are other similar testimonies of out of body experiences.[32]

Now, if their testimony is to be believed, there may be evidence that the mind can exist without the body. If the mind can exist without the body, then there is evidence of bodiless minds. However, they only provide evidence for human minds, which were once part of physical human beings, becoming temporarily separate from the bodies of these human beings. This is not the same as providing evidence of the existence of finite, created, spiritual beings that are permanently spiritual. Moreover there are psychological explanations for OBEs, which suggest that the mind never leaves the body.[33] If testimony concerning OBEs is to be believed and if alternative explanations are not seen as sufficiently convincing, then OBEs may provide limited evidence. For some this suggests that belief in the existence of angels is not irrational.[34]

A possibly more promising line of argument (responding to the assumption that belief in God is acceptable but belief in angels is somewhat bizarre) begins with the observation that God is incorporeal. God is spirit or mind and to this extent has a similar nature to the angels. The argument proceeds with the observation that there are many arguments for the existence of God.[35]

One such argument is called the argument from design. This argument is often associated with the name of William Paley (1743–1805), who introduces it like this:[36]

---

32. For further examples, see Blackmore, *Beyond the Body*, 2–5, 9, 20–21.

33. Ibid., 240–49. For another view that accepts the validity of OBEs as describing minds genuinely leaving bodies, see Heathcote-James, *After-Death*, 157–65.

34. Kreeft, *Angels*, 50.

35. For introductions to and summaries of arguments for the existence of God, see Ganssle, *A Reasonable God*, 57–116; Meister, *Philosophy of Religion*, 64–125.

36. Paley, *Natural Theology*, 1–3.

> In crossing a heath, suppose I pitched my foot against a stone, and were asked how the stone came to be there: I might possibly answer, that for any thing I know to the contrary, it had lain there forever: nor would it perhaps be very easy to show the absurdity of this answer. But suppose I had found a watch upon the ground, and it should be inquired how the watch happened to be in that place; I should hardly think of the answer which I had before given, that for any thing I knew, the watch might have always been there. Yet why should not this answer serve for the watch, as well as for the stone? Why is it not as admissible in the second case as in the first? For this reason, and for no other, viz., that when we come to inspect the watch, we perceive (what we could not discover in the stone) that its several parts are framed and put together for a purpose . . . This mechanism being observed . . . the inference, we think, is inevitable, that the watch must have had a maker; that there must have existed, at some time, and at some place of other, an artificer or artificers, who formed it for the purpose which we find it actually to answer; who comprehended its construction, and designed its use.

Although the argument has been considerably refined over the years, and modified to immunize it from some of the objections made to Paley's version, it remains essentially the same: that the way in which the universe fits together so coherently suggests that it cannot have come about by chance but rather that it must be the product of a great Mind that designed it to be like that. The argument carries some force even if it falls short of a knock down proof of God's existence. It is the argument that, in one of its more recent forms, changed the mind of one of the most notorious philosophical atheists of the twentieth century. Antony Flew found it sufficiently compelling to have decided to believe that God exists.[37] And set alongside other arguments for the existence of God a cumulative case can be made for the rationality and probability of God's existence.

If this or any other argument for the existence of God holds water, then God exists. If God exists, then bodiless Mind does exist. The existence of incorporeal spirit is no longer impossible. Belief in the existence of an incorporeal spirit is no longer irrational. Thus belief in angels is no longer irrational. Indeed given that we are much more like angels than God (we were created at a point in time, we are finite creatures, having imperfect knowledge, not being omnipresent, not being omnipotent and

37. Flew, *There is no a God*. His former critique of Christian theology appeared in a book (Flew and MacIntyre, *New Essays*) that provided a significant challenge to reasonable belief in God at the time.

so on), belief in the existence of angels ought to be easier for us than belief in the existence of God precisely because the nature of angels is closer to our experience.[38]

So returning to the embarrassing question, are angels real? Possibly. Belief in angels is certainly not as silly as it might appear to some people. There may be grounds for accepting the existence of bodiless minds from human experience—namely out of body experiences. The notion of an incorporeal spirit is not so far removed from our own reality as we might be tempted to think. In a way belief in angels is no more difficult than belief in God—after all, both beliefs require that one accepts the reality of incorporeal spirits. Besides, there are many testimonies of angel encounters. Admittedly people are going to be more convinced by reports of angel experiences from people they deem trustworthy. Not all people have access to reports of angel encounters from witnesses they deem to be trustworthy. So, how a person answers the question "are angels real?" depends who you are asking. The relationship between the witness and the enquirer is crucial to our knowledge of angels (although not crucial to their reality—they may well exist regardless of how many of us think we have any knowledge of them).

THE NATURE AND FUNCTIONS OF ANGELS

Once the work of establishing the possibility, plausibility, or likelihood of the existence of angels is over, the question becomes where do we find out about them? How can we tell what they are like—what their nature is? How can we know what they do—what their functions or operations are? Interestingly, at this point, philosophers, theologians, and others all turn to the same sources—namely ancient religious texts, which are authoritative within religious communities, and the commentaries that religious thinkers have made upon them down the ages.[39]

In the following pages, we will study some of these texts. Examining them will enable us to understand what authors in the formative years of Christianity and rabbinic Judaism thought about angels. This investigation

---

38. Williams, *Case for Angels*, 39–55.

39. For example, Adler (*Angels and Us*, 104–13) turns to Aquinas; Graham (*Angels*, 27–35) turns to the Bible; Burnham (*A Book of Angels*) turns to ancient Jewish and Christian (amongst other religious) traditions, including the Bible.

will build up a picture of how various ancients understood angels, their nature, and their role in the universe. We'll see that there were differences of opinion on angels. However, this book will not necessarily prove anything about the existence, nature, or functions of angels except for those for whom the texts we are studying are authoritative and who therefore trust that what these texts say about angels is true. Even for these people, they will only accept the testimony of a limited number of the texts studied, because very few people (if any at all) believe the Dead Sea scrolls or the writings of Josephus and Philo to be religiously authoritative or canonical. Nonetheless, the non-canonical texts of the second temple period cast light on the cultural background to and the meanings of the canonical texts. So the study will clarify what these ancient religious texts say about angels. In clarifying their meaning, the study will provide a basic introduction to the ideas of angels that were floating around ancient Judaism and early Christianity. This ought to be of some use to those who use biblical texts, or at least some of them, in order to describe what angels are like and what angels actually do. For those who do not accept these texts as canonical, the exploration will at least enable growth in knowledge of how angels have been conceived and understood in the religious traditions from which we have inherited the notion that there are angels who come and work amongst us.

2

Must Be Talking to An Angel

When disaster strikes we can find ourselves wondering why. The initial shock overwhelms us for a while but as we surface from it we begin to think through and assess all that has happened to us. At such times we can find that life does not seem to make sense. We can see no purpose in the events that have befallen us and so we search for a purpose or at least some consolation that something good might result from all the suffering. At times like these, holy people turn to prayer. But their prayer is not simply intercession. Often this prayer becomes an agonizing conversation with God as to the whys and wherefores of the crisis that has come upon them.

Such prayers are nothing new. We find these prayers in ancient literature. Consider the following prayer from the apocalyptic text 4 Ezra (an apocalyptic text is one in which the secrets of heaven are revealed to a human being).[1] It dates to the period following the destruction of Jerusalem and its temple by the Roman army in response to the Jewish revolt of AD 66–70. So 4 Ezra was written between AD 70–100 by an otherwise unknown Jewish visionary prophet, although the story of the work is set in

---

1. Although the nature of apocalyptic is debated, John J. Collins offers the following working definition, which is widely accepted: "'Apocalyptic' is a genre of revelatory literature with a narrative framework, in which a revelation is mediated by an other-worldly being to a human recipient, disclosing a transcendent reality which is both temporal, insofar as it envisages eschatological salvation, and spatial, insofar as it involves another, supernatural world" (*Apocalypse*, 9). Works providing an introduction to apocalyptic literature include Collins, *Apocalyptic Imagination*; Hanson, *Dawn of Apocalyptic*; Rowland, *Open Heaven*. 4 Ezra (sometimes called 2 Esdras 3–14) may be found in the Apocrypha or Deuterocanonical books of the Bible.

the aftermath of the destruction of Jerusalem by Babylon (the book draws a parallel between the destruction of Jerusalem by Babylon in 586 BC and the destruction of Jerusalem by Rome in AD 70).[2] Ezra begins in prayer (4 Ezra 3:1–4):

> In the thirtieth year after the destruction of the city, I was in Babylon—I, Salathiel, who am also called Ezra. I was troubled as I lay on my bed, and my thoughts welled up in my heart, 2 because I saw the desolation of Zion and the wealth of those who lived in Babylon. 3 My spirit was greatly agitated, and I began to speak anxious words to the Most High, and said, 4 "O sovereign Lord, did you not speak at the beginning when you planted the earth—and that without help—"

Ezra is troubled by the destruction of Jerusalem. He is particularly troubled by the fact that the enemies of Judah who destroyed Jerusalem are living in wealth and luxury. This is surely unfair as God promises to reward the righteous and punish sinners. So Ezra explores this problem in prayer, pointing out to God how Israel (Judah) has been much more righteous in following God's commands than gentile nations, even if the occasional individual gentile has proven remarkably holy. He ends (4 Ezra 3:30–36):

> 30 because I have seen how you endure those who sin, and have spared those who act wickedly, and have destroyed your people, and protected your enemies, 31 and have not shown to anyone how your way may be comprehended. Are the deeds of Babylon better than those of Zion? 32 Or has another nation known you besides Israel? Or what tribes have so believed the covenants as these tribes of Jacob? 33 Yet their reward has not appeared and their labor has borne no fruit. For I have travelled widely among the nations and have seen that they abound in wealth, though they are unmindful of your commandments. 34 Now therefore weigh in a balance our iniquities and those of the inhabitants of the world; and it will be found which way the turn of the scale will incline. 35 When have the inhabitants of the earth not sinned in your sight? Or what nation has kept your commandments so well? 36 You may indeed find individuals who have kept your commandments, but nations you will not find.

Ezra wonders whether God has been unjust. The unrighteous gentile nations surely deserve punishment for sin but have been rewarded with prosperity. The righteous people of Israel (despite their falling into sin from time to

---

2. For discussion of the date, authorship, and setting of 4 Ezra, see Stone *Fourth Ezra*, 9–10, 36–42.

time) have received the punishments that surely the gentiles deserve. Ezra has seen the reality of all this and believes that there is something wrong. So he brings this to God in prayer.

At this point an angel appears. The angel Uriel informs and tries to persuade Ezra that he simply does not have the ability to understand the mystery of the ways of God (4 Ezra 4:1–11). Ezra begs him to reveal why God is allowing such disasters to befall his people and Uriel begins to reveal what will happen (4 Ezra 4:22–32). On hearing that there is an end to the suffering, Ezra becomes impatient for salvation to come and Uriel calms his impatience and continues the revelation (4 Ezra 4:26–46). The vision of things to come (4 Ezra 4:52—5:13) is so shocking that Ezra wakes from his vision shaking all over and promptly faints (4 Ezra 5:14). The angel Uriel then comforts Ezra. Uriel talks with him, physically holds him, helps him to get his strength back, and gets him back on his feet (4 Ezra 5:15). Up until the point of his waking up, Ezra seems to have experienced the visitation of the angel Uriel in a vision. The vision begins with Ezra troubled while lying on his bed (4 Ezra 3:1). After this point, the angel Uriel appears physically present with Ezra.

After praying and fasting for seven days as Uriel had instructed, with embittered thoughts and questions arising within him again, Ezra begins to pray once more (4 Ezra 5:21). As he prays, God sends the angel Uriel back to him (4 Ezra 5:31). This time Uriel challenges him. Ezra has challenged God that if he really hates his people to do his own dirty work rather than sending the gentiles to do it (4 Ezra 5:28–30). Uriel acknowledges his anguish but challenges Ezra asking him who he loves more, God or Israel. Ezra admits that his grief was speaking rather than his right mind but presses Uriel for greater understanding of why God should allow such suffering. Uriel states bluntly that Ezra can never understand the mind of God (4 Ezra 5:31–35). However, Ezra presses him for greater understanding and another revelation is given (4 Ezra 5:56—6:28). So the conversation continues. Ezra prepares for further revelations, praying and fasting as instructed by Uriel (4 Ezra 6:35). Then he becomes deeply troubled again and resumes his questioning of God (4 Ezra 6:38–59). God sends Uriel, who takes Ezra through further conversations and visions (4 Ezra 7:1—9:22).

Uriel then gives Ezra some new instructions. This time he is to spend seven days in a field, eating only the flowers of the field and praying (4 Ezra 9:23–28). Having done so, Ezra is once again troubled and questions God

Angels

(9:29–37). This time he receives a vision which terrifies him (4 Ezra 9:38–10:27a). Ezra screams out for Uriel who promptly appears before Ezra, who is now lying on the ground like a dead man from fear. Uriel takes his hand, strengthens him, and gets him back on his feet (4 Ezra 10:27b–30). When all is settled, Uriel asks Ezra what happened. Ezra reproaches him for abandoning him during the vision (4 Ezra 10:29–33). Uriel explains how that vision provides the hope that Ezra has been longing for—as well as explaining that leaving Ezra in the field was for the purpose of receiving this vision (4 Ezra 10:34–54).

Then Uriel invites Ezra to enter the building he saw in his vision (the newly built Zion) and instructs him to stay in the field awaiting further dream visions (4 Ezra 10:55–59). Ezra receives further revelations of the salvation of Israel (4 Ezra 12–13). Although not mentioned by name, Uriel continues to interpret these visions (4 Ezra 12:10–39; 13:20b–50).[3] Uriel then departs the scene as the final promises and instructions are given to Ezra by God.[4]

Within the book of 4 Ezra we encounter a righteous man who is deeply troubled at the suffering of God's people, Israel. Ezra prays about what is troubling him. God answers his prayers by sending an angel and granting Ezra a series of visions. The angel talks with Ezra, enabling him to acknowledge the limitations of his understanding. Uriel acts as an interpreter of the visions. When Ezra finds himself overwhelmed or terrified, Uriel takes on a pastoral role enabling Ezra to get back both to his senses and on his feet so that he can continue receiving revelations from God. This role of the interpreting angel (sometimes referred to by the Latin phrase *angelus interpres*) is a stock part of apocalyptic texts.[5]

PASTORAL ANGELS?

When Uriel takes on something of a pastoral role towards Ezra he does something which angels are often found to do. Jonathan Macy has recently argued that the pastoral ministry of angels forms the key to understanding

3. Ibid., 365–66, 394.
4. Ibid., 410–13.
5. For background to the interpreting angel figure, see Schöpflin, "God's Interpreter," 189–203. The pastoral role of angels has been explored in a recent monograph by Jonathan Macy in *Shadow*.

angels. Understanding angels comes more easily through examining the way that angels meet people in their time of need than through studying ancient texts on the nature, roles, and functions of angels.[6] He proposes that we concentrate on what angels *do* rather than speculating about what they *are*.

He uses a model of pastoral ministry, which he draws from Clebsch and Jaekle's *Pastoral Care in Historical Perspective*.[7] Macy outlines four areas of pastoral ministry: healing, or promoting physical and spiritual wholeness; sustaining, or building a faith that can grow and last; guiding, or recognizing and making (moral) decisions; and reconciliation with both God and neighbor.[8] He studies appearances of angels of the Bible to demonstrate his thesis that angels are involved in the ministries of healing, sustaining, guiding, and reconciliation.[9]

His work is fascinating and he seems to establish that angels are involved in what we might class as pastoral ministry today. Even if we prefer to begin with a slightly different model of pastoral ministry from that of Clebsch and Jaekle, the angelic activities that he examines fall largely within the realm of pastoralia. However, this approach does not fully account for the ministry of angels. Two points in particular need making.

There are times when angels do not act according to good pastoral practice. The most striking example of this is that Mary gets no aftercare for the news that Gabriel delivers (Luke 1:38). Any competent pastor would be aware of possible fallout from such news and would make provision for dealing with the fallout. Gabriel has not come to tend Mary pastorally. He makes his announcement and then departs suggesting that Gabriel here acts as messenger rather than pastor.

There are also angelic activities that cannot be readily explained as pastoral. The angelic beings that surround the throne (Rev 4–5) praise God. Nothing they do can be described as exercising pastoral care of anyone. Likewise the angels of Michael who fight against the dragon (Rev 12:7) can hardly be described as engaging in pastoral care. It is most unlikely that Jesus envisages that the twelve legions of angels he could ask for (Matt

---

6. Macy, *Shadow*, 1–7.

7. Clebsch and Jaekle, *Pastoral.*

8. Macy, *Shadow*, 50–54.

9. Ibid., 76–142.

26:53) would administer pastoral care to the chief priests, the elders, and their thugs were he to request the Father for them.

Macy makes an important point that focusing on the actions of angels is key to understanding them. He contributes an interesting study to the discussion of angels and certainly makes the point that angels often exercise pastoral ministry. However, there is more to understanding angels than pastoral angelology.

TURNING AGAIN TO THE INTERPRETING ANGEL

The interpreting angel figure can also be found in the biblical book of Daniel. The narrative of Daniel is set in the Babylonian exile, as with 4 Ezra. Babylon has defeated Judah and taken Judeans into captivity in Babylon (Dan 1:1–4a). However, most scholars argue that the book was actually written in the second century BC when the Jewish faith was under threat from the Seleucid king Antiochus IV Epiphanes, who persecuted those Jews who remained faithful to their ancestral God and the Torah in the face of his attempt to introduce Greek culture in Palestine.[10] The setting, once again, is the suffering of the people of God at the hands of their enemies.

Daniel has a vision as he lies in bed (Dan 7:1). The vision portrays four monsters arising in succession out of the chaotic sea. The fourth monster destroys everything in its path. Thrones were set in the court of heaven and the Ancient of Days took his throne surrounded by attending angels. The court sits in judgment, imprisoning the first three monsters and putting to death the fourth. The one like a son of man enters the court on clouds and is given all authority and dominion (Dan 7:2–14).[11] This vision terrifies Daniel who approaches one of the attending angels in the court to ask what the vision means (Dan 7:15–16a). This angel interprets the vision briefly, explaining how the vision depicts the restoration of the people of God and the defeat of their enemies (Dan 7:16b–17). Daniel

10. For the persecution of faithful Jews under Antiochus IV Epiphanes, see 1 Macc 1–2 and 2 Macc 4:7—7:42. The books of 1 and 2 Maccabees may be found in the Apocrypha. For the date and setting of Daniel in the second century BC, see Collins, *Daniel*, 24–52; Goldingay, *Daniel*, 326–29; Lucas, *Daniel*, 37–42. For the date and setting of Daniel in the exile in Babylon, see Baldwin, *Daniel*, 35–46.

11. Collins, *Daniel*, 277–311. Casey (*Son of Man*, 7–50) argues that the judgment scene is set on earth rather than in heaven, in the land of Israel. For evidence against Casey, see Angel, "The Sea," 474–78.

presses the angel for further details, especially of the fourth beast and the angel provides them (Dan 7:9–27). The whole experience leaves Daniel pale and panic-stricken (Dan 7:28).

But Daniel is set to have further visionary experiences. Another vision perplexes him and he finds himself unable to understand it (Dan 8:1–15). A voice calls to Gabriel to help Daniel to understand the vision (Dan 8:15–17a) and Gabriel duly comes and interprets for him (Dan 8:17b–26). Overcome by the experience, Daniel lies sick for a few days before recuperating (Dan 8:27). Later, Daniel prays for the restoration of Jerusalem (Dan 9:3–19). As he does so, Gabriel arrives (Dan 9:21) and reveals heavenly secrets concerning the restoration of Jerusalem (Dan 9:22b–27). Another time, while mourning and fasting (Dan 10:2–4) Daniel has a vision of a great angel (Dan 10:5–8). The vision terrifies him—indeed, all those around him flee and hide themselves despite the fact that they see nothing. Daniel grows pale, loses his strength, faints, and falls to the ground (Dan 10:7–9). An angel touches him to restore him although Daniel only makes it to his hands and knees (Dan 10:10)—this angel is possibly but by no means certainly Gabriel.[12] The angel informs Daniel of the vision to come, which renders Daniel speechless and terrified. Again, the angel strengthens the seer, enabling him to receive the vision (Dan 10:11–19). The angel delivers the "vision" concerning the last days (Dan 10:20—12:4). After this, Daniel witnesses two angels having a conversation about the timing of these events (Dan 12:6–7), before one of them charges Daniel to tell nothing of what he has seen and promises him restoration and reward at the end of days (Dan 12:9–13).

Like 4 Ezra, Daniel bears witness to the interpreting angel figure, this time Gabriel, and possibly another unnamed angel. As in 4 Ezra, God sends the interpreting angel to enable the righteous man (perplexed at the suffering of God's people and praying about it) to understand heavenly secrets concerning the salvation of Israel. The angel talks with Daniel, interprets his visions, and strengthens him when he is overwhelmed and terrified by what is being revealed.

Of particular interest is the vision that Daniel receives of the throne room of heaven (Dan 7:9–10). This picture of the court and throne room of heaven is found in earlier Jewish visionary literature (1 Kgs 22:19; Isa 6; Ezek 1) and may find its roots in the religious traditions of Ugarit (an

---

12. Goldingay, *Daniel*, 291.

ancient city the remains of which are located near Ras Shamra in modern Syria).[13] The throne room of heaven is where God and the heavenly council of angels make judgments and go about the general business of heaven. For examples of this, see 1 Kgs 22:19–23, Job 1–2, and Ps 82.[14] In his vision of the heavenly council Daniel sees thrones set in the court of heaven, the majesty and glory of God (the Ancient of Days), the glory of his throne (like fiery flames with wheels like burning fire), and thousands of angelic ministers. Visions of the glory of the court of heaven, its myriads of angelic attendants, and the majesty of the one seated on the throne become something of a feature of apocalyptic literature.

One example of this is found in 1 Enoch.[15] This apocalyptic text divides into five books: the Book of the Watchers (1 En. 1–36); the Book of the Similitudes (1 En.37–71); the Book of Astronomical Writings (1 Enoch 72–82); the Book of Dream Visions (1 En. 83–90); and the Book of the Epistle of Enoch (1 En. 91–107). The Book of the Watchers begins by proclaiming the coming judgment of God (1 En. 1–5). Then it recounts the fall of the rebellious angels or watchers (1 En. 6–11).[16] The story then picks up on the Old Testament character of Enoch, who walked with God and "was not" because God took him (Gen 5:21–24), explaining that Enoch was taken by God to proclaim God's judgment on the rebellious watchers who had fallen from heaven (1 En. 12:1—13:8). Enoch ascends into the throne room of heaven (1 En. 14:8–23) where he sees the throne of God and the Great Glory seated upon it:[17]

> 8 In the vision it was shown to me thus: Look, clouds in the vision were summoning me, and mists were crying out to me; and shooting stars and lightning flashes were hastening me and speeding me along, and winds in my vision made me fly up and lifted me upward and brought me to heaven. 9 And I went in until I drew near to a wall built of hailstones; and tongues of fire were encircling them all around, and they began to

13. Cross, *Canaanite Myth*, 185–90. For an alternative view, see Handy, "Dissenting Deities," 18–35. For an introduction to the religious literature of Ugarit, see Wyatt, *Religious Texts from Ugarit*.

14. See further Mullen, *Divine Council*.

15. *1 Enoch* is found in the Pseudepigrapha.

16. See further chapter 6 below.

17. Translation from Nickelsburg and VanderKam, *New Translation*, 34–36. The parts of *1 Enoch* studied here are dated to between 300 and 250 BC (Nickelsburg, *1 Enoch 1*, 230, 293).

frighten me. 10 And I went into the tongues of fire, and I drew near to a great house built of hailstones; and the walls of this house were like stone slabs, and they were all of snow, and the floor was of snow. 11 And the ceiling was like shooting stars and lightning flashes; and among them were fiery cherubim, and their heaven was water, 12 and a flaming fire encircled all their walls, and the doors blazed with fire. 13 And I went into that house—hot as fire and cold as snow, and no delight of life was in it. Fear enveloped me, and trembling seized me, 14 and I was quaking and trembling, and I fell upon my face. And I saw in my vision, 15 and look, another open door before me: and a house greater than the former one, and it was all built of tongues of fire. 16 All of it so excelled in glory and splendor and majesty that I am unable to describe for you its glory and majesty. 17 Its floor was of fire, and its upper part was flashes of lightning and shooting stars, and its ceiling was a flaming fire. 18 And I was looking and I saw a lofty throne; and its appearance was like ice, and its wheels were like the shining sun, and the voice of the cherubim, 19 and from beneath the throne issued rivers of flaming fire. And I was unable to see. 20 The Great Glory sat upon it; his apparel was like the appearance of the sun and whiter than much snow. 21 No angel could enter into this house and look at his face because of the splendor and glory, and no human could look at him. 22 Flaming fire encircled him and a great fire stood by him, and none of those about him approached him. Ten thousand times ten thousand stood before him, but he needed no counselor; his every word and deed. 23 And the holy ones of the watchers who approached him did not depart by night, nor by day did they leave him.

Enoch falls flat on his face, terrified by his vision (*1 En.* 14:9, 13–14, 24)—like Ezra and Daniel—and requires angelic assistance to rise to his feet and receive further revelation, though his head is still bowed (*1 En.* 14:25). As he enters deeper into heaven the scenes become ever more glorious until he reaches the throne room of heaven which is indescribably glorious—but this does not prevent Enoch from describing it. Again the throne is brilliant in splendor and may even *sound* glorious (note the "voice of the cherubim" in *1 En.* 14:18, although it is difficult to discern what the text originally read here).[18] God, the Great Glory, seated upon the throne is depicted as unsurpassed in majesty with myriads of angels attending him. And the culmination of this vision is the commission Enoch receives (*1 En.* 15:1—16:4).

---

18. For the various readings and translations of this particular phrase, see Nickelsburg and VanderKam, *New Translation*, 35 n. *h*; Nickelsburg, *1 Enoch 1*, 258, 264.

Angels

After receiving his commission, angels take Enoch on a heavenly tour in which are revealed to him the secrets of the universe (1 *En.* 17–36), including such mysteries as the foundations of the earth and heaven (1 *En.* 18), the names of the archangels (1 *En.* 20), the places where disobedient stars and angels are punished (1 *En.* 21), and the paradise awaiting the righteous (1 *En.* 28–32). His tour guides are the angels Uriel, Raphael, Reuel, Michael, Sariel, and Gabriel who answer the questions Enoch asks about what he sees (e.g., 1 *En.* 21:4–5) and counsel Enoch when he falls prey to fear (e.g., 1 *En.* 21:8–10). Towards the end of this heavenly tour, Uriel also helps Enoch to write down the mysteries of the universe (1 *En.* 33:3–4). Here we see angels at work in another, related role—that of giving celestial tours.

The tour of heaven or ascent into heaven is a recognized feature of apocalyptic literature.[19] The main features of such literature are as follows. The ascender into heaven is a famous righteous figure from the past and this figure tells the story of the ascent into heaven in the first person. Angels guide the ascender and are present in the court of heaven. The ascender sees God who sometimes speaks to the ascender. The ascender passes through multiple heavenly realms and describes them in some detail. The exact number of heavens seems to differ from apocalypse to apocalypse: *2 Enoch* has ten heavens (2 *En.* 22:1); the *Apocalypse of Abraham* has seven (or possibly eight) heavens (*Apoc. Ab.* 19:4–9); the apocalypse *3 Baruch* testifies to five heavens (3 *Bar.* 11:1) although the original text possibly mentioned more; the *Testament of Levi* has three heavens (*T. Levi* 2:6–12) or perhaps seven heavens (*T. Levi* 3:1–8).[20] Regardless of the number of heavens, the ascender displays fear of entering heaven but enters and sees the throne of God. There the ascender receives a revelation of heavenly mysteries.[21]

---

19. For an introduction to the genre of celestial tours, see Himmelfarb, *Ascent to Heaven*; Himmelfarb, *Tours of Hell*; Dean-Otting, *Heavenly Journeys*; Gruenwald, *Merkavah Mysticism*.

20. See de Jonge (*Testaments*, 27) for text critical issues on the *Testament of Levi*. See Rubinkiewicz, *Apocalypse D'Abraham*, 165–67, for discussion of text critical issues concerning whether there are seven or eight heavens in the *Apocalypse of Abraham*. On *3 Baruch* and text critical issues affecting number of heavens, see Kulik, *3 Baruch*, 306–29. The *Apocalypse of Abraham*, *3 Baruch* and the *Testament of Levi* are found in the Pseudepigrapha.

21. Gooder, *Only the Third*, 151–61.

This kind of literature may cast some light on the two biblical books.[22] The Book of Revelation opens with John noting his sharing in the persecution of the early churches in Asia Minor (Rev 1:9)—the people of God are suffering. As John is in the Spirit on the Lord's day, the risen Christ speaks and appears to him (Rev 1:10–20), which appearance seems to frighten John (Rev 1:17). Then Christ delivers messages for John to deliver to the angels of the seven churches of Asia Minor (Rev 2:1—3:22). Much here is typical of the scenes we have witnessed of angels delivering messages to holy people, deep in prayer for the suffering of God's people. However, there are some notable differences. John appears not to be a person of the past but the present. More importantly God sends no angel to speak to John but Christ himself appears and delivers the prophecy John is to proclaim.[23]

Nonetheless, we are back on fairly familiar ground when the vision of heaven begins. John hears a voice calling him up to heaven and in the Spirit John finds himself in the court of heaven.[24] Here John has a vision of the throne and the One seated on the throne and describes their glory (Rev 4:2–6a). The heavenly attendants surrounding the throne and their activities are described in some detail (Rev 4:4, 6b–11). Angels play significant parts within the narrative throughout the remainder of the vision (for example, the angels of the seals, Rev 6 and 8; the angels of the trumpets, Rev 8–9 and 11; and the angels of the bowls containing plagues, Rev 16). Angels also play a part in enabling John to receive the vision (e.g., Rev 10:9–10; 17:1; 21:9—22:5) and to understand it (e.g., Rev 7:13–17; 17:6b–18). Angels also instruct John to publicize the vision (Rev 10:11; 14:13; 19:9–10; 22:10). So Revelation uses the throne room traditions of Jewish apocalyptic and draws on the now familiar figure of the interpreting angel (see particularly, Rev 22:6, 8–9, 16).

22. Although, as Gooder admits, the greater number of the apocalypses which display this pattern of heavenly ascent are later in date than the New Testament. Therefore the pattern of heavenly ascent as outlined may not have existed at the time of the writing of the NT texts (*Only the Third*, 158–61).

23. Some scholars assert that Christ appears as something of a principal angel here; so Rowland, "Risen Christ," 1–11; Collins, "Son of Man," 548–58. However for the argument that Christ is identified with God rather than an angel, see Bauckham, "Worship of Jesus," 133–40. See also Aune, *Revelation 1–5*, 60–117; Beale, *Revelation*, 205–22.

24. John does not recount his heavenly ascent in detail, so Himmelfarb (*Ascent to Heaven*, 34) judges that Revelation "is not really an ascent." Gooder (*Only the Third*, 82), noting that an ascent is implied in Rev 4:1 "come *up* here," disagrees.

These ascent traditions also cast some light on 2 Cor 12. In 2 Corinthians, Paul defends his apostleship in the face of the criticisms of those who denigrate him. At the beginning of chapter 12, Paul "competes" with these apostles in terms of revelations and visions they have received. He speaks of knowing a man who was "caught up" (2 Cor 12:2).[25] He reached the third heaven (2 Cor 12:2) or Paradise (2 Cor 12:4). In this heaven, he receives a revelation (2 Cor 12:4). Here we have three elements of the ascent to heaven: the ascent ("caught up"); the travel to heaven; and the receipt of a revelation. Paul clearly experiences some sort of heavenly ascent.

However, the tenor of the description of the vision suggests that Paul is unwilling to become too elated about the experience. He dismisses even considering the nature of the mode of ascent—"whether in the body or out of the body I do not know; God knows" (2 Cor 12:3). The description of the heavens is all but lacking. Paul does not describe the throne. There is no mention of the myriads of angels attending the One on the throne. There is no word of the content of the revelation of the heavenly mysteries (unless it is the conversation in 2 Cor 10:7b–9).[26] The cavalier way in which Paul treats the tradition of heavenly ascent tends to suggest that he wishes to play down the excitement surrounding mystical experiences and bring home the truth that God's power is made perfect in the weakness of Christ's disciples (2 Cor 12.9).[27]

So angels are found in visions. When holy and righteous people seek the wisdom of God in order to understand their suffering or the suffering of the people of God, God may send an angel to enable them to understand what is happening. The angel may, to some extent, look after the visionary in his or her distress. The angel enables the seer to understand the visions of the heavenly mysteries that God grants them, and strengthens them when these revelations become overwhelming. The angels may also guide the

25. For the identity of the man as Paul himself, see Thrall, *Second Corinthians*, 2:778–79.

26. As argued by, e.g., Gooder, *Only the Third*, 190–211.

27. Gooder (ibid., 165–211) argues that Paul experienced a failed ascent, foiled by the intervention of Satan who prevented Paul moving to a higher heaven than the third. However, the fact that Paul receives a revelation suggests the success of the ascent. Moreover, the third heaven might be the highest in Paul's heavenly cosmology—after all, it appears that different apocalyptists had different ideas about how many heavens there were. Nonetheless, the basic insight that Paul does not depict his ascent in the regular way seems sound.

prophet on a heavenly tour of the secret things of the cosmos as part of this process. Various biblical texts draw on and use these traditions but Paul seems to suggest that the Christian disciple ought not to get too drawn into visionary experiences, either for their own sake or for the sake of status.

3

What Do Angels Do All Day?

That angels are said to dwell in the heavens is nothing new to most of us. That angels are sent to earth on missions is equally familiar. But when angels are not occupied with any such task, what do they do in heaven all day? Stereotypical angels in popular culture live on clouds, sometimes playing harps and at other times gazing wistfully into the middle distance. However, this is not exactly the picture of angels in heaven that we find in the ancient documents.

The ancient texts depict heaven as an orderly and active place, and the angels within it are accordingly ordered and active. As in an army, angels are organized according to rank and assigned tasks accordingly.

> 1 These are the names of the holy angels who watch. 2 Uriel, one of the holy angels, who is in charge of the world and Tartarus. 3 Raphael, one of the holy angels, who is in charge of the spirits of men. 4 Reuel, one of the holy angels, who takes vengeance on the world of the luminaries. 5 Michael, one of the holy angels, who has been put in charge of the good ones of the people. 6 Sariel, one of the holy angels, who is in charge of the spirits who sin against the spirit. 7 Gabriel, one of the holy angels, who is in charge of paradise and the serpents and the cherubim. 8 Remiel, one of the holy angels, whom God has put in charge of them that rise. 8 The names of the seven archangels.
>
> (*1 En.* 20:1–8)

This example of angelic organization lists the seven archangels and describes their respective spheres of influence. A number of texts suggest that the celestial hierarchy is headed by archangels. Raphael identifies himself as one of the seven archangels in Tobit (Tob 12:15). The *Songs of the Sabbath Sacrifice* from Qumran (the Dead Sea Scrolls were the library of the community at Qumran) speak of seven chief angelic princes (4Q403 1 i 10–25).[1] Some texts suggest that there are four main archangels: Michael, Sariel, Raphael, and Gabriel (*1 En.* 9–10; 1QM 9:15–16); or perhaps, Michael, Raphael, Gabriel, and Phanuel (*1 En.* 71:9–13). There is not complete agreement as to the identity of the archangels.

Nor is there unanimity as to the identity of the principal angel. Some texts suggest that there is one prince and chief amongst the angels who acts as "right-hand man" to God. Many of these texts identify the principal angel as Michael (1QM 17:6–8; *2 En.* 22:6; *3 Bar.* 11:4; *T. Ab.* 14:5) who may be identified with the angelic Prince of Light (1QM 13:10) and Melchizedek (11QMelch).[2] The *Prayer of Joseph* identifies the principal angel as Jacob and Israel, who is also Uriel (*Pr. Jos.* 1, 7–8).[3] The *Apocalypse of Abraham* identifies the principal angel as Iaoel (*Apoc. Ab.* 10:1–17).[4] But for all the disagreements as to the identity of the principal angel and the archangels, there seems to be a consensus that there is organization and rank among the angels in heaven.[5]

Angels are given particular tasks to perform. Some are particular tasks for a particular situation. Thus, the four archangels (Michael, Sariel, Raphael, and Gabriel) are required to punish the fallen angels and restore the earth after the events of Gen 6:1–4 (*1 En.* 9–10). Others are more general tasks. In the heavenly ascent texts angels guide the visionaries around heaven and interpret for them the meaning of the events they witness there. Certain angels of the LORD sit at the gates of heaven observing and recording the deeds of the righteous in manuscripts that are then taken to the Almighty who writes the names of these righteous in the Book of the Living (*Apoc. Zeph.* 3:6–7).[6] Meantime their counterparts, the angels of the

---

1. For an introduction to angels in the Dead Sea Scrolls, see Davidson, *Angels at Qumran*; Wassen, "Angels," 499–523.

2. For a detailed study of Michael, see Hannah, *Michael and Christ*, 25–121. *2 Enoch* and the *Testament of Abraham* are found in the Pseudepigrapha.

3. The *Prayer of Joseph* is found in the Pseudepigrapha.

4. On principal angels, see further Segal, *Two Powers*, 182–205; Hurtado, *One God*, 71–92; Barker, *Great Angel*, 70–96. For such angels in the Dead Sea Scrolls, see Collins, "Powers in Heaven," 9–28.

5. On the angelic hierarchy, see Kuhn, "Angelology," 221–25.

6. The *Apocalypse of Zephaniah* is found in the Pseudepigrapha.

accuser, write down all the sins of human beings and their notes are taken to the heavenly Accuser who holds their sins against them when they die (*Apoc. Zeph.* 3:8–9). Angels intercede, pray to, and petition God on behalf of the people of God (*1 En.* 39:5)—an idea which Paul may have in mind when stating that Christians have but one mediator in heaven, Jesus Christ (1 Tim 2:5) and not the kind of interceding angel we encounter here or elsewhere (*1 En.* 40:6; *T. Dan* 6:2).[7] Jubilees depicts angels being created for particular tasks in organizing the universe:

> For on the first day he created the heavens, which are above, and the earth, and the waters and all of the spirits which minister before him: the angels of the presence, and the angels of sanctification, and the angels of the spirit of fire, and the angels of the spirit of the winds, and the angels of the spirit of the clouds and darkness and snow and hail and frost, and the angels of resoundings and thunder and lightning, and the angels of the spirits of cold and heat and winter and springtime and harvest and summer, and all of the spirits of his creatures which are in heaven and on earth.
>
> (*Jub.* 2:2)[8]

The text suggests that certain angels are assigned to order particular aspects of creation (so also *1 En.* 60:11–22; *2 En.* 19). The Astronomical Book or Book of the Luminaries (*1 En.* 72–82) paints a similar picture. Uriel is set over the sun, moon, and stars—indeed, all the heavenly lights (*1 En.* 75:3). Some of this work is delegated to the angelic leaders of the heads of the thousands (*1 En.* 75:1; 80:1, 6). This work names some of the angelic leaders of the different parts of creation—so, for example, Milkiel, Helememelek, Mele'eyel, and Narel are the angels in charge of the four seasons (*1 En.* 82:13).

In addition to governing and ordering creation, the angels live and model the holy life in the presence of God in heaven. Angels keep the Torah. They keep the Sabbath and have done so in heaven since before the Sabbath was made known to anyone on earth (*Jub.* 2:18, 30). They celebrate Shavuot or the Feast of Weeks, having done so since the day of creation (*Jub.* 6:18).[9] The angels of the presence, the archangels and angels of holiness

7. Fiore, *Pastoral Epistles*, 60. The *Testament of Dan* is found in the Pseudepigrapha.

8. The book of *Jubilees* is found in the Pseudepigrapha.

9. For a summary of the roles of angels in *Jubilees*, see VanderKam, "Angel of the Presence," 379.

are circumcised, having been created this way: "Because the nature of all the angels of the presence and all of the angels of sanctification was thus [circumcised] from the day of their creation. And in the presence of the angels of the presence and the angels of sanctification he sanctified Israel [i.e. circumcised their males] so that they might be with him and with his holy angels" (*Jub.* 15:27).

The angels model the holy life and certain ancient Jewish groups believed that the people of God were to imitate it—so that they might enjoy fellowship with God and the holy angels. This angelic modeling of the holy life in heaven is discernable in the texts of the Qumran community. Both the angels and the Qumran community (4Q400 1 i 2–6; 1QS 1:1–15; 8:5–16) formed a special community. Both the angels and the community had a covenant with God (4Q400 1 i 2–7; 1QS 1:8, 16—2:25). Both the angels and the community were given special laws to follows (4Q400 1 i 15; CD 3:14; 6:2–11). Both the angels and the community offered bloodless sacrifices (11Q17 1–3; 1QS 8:9–10; 9:4–5). Both the angels and the community were to live in perfect purity (4Q400 1 i 14–15; 1QS 3:4–10). Neither the angels nor the community were permitted any sinfulness or evil in their midst (4Q511 1 6; 1QS 1:16–28). Both the angels and the community praise God (1QM 12:1–2; 1QS 1:21–22; 11:15). Both the angels and members of the community possessed divine wisdom (4Q401 17 4; 1QH 1:21). And just as the angels were tasked to teach each other the things of God so members of the community were to teach each other wisdom and godliness (4Q400 1 i 17; 1QS 3:13).[10]

Many scholars see this desire to imitate the angels and to live in fellowship with the angels as the reason behind the strict purity rules of the Qumran community. The angels are holy and so religious people must be strict about maintaining their holiness. This may also explain why the Qumran community was male and celibate (as angels seem to be male— note some are circumcised—and they have no need of marriage).[11] The idea of fellowship with the angels extended to the belief that angels might be present at public worship (see further below). This particular notion may lie behind one of the more obscure passages in Paul. Paul urges women

10. Dimant, "Men as Angels," 93–103.

11. Ibid., 102. Cecilia Wassen ("What do the Angels," 115–29) proposes that the strict purity rules actually relate to being prepared to fight in the eschatological battle against the sons of darkness.

to cover their heads in worship because of the angels (1 Cor 11:10). The angels are utterly holy and so there must be no unclean thing in their presence (1Q28a 2:3–10; 1QM 7:4–6; cf. the purity rules in Lev 21:17–23). The angels are present at public worship and as the uncovered head of a woman is a "disgrace," no woman may uncover her head in worship.[12]

Angels also worship God and serve as priests in the heavenly temple. The *Songs of the Sabbath Sacrifice* (4Q400–4Q407) depict the heavenly worship of the angels. The angels act as priests in the inner sanctuary of heaven (4Q400 1 i 19–20) who offer perfect sacrifices by which they perpetually purify themselves and appease God in favor of all people who turn from sin (4Q400 1 i 14b–16). They extol the glory and majesty of God continually (4Q400 2 1; 4Q403 1 i 1–29) with psalms of praise and exaltation and blessings: "Blessed be the Lord, the King of all, above all blessing and praise. And may he bless all the holy ones who bless him, and proclaim him just in the name of his glory. And he will bless those permanently blessed" (4Q403 1 i 28–29).

Some of the songs are a mixture of praise and calls to the heavenly host, or particular members or groups within the heavenly host, to praise God: "Praise the God of the heights, you exalted ones among all the divinities of knowledge. May the holy ones of God magnify the King of glory, who makes holy with holiness all his holy ones. Chiefs of the praises of all the gods, praise the God of majestic praises, for in the magnificence of the praises is the glory of his kingdom" (4Q403 1 i 30b–32a).

The songs picture the actions of various groups of angels worshipping God on the throne-chariot (4Q405 20–22 ii 7b–13):

> 7 The cherubs fall down before him, and bless. When they rise the murmuring sound of gods [i.e. angels] 8 is heard, and there is an uproar of exultation when they lift their wings, the murmuring sound of gods. They bless the image of the throne-chariot, which is above the vault of the cherubs, 9 and they sing the splendor of the shining vault, which is beneath the seat of his glory. And when the ophanim move forward, the holy angels return; they emerge from between 10 its glorious wheels with the likeness of fire, the spirits of the holy of holies. Around them is the likeness of streams of fire like electrum, and a luminous substance 11 gloriously multi-colored, wonderful colors,

---

12. Fitzmyer, "Feature," 187–204. For an alternative view, see BeDuhn, "Because of the Angels," 295–320. For a response to BeDuhn, review of alternative proposals and restatement of his view, see Fitzmyer, *First Corinthians*, 417–19.

purely blended. The spirits of living gods move constantly with the glory of the wonderful chariots. 12 And there is a murmuring of blessing in the uproar of their motion, and they praise the holy one on returning from their paths. When they rise, they rise wonderfully; when they settle, 13 they stand still. The sound of glad rejoicing becomes silent and there is a calm blessing of gods in all the camps of the gods.

The praise of the angels is a riot of movement and color. They raise their wings in exultation as their music crescendos towards a climax. The cherubim are beneath the throne of God, singing his glory. The holy angels appear to be flying in and out of the wheels of the chariot, emerging from them with the fire of the glory of the chariot. All around the spirits of heaven are glorious colors (or, on another translation, the spirits themselves are beautiful colors).[13] Either way, these colors fill the court of heaven with beauty and wonder. As the angels move, they sing spreading their praises around the spacious and glorious vault of heaven in music and movement. When they come back to their places they continue in praise. And at times their praises move to deeply worshipful silence.[14] For anyone who knows and enjoys both the transcendence and sublimity of worship and praise of God, the scene is magnificent.

And the beauty of the worship of the angels attracted people. There is some evidence that the Qumran community believed that its members worshipped in the company of the angels (4Q400 2 1–8; 4Q405 8–9 1–5). There was an acknowledgement of the paucity of human worship in comparison with that of the angels: "how will it be regarded amongst them [the angels]? And how is our priesthood in their residences? And . . . their holiness? What is the offering of our tongue of dust compared with the knowledge of the divinities?" (4Q400 2 6–7). The worship of humanity is not on a par with the worship of angels.[15] This probably only served to make the worship of angels all the more attractive.

This kind of angelic worship probably serves as the background to another puzzling phrase in Paul. He warns the Colossians against the worship of angels (Col 2:18). This phrase has often been understood to refer to the human worship of angels as opposed to the worship of God.[16]

13. For an alternative translation, see Davila, *Liturgical Works*, 147.

14. Ibid., 147–53.

15. Chazon, "Liturgical Communion," 95–105.

16. And this viewpoint has been defended recently by Clinton E. Arnold (*Colossian*

Angels

However, there is a growing consensus that Paul does not refer to the human worshipping of angels here but to angels themselves worshipping. In other words, the Colossians were eager to engage with the angels in their heavenly liturgy.[17] This fits the context of self-abasement (as fasting sometimes precedes ascents into heaven) and dwelling on visions, which was presumably the medium through which such worship was experienced (Col 2:18). It also fits the context of observing Jewish food regulations and festivals (Col 2:16) as the ascent into heaven was clearly part of the mystical side of second temple Judaism. Paul associates this practice with growing arrogance and distancing from Christ (Col 2:19), neither of which he wishes to encourage. So he discourages the Colossians from seeking to participate in such worship.

Paul displays a similar attitude towards the charismatic gift of speaking in tongues, sometimes called *glossolalia*. In 1 Cor 12–14, Paul discusses a number of spiritual gifts that the members of the Corinthian church practice as gifts from God. One of these seems to have been particularly popular, the gift of speaking in tongues. Speaking in tongues involves speaking in the other languages, which the speaker has not learned. The speaker is able to speak in these languages by the power of the Spirit of God. Paul states that these languages are sometimes the foreign human languages and at other times the languages of angels (1 Cor 13:1). The author of the *Testament of Job* seems to be aware of the same phenomenon.[18] Towards the end of the book, Job gives each of his three daughters (Hemera, Kasia, and Amaltheia's Horn) a heavenly sash of many colors, which shimmered like the sun, giving off sparks of fire (*T. Job* 46:5–9). He instructs them to put on the sashes as they will protect them from Satan, heal them, and lead them into a better heavenly world (*T. Job* 47:2–11). As the daughters put on their sashes their hearts are changed towards focusing on heavenly rather

---

Syncretism). However, his argument against taking "worship of angels" as a subjective genitive is weak (Josephus, *Ant.* 12.5.4§253 and 4 Macc 5:7 do use "worship" in subjective genitive compounds), and his reduction of "worship" to "veneration" is not convincing—not least as his evidence does not generally support veneration of angels so much as invocation of them to perform favours. However, some accept his argument, e.g., MacDonald, *Colossians and Ephesians*, 112–13. 4 Maccabees is found in the Apocrypha.

17. Francis, "Humility," 163–95; Yates, "Worship of Angels," 12–15. More recently Dunn, *Colossians and Philemon*, 178–85.

18. The *Testament of Job* is found in the Pseudepigrapha.

than earthly things, and they begin to praise God in the tongues of angels (*T. Job* 48–50). Speaking in these heavenly languages was a highly prized gift among the Corinthians and Paul tries to persuade the Corinthians to enjoy the gift but to think about which gifts will really serve the purposes of building up the church and helping people to find salvation and healing in Christ (1 Cor 14:1–19). He enjoys and values the gift but urges the Corinthians not to use it in such a way that they focus on self-fulfillment and self-realization. Instead they should use all these spiritual gifts lovingly, preferring the interests of others to their own (1 Cor 14:17–19). The gift of praising with the tongues of angels may be wonderful but the focus must be on living the life of love to which Christ calls us.[19]

And this does not seem so far away from reported angel experiences today. The following testimony is but one of many accounts of experience of angels being present at worship where the worshippers are speaking or singing in tongues. The person who reported the experience informs me that it took place in Gillingham, UK, in 1984 during a Christian conference at which they were present: "During the worship one evening, the whole congregation had been singing in tongues. A sudden silence came over the congregation as people became aware of an angelic presence and the sound of angels singing. It was so pure, so sweet that it was not human or natural. Members of the congregation could not believe their ears." Although anecdotal, it is probably not unreasonable to note that within the Christian movement of charismatic renewal there are groups of worshippers who seek out such experiences as somehow more authentic than everyday Christian living and who can dismiss worship that seems less exciting. Susan Garrett suggests that there is an equivalent tendency in New Age spirituality. Rather than confession of sin and reconciliation with God in Christ, the goal becomes moving out of ignorance by realizing one's inner self in mystical communion with angels. Self-fulfillment and self-affirmation replace humility and love as the heart of spirituality.[20]

So far from gazing wistfully into the middle distance, angels are anything but idle. They manage the workings of the cosmos. They perform special tasks at particular times, as required by the Almighty. They intercede, pray for, and petition the Lord on behalf of humanity (but the likelihood is

19. See further on spiritual gifts in 1 Cor 12–14 the discussion in Collins, *First Corinthians*, 441–525.

20. Garrett, *No Ordinary Angel*, 40–76.

that this role was taken over by Jesus according to early Christians). They lead exemplary lives in heaven, modeling holiness to humanity. But pictures of angels with harps are not wholly wide of the mark. The chief role of angels is to worship God and in this they model the primary calling of all people. Indeed their worship was understood to be so enthralling that some ancient Jews and Christians sought to join in the heavenly worship, but one of their number—the early Christ-follower, Paul—saw how the eagerness for experience was leading to arrogance rather than godliness and urged his fellows to worship instead in humility and truth.

4

Angels from the Realms of Glory

The biblical book of Hebrews asks (Heb 1:14): are not all angels spirits in the divine service, sent to serve for the sake of those who are to inherit salvation? The answer to this question is surely: indeed, but not only that, if the "being sent for the sake of" merely refers to rescuing people from tricky situations. Many biblical and modern accounts of angels are indeed about the rescue of people from difficult situations but this is not the whole story. Angels have been given various tasks to perform on earth and this chapter will outline three: ministering spirits, angels of death, and angels as mediators of the covenant with Israel at Sinai.

MINISTERING SPIRITS

This task is probably the one with which we are most familiar—and almost certainly the central theme of most of the stories of angel encounters today. The scenario works something like this. Events have spiralled out of control and seem beyond repair. A stranger appears, seemingly from nowhere. The stranger sorts out the crisis. The stranger disappears back whence they came. The stranger may or may not reveal their angelic identity. To illustrate this it may be best to tell the story of Tobit, a popular story from the second temple period.[1]

Tobit begins with his story of riches to rags despite his righteous actions. Living in Nineveh and reduced to poverty by a pagan ruler, all he has left to him is his wife Anna and their son Tobias. He then goes blind

---

1. The book of Tobit is found in the Apocrypha.

(bird droppings in his eyes and poor medical attention) and his wife goes out to work to support them. After one embittered argument with Anna, Tobit asks God to let him die. Meanwhile in Ecbatana, another family suffers equally badly. Sarah has been widowed for the seventh time—each of her husbands dying at the hand of the demon Asmodeus on their wedding nights. To add insult to injury, her maid accuses Sarah of killing them. She goes up to her room to hang herself, drawing back from the brink only because she fears her suicide might kill her father Raguel. She too turns to prayer. God hears their prayers and sends the angel Raphael to heal Tobit of blindness and to bring honor and happiness to Sarah by giving her in marriage to Tobias, and freeing her from the power of the demon Asmodeus.

Preparing for his death, Tobit remembers some money he has left on trust with a friend in Rages (near Ecbatana) in Media. Tobit gives Tobias some good advice on righteous living and sends him for the money. Tobias looks for a guide to help him with his journey and teams up with the angel Raphael who, appearing as a young man, introduces himself as Azariah, a distant relative. On the journey Tobias is attacked by a fish, which he catches as Raphael instructs him, for the gall, heart, and liver act as good medicine (gall heals blindness, and burning the heart and liver gets rid of demons).

As they enter Media, Azariah (alias Raphael) suggests to Tobias that they spend the night with another distant relative, Raguel and his daughter Sarah. He explains Sarah's predicament to Tobias but counsels him to marry her, instructing him as to how to rid her of the demon Asmodeus. Tobias sorts out the marriage contract with Raguel and marries Sarah. On entering Sarah's bedroom, Tobias places the fish liver and heart on the incense burning there. This creates a sufficiently repellent odor to repel Asmodeus to the nether regions of Egypt, where Raphael follows him and binds him hand and foot. Raguel digs another grave (just in case), and sends a maid to fetch the corpse of Tobias (to bury him at night to avoid further public humiliation). To everybody's delight Sarah and Tobias are found sleeping soundly (and further servants are sent to fill the grave before daybreak).

After fourteen days of wedding feasting Tobias returns to Nineveh with his bride and the money. Azariah instructs Tobit to smear the fish gall on his father's eyes. He does so and Tobit sees again. The family has much to celebrate and there follow a further seven days of wedding feast. Tobit and Tobias attempt to pay Azariah for his services. Azariah reveals that he is really Raphael, one of the seven angels who stand before God. He took the prayers of Sarah to God, and God sent him to rescue Sarah and to heal Tobit. He urges them to praise and bless God, and returns to heaven.[2]

Although maybe not quite as colorful, we find stories of angelic intervention to rescue the righteous in the biblical book of Acts. Peter and John have been held overnight in custody and intimidated for preaching the gospel (Acts 4:1–22). They preach again and are imprisoned (Acts 5:12–18). An angel releases them from prison, charging them to continue preaching—which they do (Acts 5:19–21). They are arrested again and flogged (Acts 5:26, 39b–40). Later, Peter is imprisoned yet again—the church praying fervently for him as Herod has just executed another apostle, James (Acts 12:2–5). Probably in order not to run the risk of further jailbreaks, Peter is bound in two chains with two guards beside him in his cell and further soldiers outside the door. An angel of the Lord appears, taps him on the shoulder, and tells him to get up and dressed. Peter's chains fall off. He follows the angel (all the while thinking that he is having a vision). The angel takes him past the guards and out of the iron gate into the city, which opens of its own accord. The angel leaves suddenly and it is only as Peter walks along this backstreet alone that he realizes that he has been party to an angelic escape from prison rather than an heavenly ascent or some other kind of vision with an angelic guide (Acts 12:6–11).

The detail of Peter needing space to accept that an angel had rescued him from jail (Acts 12:9, 11) suggests that the author of Acts recognizes how incredible this story must appear to the reader, yet he wants them to accepts it as true.

The Chinese house church pastor Brother Yun evidently feels the same in relating his own experience:[3] "What happened next is not possible from a human perspective, yet God is my witness that what I am about to tell you is the truth." The story Brother Yun narrates concerns his first escape from a Chinese jail. He has been imprisoned and tortured for preaching Christianity. Prior to his imprisonment he had a vision of a horrible black creature sit on him, choke him, and try to silence him. As he stopped breathing a great and strong angel carried him away to safety. In jail he was tortured for preaching Christ and in an attempt to make him give over the names of others in the Chinese house church movement. Bloodied and

2. See further, Nowell, "Archangel Raphael," 228–38.
3. Yun and Hattaway, *The Heavenly Man*, 65.

bruised in the interrogation room he reports that the Holy Spirit told him that the God of Peter was his God also. The rope tying his hands behind his back snapped. He kept the ropes in place and made off towards the toilet block as if he had need of it. In the toilet block he took the ropes off his hands and body and decided to escape over the eight foot high cement wall (with glass embedded on the top). He pulled himself up as high as he could and noticed a ten-foot wide, open septic tank on the other side. At this moment he felt somebody pick him up and throw him over—so far that he not only cleared the wall but also the septic tank. Brother Yun reports his belief that the angel he saw in his vision helped him over the wall.[4]

Many other stories could be added to this one. Brother Yun himself has many other remarkable stories, including further miraculous escapes from prison. The popular literature on angels in both the modern Christian and contemporary spirituality traditions attests many extraordinary experiences of angels coming to rescue people when they have lost hope.[5] However, these stories of angelic encounters focus on only one aspect of the ministry of angels as reported in the second temple Jewish and early Christian literatures.

ANGELS OF DEATH

Another role that angels fulfill is that of psychopomp, that is a guide to the world of the afterlife. Angels may be sent by God to gather the soul of a person whose time has come. This angelic role is best illustrated in a story. The *Testament of Abraham* tells the story of the angels Michael and Death being sent by God to perform this function.[6]

Abraham has led a righteous life and the time has come for him to shed this mortal coil. Having been blessed as the stars of heaven and the sand on the seashore during life, Abraham now has abundant wealth. Knowing this, God commands Michael, his angelic commander-in-chief, to inform Abraham of his impending demise so that he may put his affairs in order. So Michael appears to Abraham who welcomes him warmly and seemingly cheerfully throws a feast for him. (We are led to suspect that

4. Ibid., 60–65.

5. For examples, Anderson, *Where Angels Walk* and Hickey, *Angels All Around*.

6. What follows is a summary of the *Testament of Abraham* recension A which may be found in the Pseudepigrapha.

Abraham knows what this is all about as he hears a cypress tree praising God who "is summoning those who love him," and he hopes that Michael has not heard.) Michael is so overwhelmed by Abraham's hospitality that, with the excuse of needing to relieve himself, he disappears back to the court of heaven to tell God that he cannot go through with delivering the message as such a righteous man does not deserve to die, at least yet. God commands him to go through with it all the same.

After dinner, Isaac is sent to bed and all fall asleep, including Abraham and Michael. God sends Isaac a dream of Abraham's impending death. Isaac runs to Abraham, tells him of his dream, and crying he hugs and kisses his father. Sarah rushes in assuming Lot has died and is put straight on that by Michael who still fails to deliver the news. Sarah takes Abraham aside, recognizing Michael from the incident at Mamre (Gen 18:1–15). Then Sarah asks Isaac to explain his crying. Isaac recounts his dream, which Michael interprets—finally delivering the news. Abraham listens and accepts that Michael has a job to do. However, he refuses to go with him.

Michael becomes invisible and ascends to the court of heaven again. He asks the Almighty what he should do. God commands Michael to remind Abraham of his goodness to him and to instruct Abraham to follow Michael. Michael does as he is commanded. Abraham agrees to follow Michael if he takes him on a tour of the world. Michael does this. However, he has to cut the tour short as every time Abraham sees people sinning he destroys them. Instead they ascend into and tour the heavens. After the tour Michael requires Abraham to keep his side of the bargain. But Abraham refuses to go.

Michael ascends to heaven once again to complain of the difficulty of his task. The Most High summons Death whom he sends to receive the soul of Abraham. Abraham refuses to go with Death and so Death follows Abraham everywhere he goes—much to the annoyance of Abraham. Angrily Abraham tells Death that he will not go with him; he will only go with Michael. While the family surround Abraham, mourning his imminent demise, Death deceives Abraham into kissing his hand. Immediately his soul cleaves to death. Michael appears with multitudes of angels and they bear his precious soul into heaven with songs of praise.

Examples of angels in this role may be found in biblical literature. Jesus has angels in this role in his parable of Lazarus and the rich man:

> 19 There was a rich man who was dressed in purple and fine linen and who feasted sumptuously every day. 20 And at his gate lay a poor man named Lazarus, covered with sores, 21 who longed to satisfy his hunger with what fell from the rich man's table; even the dogs would come and lick his sores. 22 The poor man died and was carried away by the angels to be with Abraham.
>
> (Luke 16:19–22)

Lazarus dies and the angels take him to be with Abraham—that is, to eternal rest.[7] Again, we find the archangel Michael in this role in Jude 9: "But when the archangel Michael contended with the devil and disputed about the body of Moses, he did not dare to bring a condemnation of slander against him, but said, 'The Lord rebuke you!'" This text clearly refers to a story known to the recipients of the letter, although it is difficult for us to reconstruct it. However, it seems to have gone something like this. Moses dies and God sends Michael to bury him. Satan arrives at Mount Nebo and demands the body of Moses, accusing him of murder (cf. Exod 2:12). Michael calls this accusation slander and rebukes Satan. The devil was silenced and Michael took Moses body for burial.[8] When in the role of psychopomp, Michael appears to have found that things did not always go as smoothly as he might hope.

MEDIATORS OF THE COVENANT?

Another role which angels are said to have performed was the giving of the Torah on Mount Sinai. There is no reference to angels giving the Law in Exodus 19–20; indeed, *God* clearly gives the Law here. However, there seems to be some evidence that Jews in the second temple period believed that the angels were involved in the giving of the Torah. The New Testament refers to it four times:[9]

> 38 He is the one who was in the congregation in the wilderness with the angel who spoke to him at Mount Sinai, and with our ancestors; and he

7. On the location of Abraham's bosom, see Fitzmyer, *Luke X–XXIV*, 1132; Bock, *Luke 2*, 1368.

8. Bauckham, *Jude, 2 Peter*, 47–48, 65–76.

9. On Acts 7:38, 53, see Fitzmyer, *Acts*, 380, 385–86; Bock, *Acts*, 297, 306. On Gal 3:19, see Bruce, *Galatians*, 176–77; Martyn, *Galatians*, 356–57. On Heb 2:2, see Attridge, *Hebrews*, 64–65; Koester, *Hebrews*, 205. For a summary of the theory and evidence, see Langton, *Angel Teaching*, 91–94.

received living oracles to give to us ... 53 You are the ones that received the law as ordained by angels, and yet you have not kept it.

(Acts 7:38, 53)

19 Why then the law? It was added because of transgressions, until the offspring would come to whom the promise had been made; and it was ordained through angels by a mediator.

(Gal 3:19)

2 For if the message declared through angels was valid, and every transgression or disobedience received a just penalty

(Heb 2:2)

Certain Jewish texts have also been purported to bear witness to this tradition of angelic mediation of the Torah, most notably Josephus, *Ant.*15.5.3§136: "And for ourselves, we have learned from God the most excellent of our doctrines, and the most holy part of our law, by angels or ambassadors; for this name brings God to the knowledge of mankind, and is sufficient to reconcile enemies one to another." Some scholars dispute whether there is a body of Jewish texts bearing witness to this tradition and suggest that the word translated "angels" here in Josephus may refer to prophets (as Josephus uses it of both angels and prophets).[10] Andrew J. Bandstra offers a strong rebuttal of their arguments, asserting some kind of angelic mediation of the Torah in *Ant.* 15.5.3§136.[11] Moreover, there is no doubt that there is a body of tradition within Jewish literature from the earliest texts of the Hebrew Bible to late rabbinic texts that speaks of angelic presence at the giving of the Torah.[12] One example of such a text is found in Pseudo Philo's *Liber Antiquitatum Biblicarum* 11:5:[13]

10. Davies, "Note on Josephus," 135–40; Silberman, "Prophets/Angels," 91–101; Gaston, "Angels and Gentiles," 65–75.

11. Bandstra ("The Law and Angels," 225–29) reveals the flaws in the argument of Silberman and Gaston, demonstrating that Josephus does refer to the Jewish Law here and not international law as they suggest. Bandstra ("Law and Angels," 229–33) also reveals the inadequacies of Davies' arguments.

12. Silberman ("Prophets/Angels," 91–101) notes its presence in Deut 33:2 LXX, Mekhilta to Exodus 20:18, Babylonian Talmud tractate Shabbat 88a, Pesikta Rabbati 21 and Midrash Song of Songs Rabbah 21—although he notes that most of these texts are later than the New Testament.

13. The presence of the angels at the giving of the Law on Sinai is also mentioned

> And behold the mountains were ablaze with fire, the earth trembled, the hills shook, and the mountains were rolling themselves about, and the depths boiled, all the habitable world was shaken, the heavens folded up, the clouds dripped water, flames of fire burned, thunder and lightning abounded, winds and storms roared, the stars assembled, and angels ran ahead, until God should give the Law of his eternal covenant to the children of Israel and give everlasting commandments that will not pass away.

So even if angels are not involved directly in the giving of the Torah, they are certainly present at Sinai when it is given to Israel. Reviewing the scholarly debate on this issue, Darrell Hannah concludes:[14]

> Silberman ("Prophets/Angels") has questioned whether there was a Jewish tradition that the law was mediated by angels. He has quite rightly pointed out that all, bar one, of the rabbinic texts cited by Strack-Billerbeck in support of angelic mediation of the law in fact only attest angelic presence at the giving of the law. The one rabbinic text which could support the existence of such a tradition, CantR 1:2 (R. Yohanan [pA2]), is both late and obscure. Silberman, however, ignores entirely Acts 7:38, 53 and Gal 3:19, and proposes a reading of Heb 2:2 which will not stand scrutiny. In the end, he has missed the cumulative effect which results from reading Jub. 1:27–2:1; Apoc.Mos. preface; Acts 7:38, 53; Gal 3:19; Heb 2:2 and CantR 1:2 together. If the existence of the tradition cannot be said to be certain, it is nonetheless likely.

So angels were clearly present at the giving of the Law at Sinai in Jewish tradition and were most likely been party to its meditation.[15] Besides which, the fact that angelic mediation of the Torah may not be prominent in extra-biblical Jewish literature does not mean that it is not present in the New Testament—and it is difficult to read Acts 7:53 and Gal 3:19 any other way.

In some ways the roles of angels reviewed above are very familiar. Modern angel accounts frequently recount stories of rescue from imminent danger or the bringing of healing into situations that are past hope. They also provide accounts of the presence of angels at death. In these two kinds of story the ancient and biblical literature portray the role of the angels

---

in *L.A.B.* 23:10. This text most probably dates to the first century AD or soon after, see Harrington, "Pseudo-Philo," 2:300; Jacobson, *Pseudo-Philo*, 210–22. The *Liber Antiquitatum Biblicarum* is found in the Pseudepigrapha.

14. Hannah, *Michael and Christ*, 124 n. 5.

15. So also Najman, "Angels at Sinai," 313–33.

in very much the same way as the modern literature. However, there is a distinct difference when it comes to angels as mediators of the Law. As Susan Garrett suggests, much contemporary spirituality sees the problem from which angels are said to deliver people as ignorance rather than sin.[16] The idea that angels might enable people to know their own sinfulness and to become obedient to God is quite foreign to the modern spirit, although it is clearly there in the New Testament and probably also in other ancient Jewish literature. Although this may be the mediatorial role of angels against which the New Testament reacts (Gal 3:19; 1 Tim 2:5), Paul hardly encourages moral license or the centrality of self-realization to Christian spirituality. The New Testament authors emphasize the role of Christ as the one mediator (1 Tim 2:5) and the one who teaches obedience to the commands of God (e.g., Matt 23:8–10; John 14:21; Rom 6:17–18; 1 Cor 9:21; Gal 6:2). Far from enabling people to escape legalism or moral authority, angels appear to have helped to institute the commandments of God as the basic structure of the spiritual life—and the New Testament transfers this role to Christ and the Spirit.

16. Garrett, *No Ordinary Angel*, 41–46.

5

What Do Angels Look Like?

Art portrays angels in a variety of ways. In his "Angel of the Annunciation" Melozzo da Forlì paints Gabriel as a model of classical beauty—and the result is the rather effeminate male angel familiar to us from much art from the renaissance onwards.

In his "Adoration of the Shepherds", Philippe de Champaigne depicts three chubby cherubs hovering playfully above the group of shepherds who stare in wonder at the Christ child. Edward Burne-Jones creates angels who combine strength and delicacy with a distant air in his tapestry "Angeli Laudantes" ("Praising Angels").[1] And some contemporary photography portrays angels as sensitive muscular males with large feathered wings.[2] Effeminate males and chubby cherubs, both often winged, are two of the most popular images of angels in our culture—largely on account of the influence of artistic depictions. But what exactly do angels look like?

To answer the question we need to ask more about the nature of angels. Tradition asserts that angels are created. However the Old Testament can give the impression that angels were present before the creation of the world. So on one reading of the text, God suggests to the divine council on the sixth day of creation that they make humankind in their image (Gen 1:26).[3] God enters similar deliberations with the angels in the

---

1. For all these pictures, see Wilkinson, *Angels in Art*, plates 9, 16, and 19 respectively.

2. For example, "Fernando with Wings, 1993" by Blake Little, "Jason, 1995" by Kelly Grider, and "Untitled" by Giacomo Bianco in Bloncourt and Engelmann, *Visions of Angels*.

3. Wenham, *Genesis 1–15*, 27–28. See further Day, *God's Conflict*, 54–56; Gunkel,

divine council elsewhere (Gen 3:22; 11:7).[4] In the biblical book of Job, God asks Job the question: "Where were you when I laid the foundation of the earth? Tell me, if you have understanding. Who determined its measurements—surely you know! Or who stretched the line upon it? On what were its bases sunk, or who laid its cornerstone when the *morning stars* sang together and all the *heavenly beings* shouted for joy?" (Job 38:4–6). The angels again appear to be present at creation. Thus some scholars conclude that early Israelite images of the divine council picture angels (or the minor gods) as present at the creation of the world.[5] Elsewhere the Old Testament and Apocrypha attribute the creation of all in heaven including the heavenly hosts to God (Neh 9:6; 2 Macc 7:28; Sg Three 3:35–37, 39).[6] This problem of when the angels were created may be partially solved by the traditions we find in the book of Jubilees where the angels are created on the first day, immediately after the creation of heaven and earth (*Jub.* 2:2), enabling them to bless and praise God for establishing the foundations of the world as they do in Job (*Jub.* 2:3). The same kind of tradition is present in 4 Ezra 6:3 and 2 Bar. 21:6.[7]

Angels are created spirits. They are essentially incorporeal, they have no bodies. This is illustrated by the dilemma the archangel Michael reports to the LORD when Abraham has prepared a sumptuous feast for him (*T. Ab.* 5:9): "And the Commander-in-Chief [Michael] said, 'Lord, all the heavenly spirits are incorporeal, and they neither eat nor drink. Now he [Abraham] has set before me a table with an abundance of all the good things which are earthly and perishable. And now, Lord, what shall I do? How shall I escape his notice while I am sitting with him?'" Again, the book of *Jubilees* identifies the various angels, created on the first day of creation (angels of the presence and sanctification, and the angels in charge of various meteorological phenomena) as *spirits* who minister before God (*Jub.* 2:2a).

Creation and Chaos, 8–9.

4. Wenham, *Genesis 1–15*, 85, 241.

5. E.g., Day, *God's Conflict*, 54–56.

6. Heidt, *Angelology*, 23–25. See also Sollamo, "Creation of Angels," 277–82. Interestingly, she argues that the LXX of Job 38:6–7 is unclear as to whether angels were present on creation or sang on being created, ibid., 286–87. Possibly, Job 38:6–7 LXX bears witness to the same tradition concerning the creation of angels we find in *Jub.* 2:2–3 in the second temple period. 2 Maccabees and the Song of the Three are found in the Apocrypha.

7. Stone, *Fourth Ezra*, 156–57. 2 Baruch is found in the Pseudepigrapha.

Angels

As spirits, angels are not only incorporeal but also invisible—at least to humans and under normal circumstances. The biblical story of Balaam portrays this beautifully. Balaam has saddled his donkey and gone to curse the people of Israel on behalf of king Balak of Moab (Num 22:1–21). The angel of the LORD blocks his way but only the donkey can see him—initially neither Balaam nor his two servants see the angel (Num 22:22–30). The donkey tries to avoid the angel, who wields a drawn sword, and scrapes Balaam's foot in the attempt. The angel outmaneuvers the donkey who finally gives up and sits down. Balaam is furious and strikes the donkey, who retorts that the punishment is unjust as he is a very faithful donkey (Num 22:27–30). The LORD then opens Balaam's eyes and he sees the angel who berates him for striking the donkey and instructs him as to how he must prophesy (Num 22:31–35). Pseudo Philo recounts the story briefly in his early history of Israel but may have the angel open the eyes of Balaam (*L.A.B.* 18:9).[8] In his account of the same tale Josephus has the angel reveal himself to Balaam (*Ant.* 4.6.3§110). Regardless of who reveals the angel to be such, the original story and its retellings in the second temple period demonstrate that angels are invisible to people under normal circumstances but can be revealed such that people can see them.

Contrary to one stream of popular mythology, angels are not asexual. They do have gender so far as we can tell. Angels appear to be male and not simply in the way they appear to people on earth but in their essential heavenly nature. *Jubilees* depicts the angels of holiness, the angels of the presence, and the archangels as created circumcised (*Jub.* 15:27). This suggests that those angels are male in gender. The apocalyptic vision of 1 *En.* 83–90 depicts rebellious angels as having penises like those of horses (1 *En.* 86:4), which again depicts these angels as male. Although there are only a few second temple texts that depict angels as men, there are none that depict angels as women.[9] Nor are there texts that specify that angels are asexual. Although there are texts that depict angels as male, these texts do not depict *all* angels as male. Nonetheless the evidence we possess in the early Christian and Jewish texts suggests that the angels in heaven are created male. Angels are male spirits.[10]

---

8. Harrington, "Pseudo-Philo," 2:325 n. m; Jacobson, *Pseudo-Philo*, 592.

9. Sullivan, "Gender of Angels," 214–18.

10. Ibid., 211–28.

ENTERTAINING ANGELS UNAWARES

The biblical book of Hebrews counsels people to show hospitality to strangers for in doing so some have entertained angels unawares (Heb 13:2). The assumption in this instruction is that angels appear to be human—otherwise their angelic identity would surely be obvious.[11] There are plenty of stories in the biblical and extra-biblical literature where angels do appear as human beings.

In the story of Tobit the angel Raphael appears as a human being—Azariah, who claims to be a distant relative of Tobias and Anna (Tob 5:4–14). None of the main characters of the book (Tobias, Anna, Tobit, Raguel, or Sarah) seem to notice that this character is anything other than human until Raphael reveals himself to be one of the seven principal angels who stand before God (Tob 5:4b; 12:11–15). In the *Testament of Abraham* Michael appears as a human being to Abraham and his family. In the story of the three angels appearing to Abraham at the oaks of Mamre (Gen 18:1–15), the angels appear as human beings in both the biblical account and in Josephus (*Ant.*1.11.2§196–98)—except Josephus, unlike the biblical account, has the strangers reveal their identity as angels of God when Sarah laughs (*Ant.* 1.11.2§198).[12] In the biblical story of the birth of Samson, Manoah does not recognize the angel as such although his wife may suspect this, referring to the man of God she meets as looking like an angel (Judg 13:6, 16).[13] Pseudo Philo presents Manoah's wife as knowing that the visitor is angelic (*L.A.B.* 42:4) but Manoah himself is skeptical and does not believe that this stranger is a visitor until the angel has fire devour the sacrifice that Manoah lays upon his altar (*L.A.B.* 42:5a, 10). Josephus paints Manoah as a jealous husband who becomes suspicious when his wife tells him of the appearance of an angel who was remarkably good looking. Manoah does not accept that this beautiful visitor is anything other than a young man until the angel burns his sacrifice and ascends into heaven before their very eyes (*Ant.* 5.8.2–3§276–84). Within the biblical and extra-biblical writings angels appear in the form of human beings.

11. Attridge, *Hebrews*, 386.

12. *Jubilees* does not mention whether the angels were mistaken for humans by Abraham and Sarah (*Jub.* 16:1–4).

13. Butler, *Judges*, 326–29.

Angels

Interestingly not only do angels appear as young men (and never as women) but they often appear as very handsome young men. Josephus has the angel who appears to Manoah and his wife as sufficiently good-looking to provoke considerable jealousy and concern in Manoah (*Ant.* 5.8.2–3§276–84). In recounting the tale of Heliodorus attempting to misappropriate money set aside in the Jerusalem temple for sacrifices, the book of 2 Maccabees recounts how three angelic warriors prevented him following through his plan (2 Macc 3:1–30).[14] Two of these angelic warriors are described as extraordinarily strong, gloriously handsome, and well dressed (2 Macc 3:26). When Michael comes to inform Abraham of his impending demise, Abraham is clearly struck by how good looking he is, describing him as bright as the sun and very handsome, indeed more handsome than any other man on earth (*T. Ab.* 2:4–5). Michael also appears as a soldier (*T. Ab.* 2:2). So angels appear as handsome young men and often as good-looking military men.

There remains the question as to whether these angels actually *become* human beings or only *appear* as human. The test case for this appears to be whether angels eat or not. The manna of Exod 16 is described as angels' food in Ps 78:23–25.[15] However, there is little evidence outside of rabbinic tradition that angels eat (and even within rabbinic tradition it was debated).[16] Although Gen 19:3 has the three angels eat the food which Abraham prepared (which would suggest their having become physically human in some sense or other), the interpreters of the second temple literature and early Christianity disagreed. The Jewish philosopher Philo maintains that the angels only appeared to eat (*Abr.* 1:118). Josephus agrees that the angels only made a show of eating (*Ant.* 1.11.2§197). The early Christian writer Justin Martyr admits of some kind of eating but is keen to point out that it is not an earthly or human kind of eating (*Dial.* 57).[17] The dilemma that Michael presents to the LORD in the *Testament*

14. Goldstein, *2 Maccabees*, 212–13. The book of 2 Maccabees is found in the Apocrypha.

15. Hossfeld and Zenger, *Psalms 2*, 296. The LXX translates the Hebrew as "food of angels" retaining the tradition in the second temple period.

16. David Goodman, "Do Angels Eat?" 160–75. Rabbi Aqiba (*b. Yoma 75b*) supported the idea that angels ate but the majority of rabbis disagreed.

17. Ibid., 171. Only the later rabbinic work *Gen. Rab.* 48:14 seems to interpret Gen 19:3 as actual eating.

of Abraham (how can he remain incognito at a banquet given that angels do not eat?) is solved by the Most High, who sends an all-devouring spirit to consume the food that Michael *pretends* to eat (*T. Ab.* 4:10). When departing the family of Tobit for heaven, Raphael explains: "Although you were watching me, I really did not eat or drink anything—but what you saw was a vision" (Tob 12:19). Raphael makes it clear that what looked like eating was really a vision. Although the events were taking place on earth (rather than in a vision or dream, such as encounters with angels in ascents to heaven), the angel in physical form was seen as in a vision rather than actually taking on physical form.

There is a possible exception to this rule, which appears in the romantic novel of *Joseph and Aseneth*. This story explains how the righteous Joseph could possibly have married Aseneth, the daughter of the heathen Potiphera, priest of On (Gen 41:45)—the reason being that she converted, as the novel relates.[18] An angel visits Aseneth and eats honeycomb (*Jos. Asen.* 16:15). However this honeycomb is the only part of the meal that Aseneth prepares for her visitor (*Jos. Asen.* 15:14–15; 16:1–2, 15). The angel specifically requests the honeycomb and makes it appear in the larder miraculously (*Jos. Asen.* 16:2–11). The angel explains that this is heavenly food (*Jos. Asen.* 16:14). This angel does not eat earthly food and so is no exception to the rule. As there are therefore no exceptions to the rule, it is reasonable to conclude that angels do not take on the physical form.

So angels *appear* in human form but do not *become* human. In this, they are very different to the Word (John 1:14). One reason that Luke is keen to depict the risen Jesus as eating (Luke 24:37–43) may be so that the risen Christ is understood to be a *human* person, Jesus, risen from the dead and *not an angel*.[19] Angels do not eat—or, at least, that was the ancient general consensus. However they appear human. Where they are described in detail, they appear as young men and often as very handsome soldiers.

ALL GLORIOUS BELOW

Angels also appear to human beings in their heavenly glory. Such an appearance is sometimes described as an angelophany. There are various accounts of angelophanies in both the biblical and extra-biblical literature. In

18. *Joseph and Aseneth* is found in the Pseudepigrapha.
19. Goodman, "Do Angels Eat?" 168.

his heavenly ascent Zephaniah sees the angel Eremiel, the angel over the abyss and Hades: "Then I arose and stood, and I saw a great angel standing before me with his face shining like the rays of the sun in its glory since his face is like that which is perfected in its glory. And he was girded as if a golden girdle were upon his breast. His feet were like bronze which is melted in a fire" (*Apoc. Zeph.* 6:11–12).

The angel Iaoel, who guides Abraham through his heavenly ascent, appears in glorious form to Abraham: "The appearance of his body was like sapphire, and the aspect of his face was like chrysolite, and the hair of his head was like snow. And a *kidaris* [headdress] was on his head, its look like that of a rainbow, and the clothing of his garments was purple; and a golden staff was in his right hand" (*Apoc. Ab.* 11:2–3).

The angel who appears to Aseneth, again manifests himself in glorious form: "And Aseneth raised her head and saw, and behold, there was a man in every respect similar to Joseph, by the robe and the crown and the royal staff, except that his face was like lightning, and his eyes like sunshine, and the hairs of his head like a flame of fire of a burning torch, and hands and feet like iron shining forth from a fire, and sparks shot forth from his hands and feet" (*Jos. Asen.* 14:9).

The book of Daniel also contains a similar vision of a glorious angel: "I looked up and saw a man clothed in linen, with a belt of gold from Uphaz around his waist. His body was like beryl, his face like lightning, his eyes like flaming torches, his arms and legs like the gleam of burnished bronze, and the sound of his words like the roar of a multitude" (Dan 10:5–6). So it is clear that in the literature Angels sometimes appear to human beings—not least before some revelation of heavenly mysteries and particularly an ascent into heaven—in their heavenly glory, an appearance which generally terrifies the beholder.

Given the glorious way in which angels appear to people in the Old Testament and extra-biblical literature, what is intriguing about the ange-lophanies of the New Testament is how low key they are by comparison. Although the beholders are often clearly afraid, the appearance of the an-gel is either not described or hardly described. When Gabriel appears to Zechariah (Luke 1:11) and Mary (Luke 1:26–27), there is no description of his appearance. When the angel of the LORD appears to the shepherds, the shining of the glory of the LORD is mentioned but no description of the glory of the angel. Similarly, the angel who appears to Cornelius is not described (Acts 10:3). And the second time an angel appears to rescue Peter from jail, an accompanying light shines in the prison cell but there is no real description of the angel (Acts 12:7a). In fact, the nearest we get to an angelophany of any description is in Matthew's account of the resurrection. As the women come to the tomb an angel descends from heaven with a great earthquake, Matthew describes his appearance: "His appearance was like lightning, and his clothing was white as snow" (Matt 28:2). This is not a great deal of information for an angelophany and it is hardly the most glorious angelophany in the literature. One suspects that Matthew might even be slightly light-hearted in his use of the tradition as he paints the rather casual picture of the angel sitting on the stone which covered the entrance to the tomb after rolling it back—not the most majestic action an angel could perform.[20] There may be a reluctance amongst the NT writers to use the angelophanic traditions of second temple Judaism just as Paul is reluctant to recommend the search for spiritual experiences such as heavenly ascents. The focus is to be on *Christ*, instead. Indeed it is probably not a coincidence that the nearest we get to an angelophany in the New Testament is the vision of Christ in Rev 1:12–16.[21]

WHAT CHERUBIM ARE REALLY LIKE

Not all angels take human form, however. The now traditional way of depicting cherubs in western art as cute little children with wings is a far cry from the picture in the OT and the second temple literature. The cherubim of the OT are indeed winged creatures (1 Kgs 6:23–35). Ezekiel pictures them as creatures with four faces and four wings that sparkle like bronze. They have straight legs, calves' hooves for feet and human hands under

20. For the angelophany here see Davies and Allison, *Matthew*, 3:660–61, 665–66. However, I cannot agree that that the motif of the angel seated on the rolled away tombstone is "an elevated posture of triumph" (ibid., 3:665)—rolling away a tombstone is hardly comparable to military victory for a heavenly warrior, surely? And the angel did not raise Jesus from the dead so he cannot claim that victory either.

21. For a discussion of this text as drawing on angelophanic traditions, see Rowland, "Risen Christ," 1–11, and Collins, "Son of Man," 548–58. For the form of the text as a christophany (revelation of Christ) identifying Christ with God, see the majority of commentators, e.g., Beale, *Revelation*, 205–22. Collins ("Son of Man," 548–58) suggests that reading Christ as divine here involves downplaying the angelic elements. She reads Christ as a principal angel figure here but arguably only achieves this reading by downplaying the divine elements of the christophany.

their wings. They each have the face of an eagle, of a lion, of an ox, and of a human being (Ezek 1:5–12; for their identification as cherubim, Ezek 10:15). Elsewhere Ezekiel describes cherubim as having two faces, the one of a young lion and the other of a human being (Ezek 41:18–19). Clearly there were different sorts of cherubim in the OT. However, they are all composite creatures or mixed beasts. They look like they are made of up different limbs from various different animals and human beings.[22]

The depiction of the cherubim as mixed beasts continues into the second temple period. Drawing on the image of the cherubim as the throne-chariot of the LORD (2 Sam 22:11; Ezek 1:4–28), the *Ladder of Jacob* proclaims: "LORD God of Adam your creature and LORD God of Abraham and Isaac my fathers and of all who have walked before you in justice! You who sit firmly on the cherubim and the fiery throne of glory . . . and the many eyed ones just as I saw in my dread, holding the four-faced cherubim, bearing also the many-eyed seraphim" (*Lad. Jac.* 2:6–8).[23]

The LORD is seated upon the cherubim as his throne-chariot and they remain many-faced. The same tradition seems to inform the picture of the living creatures around the throne in the vision of John on Patmos (Rev 4:6–8):

> Around the throne, and on each side of the throne, are four living crea-
> tures, full of eyes in front and behind: 7 the first living creature like a
> lion, the second living creature like an ox, the third living creature with a
> face like a human face, and the fourth living creature like a flying eagle.
> 8 And the four living creatures, each of them with six wings, are full of
> eyes all around and inside. Day and night without ceasing they sing,
> "Holy, holy, holy, the Lord God the Almighty, who was and is and is to
> come."

Although the creatures do not have four faces each like their counterparts in Ezekiel, the parallels with the living creatures of Ezekiel 1 are sufficiently strong to suggest that these creatures are modeled on them and so are likely cherubim.[24]

By way of summary, angels appear in many forms. The most common way in which they appear to people is in human form. However they appear

---

22. Hartenstein, "Cherubim and Seraphim," 155–88. For an intriguing discussion of the angels of Rev 4:1–11 as stars, see Malina and Pilch, *Revelation*, 75–76, 85–86.

23. The *Ladder of Jacob* is found in the Pseudepigrapha.

24. Beale, *Revelation*, 328–31.

human rather than taking on human nature. Their appearance is, in a sense, visionary even when they are seen in the cold light of day rather than in dream visions. They sometimes appear in heavenly majesty and often when they are to announce a great heavenly mystery or take a righteous person on a tour of heaven. Angels are spirits but not spirits as we know them. They are spirits of the male gender with some kind of discernibly bodily form. This may explain why they always appear as men on earth—and, as we have observed, often as very handsome warriors.

6

Do Angels Have Sex?

This question may come as something of a surprise. Many people simply assume that angels do not have sex. This assumption goes with the equivalent assumption that angels do not have gender. At one level these assumptions seem to make sense. If angels are everlasting (and there is little to suggest that angels die), then they have no need to procreate. If they have no need to procreate, then they have no need for gender. The idea that angels might engage in sex purely for pleasure seems quite foreign to many people. Angels are different from human beings in this regard.

This set of assumptions ought at least to be questioned. The ancient texts provide a rather different picture. That angels are male comes as a surprise to many people given the common assumption that angels are asexual, but male they are. The question of whether angels are asexual and sexually inactive ought to be asked of the ancient texts. The prevalence of this view may be partly the result of the dominance of the teaching of Jesus in this respect. In a debate with the Sadducees about the resurrection of the dead, Jesus declares of the resurrected righteous: "When they rise from the dead, they *neither marry nor are given in marriage*, but are *like angels in heaven*" (Mark 12:25). The general consensus seems to be that this text suggests that there is no sexual activity either amongst the resurrected dead or amongst the angels in heaven.[1] Recently Ben Witherington has suggested another reading, that Jesus does not suggest that marriage ceases to exist in the resurrection but rather that levirate marriage ceases to exist (the form

---

1. France, *Mark*, 474; Marcus, *Mark 8–16*, 833–34, cf. Davies and Allison, *Matthew*, 3:229. See also, Flusser, "Resurrection and Angels," 568–72.

on marriage in which if a man dies childless his brother marries his wife to produce children for his brother and so keep the family line going). In the resurrection there will be no death and so levirate marriage becomes unnecessary.[2] Whether or not Witherington is correct, the general interpretation has certainly made its mark on the popular consciousness, which assumes that angels do not have sex.

So do angels have sex? Only the wicked ones. There is an ancient tradition that as angels are everlasting they have no need of procreation. The judgment speech that God commissions Enoch to pronounce on some fallen angels includes this: "But you originally existed as spirits, living forever, and not dying for all the generations of eternity; therefore I did not make women among you" (*1 En.* 15:6–7a). The angelic ideal here suggests that angels have no need of sexual activity or female partners as there is no need to procreate to repopulate the angel world after the deaths of angels because, once created, angels do not die. (Incidentally the text is further evidence that angels are male as God created no women amongst them).[3] However, as the judgment speech notes, not all angels kept to this original plan.

The story of the Fall of the Watchers tells of angels who left their heavenly abode to have sex with the daughters of men, whom they found attractive. The story begins with an odd little text in Genesis:

> When people began to multiply on the face of the ground, and daughters were born to them, 2 the sons of God saw that they were fair; and they took wives for themselves of all that they chose. 3 Then the LORD said, "My spirit shall not abide in mortals forever, for they are flesh; their days shall be one hundred twenty years." 4 The Nephilim were on the earth in those days—and also afterward—when the sons of God went in to the daughters of humans, who bore children to them. These were the heroes that were of old, warriors of renown."
>
> (Gen 6:1–4)

The sons of God are most likely the angels.[4] Certainly they were interpreted as angels in second temple literature where we find this myth retold a number of times and in a variety of interpretations.[5]

2. Witherington, *Jesus Quest,* 169.

3. Nickelsburg, *1 Enoch 1,* 272.

4. See Wenham, *Genesis 1–15,* 139–41 for a discussion of the interpretations of the phrase.

5. For a discussion of various accounts of this myth, see Stuckenbruck, "'Angels' and

Angels

Probably the earliest retelling of this story is found in the Book of the Watchers.[6] *1 Enoch 6–11* recounts how humanity multiplied on earth and the beauty of their daughters attracted the attention of the (angelic) Watchers in heaven. Under their leader Shemihazah they made a pact to go to earth and take wives from these beautiful human women. They did so, and taught their brides sorcery and magic. The children of these marriages were giants who soon began to wreak havoc on earth. The fallen angels taught all humanity heavenly secrets which led to the spread of godlessness on earth. The four archangels Michael, Sariel, Raphael, and Gabriel bring news of the chaos on earth (the angel marriages, and the angels teaching sorcery and heavenly mysteries to humanity) to the Most High. By way of response the Most High commissions the angels: Sariel to tell Noah to prepare for the coming flood; Raphael to bind up Asael (who was particularly implicated in the teaching of secrets) and cast him into outer darkness until the day of judgment, and to heal the earth; Gabriel to destroy the giants by setting them at war against each other; and Michael to bind up Shemihazah and his associates ready for punishment in the fiery abyss on the day of judgment, and then to renovate the earth.

A variation of the myth appears in the Animal Apocalypse (*1 En.* 86:1—89:1).[7] A star falls from heaven to earth and pastures amongst the cattle of earth. Many other stars follow its example and fall from heaven to pasture amongst the cattle of earth. Then these stars become bulls and mount the cows, who conceive, bearing elephants, camels, and asses. These animals then begin to devour the (earthly rather than angelic) bulls, which turn and flee in fear. Then four white men emerge from heaven with three others, which three lift Enoch (the seer) to a high tower to observe what happens next. One of the four white men catches the original fallen star and throws it bound into the abyss. Another gives a sword to the elephants, camels, and asses, which proceed to kill one another. Another gathers and binds all the other star bulls and throws them into the abyss.

'Giants,'" 354–77.

6. Nickelsburg dates this texts to 323–302 BC (*1 Enoch* 1, 169–71). For discussions of the historical setting of the myth, see Hanson, "Rebellion in Heaven," 195–233; Nickelsburg, "Apocalyptic and Myth," 383–405; Suter, "Fallen Angel, Fallen Priest," 115–35.

7. Nickelsburg, *1 Enoch* 1, 372–74. He dates the texts to 165–163 BC (ibid., *1 Enoch* 1, 360–61).

The last white man informs another white bull of a mystery and that bull builds a boat. The storyline is essentially the same except that it is told in full mythological color.

The book of *Jubilees* recounts the story similarly—only with certain extra details (*Jub.* 5:1–11; 7:21–24; 10:5–14). Attracted to the daughters of human beings, certain angels descended to earth and took them as wives. They bore children, the giants or Naphidim. The giants all killed each other and humankind. Injustice and violence increased upon earth, affecting all species. Humanity harbored nothing but evil desires and lawlessness reigned. The LORD looked down and saw the injustice of the earth. God had the fallen angels bound and cast into the abyss. The giants were set to war against each other until they killed each other—their parents looking on all the while from the places they were kept pending the judgment. The souls of the giants became the evil spirits or demons. Nine tenths of these were sent to the place of judgment but Mastema, the chief of the demons, was allowed to keep one tenth to help him do hit work amongst human beings.[8]

Fragments of the story appear elsewhere in the literature of the period. In an ascent into heaven in the *Book of Parables* (*1 En.* 37–71) Enoch is shown the angels who descended to the earth and taught them the heavenly mysteries, leading them astray (*1 En.* 64:1–2). In the *Genesis Apocryphon*, Lamech (the father of Noah) worries that Noah is not really his son but the progeny of the Watchers.[9] He approaches his wife Bitenosh and asks her frankly if the child is his. Understandably, Bitenosh becomes angry and tells Lamech in no uncertain terms that the child belongs to him and reproaches him for the mood that has brought this on (*1QapGen ar* ii 1–17). Lamech asks his father Methuselah who in turn consults Enoch to discover the truth (*1QapGen ar* ii 19–26). Enoch replies that the boy is definitely the son of Lamech and not of one of the Watchers (*1QapGen ar* v 1–4). The same story may be found in the final sections of *1 Enoch*, prefacing a prophecy of the flood (*1 En.* 106:1–18).

Another fragmentary use of the story is found in an exorcistic text amongst the Dead Sea Scrolls.

---

8. This story explains the origin of demons, cf. Alexander, "Demonology," 2:331–53—although Andrew Reimer questions whether this works as an aetiology for all demons ("Rescuing the Fallen Angels," 334–53).

9. The *Genesis Apocryphon* is found in the Dead Sea Scrolls.

> An incantation in the name of YHWH. Invoke at anytime 5 the heavens. When he comes upon you in the night, you shall say to him: who are you, oh offspring of man and of seed of the holy ones? Your face is a face of 7 delusion, and your horns are horns of illusion. You are darkness and not light, 8 injustice and not justice, . . . the chief of the army. YHWH will bring you down 9 to the deepest Sheol, he will shut the two bronze gates through which no 10 light penetrates. On you shall not shine the sun, which rises 11 upon the just man to . . .
>
> (*11Q11* v 4–11)

The addressee is assumed to be plagued by visitations from a demon. The demon is the result of the angel marriages—offspring of humanity and angelic seed.

It has been suggested that one of these fragmentary references to the story may be found in Paul in 1 Cor 11:10. Paul argues that in worship women ought to cover their heads "because of the angels." One explanation of this phrase was that women must cover their heads because uncovered heads are a disgrace that would offend the angels who are present at the public worship of the church. Another explanation of this difficult phrase is that the women must cover their heads so as not to attract the angels, to avoid a repeat of the kind of problems that we find in the Watchers myth.[10]

The Watchers myth provides the closest thing to a plausible background to another tricky text in 1 Corinthians. Paul admonishes members of the congregation for taking each other to court, arguing that they ought to have the wisdom to settle their disputes between themselves (1 Cor 6:1–7). Drawing on the tradition that the people of God have always settled disputes within the community, he asks why they would want to take their disputes before people from outside the community of faith. Paul asks the Corinthians whether they realize that they will judge the nations and that they will judge angels (1 Cor 6:2–3). This judgment of angels takes place on the Day of Judgment. The Watcher myth has Enoch sent by God to admonish the angels and pronounce the judgment of God on them (*1 En.* 12–16; 4Q204 1 vi 14–15) and it has the Watchers judged on the Day of Judgment (4QEnoch 1 iv 22–23). There is no explicit mention of Enoch meting out judgments on that Day so the parallel is not exact. However, it seems to be the nearest parallel to the judgment of angels by humans (1 Cor 6:3) and

10. Lietaert Peerbolte, "Man, Woman, and the Angels," 76–92.

demonstrates that such a notion was not foreign to second temple Judaism and early Christianity.[11]

In a rather different vein, Philo uses the story as moral exhortation (*Giants* 1:6–19). His commentary on Gen 6:2 identifies the sons of God as angels and compares them to human souls, or what his contemporaries in Greek philosophy called *daemons*. Just as there can be good souls and bad souls, or good and evil daemons, so there can be good and evil angels— Philo argues that angels exist and that the story must not be dismissed as a fable. The good angels remained in heaven where they served God in administrating the affairs of humanity. The evil angels were overtaken by attraction for these human women and married them, "some choosing them by the sight, and others by the ear, others again being influenced by the sense of taste, or by the belly, and some even by the pleasures below the belly" and so they fell from their higher calling (*Giants* 1:18). Although Philo takes the story seriously as part of Torah, he deals with it not so much as an episode in ancient history or prehistory as a moral tale from which his contemporaries can learn the virtue of the pursuit of truth and wisdom and the shunning of physical pleasures.[12]

One suggestion concerning the evident widespread popularity of this myth in both Jewish and early Christian traditions is that it acts as an aetiology, or explanation of the origin, of evil. If the myth of the fall of the Watchers stems from the third century or fourth century BC, then it may predate the times when the story of Adam and Eve was interpreted as the origin of evil.[13] As an aetiology of *angelic* evil, this makes sense. However, the suggestion that this is an aetiology of *evil itself*, which replaces the narrative of Gen 2–3 as an explanation of human sin, is less convincing. In all likelihood the Genesis narrative is earlier than the Watchers myth, and the Genesis narrative has Eve and Adam disobey the command of God (Gen 3:3, 11) for which God curses them (Gen 3:14–19). It is difficult to read disobedience towards God as anything other than evil, especially when it evidently incurs God's displeasure. The explanation of the myth as a way of coming to terms with the violence which scarred Palestine during the wars of the Diodochi (323–302 BC) seems to make more sense of the myth. The warring Macedonian chieftains regarded themselves as sons of the gods,

11. Fitzmyer, *First Corinthians*, 252.

12. See further Dillon, "Philo's Doctrine of Angels," 197–205.

13. Reed, *Fallen Angels*, 24–57.

parodied in the myth as sons of evil angels whose work did little but wreak havoc and violence. However, as Nickelsburg notes, the identification of the historical setting of the work is hypothetical and so remains tentative.[14]

Less speculative is the use to which the myth was put in the *Testaments of the Twelve Patriarchs*.[15] Reuben urges his children to stay chaste despite the predilection of youthful ignorance towards sexual promiscuity (*T. Reu.* 2:8–9). He particularly warns against being seduced by the charms of beautiful women, noting how in the Watchers myth this only led to evil (*T. Reu.* 5:5–6). Naphtali gives similar advice to his offspring, warning them not to behave like the Watchers and the inhabitants of Sodom and Gomorrah (*T. Naph.* 3:4–5). The myth is used as a warning against sexual immorality in humans. The biblical book of Jude uses the myth similarly. Certain new members of the congregation appear to indulge in sexual immorality and believe their faith can accommodate such behavior (Jude 4, 7–8). Jude warns the congregation: "And the angels who did not keep their own position, but left their proper dwelling, he has kept in eternal chains in deepest darkness for the judgment of the great Day" (Jude 6). The story is easily recognized. The proper abode of the angels is heaven and the keeping in chains awaiting the Day of Judgment appears in the myth as told in both *1 Enoch* and *Jubilees*. Jude refers to the story to encourage the congregation not to imitate the licentious behavior of these new members of the church.[16]

2 Peter uses the story similarly. The context is a warning that false prophets will infiltrate the congregation with their arrogance, deceitful teaching, and licentious behavior. Then comes the warning:

> For if God did not spare the angels when they sinned, but cast them into hell [Gk. *tartaros*] and committed them to chains of deepest darkness to be kept until the judgment; 5 and if he did not spare the ancient world, even though he saved Noah, a herald of righteousness, with seven others, when he brought a flood on a world of the ungodly . . . 10 Bold and willful, they are not afraid to slander the glorious ones, 11 whereas angels, though greater in might and power, do not bring against them a slanderous judgment from the Lord. 12 These people, however, are like irrational animals, mere creatures of instinct, born to be caught and

14. Nickelsburg, *1 Enoch 1*, 170.

15. The *Testaments of the Twelve Patriarchs* (including the *Testament of Reuben* and the *Testament of Naphtali*) are found in the Pseudepigrapha.

16. Bauckham, *Jude, 2 Peter*, 50–53. See also Charles, "Angels under Reserve," 39–48; Suter, "Fallen Angel, Fallen Priest," 134.

killed. They slander what they do not understand, and when those creatures are destroyed, they also will be destroyed, 13 suffering the penalty for doing wrong.

(2 Pet 2:4–5, 10–13)

Again the story is recognizable from the reference to angelic sin and punishment in being cast into hell (Gk. *tartaros*) to await the judgment—and not least from its position before the story of Noah (the author takes the stories in the biblical order in 2 Pet 2). 2 Peter uses the story to assure the faithful that the false prophets that are plaguing the church will receive the punishment due on the Day of Judgment.[17]

So angels are probably male and thus have gender. However, as beings that are created everlasting (at least according to *1 Enoch*), they have no need of sex as they have no need of procreation to repopulate their numbers as a result of death. Nonetheless, some angels preferred to pursue their desires rather than to worship God by showing obedience to the commands of God. This theme in the myth is used by Jude to encourage Christian believers to follow the path of obedience to God over and above the path of the pursuit of desire—even though some of their number clearly believe and recommend that one can do both. Such themes are not far from modern spirituality. There is a stream of contemporary angelology that teaches that knowledge of angels is about finding the fulfillment of one's desires.[18] Although they may not claim angelic revelation as the root of their doctrine, there are streams within the modern churches that teach something similar in presenting the Christian faith primarily in terms of self-fulfillment and achieving wholeness. Unfashionable today as it seems to have been then (at least amongst some), Jude prefers to warn his readers that following the path of self-fulfillment over and above the path of obedience to Christ puts them under judgment. Conversely obedience brings ultimate healing.

---

17. Bauckham, *Jude, 2 Peter*, 248–49.

18. See the superb discussion and critique in Garrett, *No Ordinary Angel*, 70–102.

7

Do People Become Angels When They Die?

From time immemorial people have asked the question of whether there is any life after death. One popular notion is that our souls become angels and live with God in heaven for eternity. Flowers given to commemorate the death of a loved one often contain cards that suggest that the angel of the deceased now watches over us from heaven. Folk religion assumes that we become angels when we die.

Traditionally Judaism and Christianity have asserted that angels are different from human beings. Angels do not become human and humans do not become angels. The story of creation in *Jubilees* has angels created on the first day of creation as eternal spirits who administer heaven (*Jub.* 2:2) and human beings created on the sixth day of creation as physical people who rule over earth (*Jub.* 2:14). The two species, angels and humans, are different from each other, are created to perform different roles, and were created at different times. This echoes the LXX translation of Ps 8, which claims that God has created humankind "a little lower than *the angels*" (Ps 8:6 LXX).[1] The two species of angels and humans are different and one does not become the other. Therefore, people are unlikely to become angels when they die.

However, the ancient Jewish and Christian literature that we are examining is not as clear cut as one might wish. There is quite a bit of discussion

1. Ps 8:5 in the English translation. For a brief discussion of how the different early translations of the OT understood and so translated the Hebrew text here, see Craigie, *Psalms 1–50*, 108. It is worth noting that the Hebrew text reads "a little lower than the *elohim*" which is almost certainly refers not to God but to the divine council (hence the LXX translation as "the angels").

and debate about these issues amongst the scholars who study these texts, and the texts are by no means easy to interpret—at least to the satisfaction of all concerned.

BECOMING ANGELS

Currently there is much discussion over whether there is such a rigid distinction between angels and human beings. Some scholars assert that the Jewish and Christian literature we are examining bear witness to certain human beings who become angels—they often refer to this as angelomorphism (turning into an angel). They also bear witness to angels becoming human.[2] If the line between angels and humanity is thinner than tradition makes out, then maybe there is some evidence in the ancient texts for the idea that people become angels when they die.

Angels certainly appear to have human form, or aspects of human form. Angels appearing in glorious angelophanies have some human features too. An example of this is the angel in Daniel 10 whom Daniel describes as a man, having face, body, waist, arms, and legs like a man. However, his body is like the jewel beryl, his face was like lightning, his eyes like torches, and his arms and legs shining like bronze. This "man" is clearly not a normal human being and this angel can hardly be described as such. Rather this angel has the outline of a human form but its body is of a different order. The angel appears in a vision in its heavenly glory, which glory signals that it is not a human but a heavenly being. It would be a mistake to interpret the language of human form as suggesting that the angel appears

---

2. The scholarly debate over angelomorphism is principally about the nature of heavenly beings, and particularly about the nature of Christ (did the earliest Christian disciples think he was God or an angel or the principal or chief angel? And why did they worship him?) and less about whether human beings become angels when they die. However, its relevance to the question is clear—if humans can become angels, then they may become angels on death. Key texts in this debate include: Charlesworth, "Portrayal of the Righteous," 135–51; Fossum, *Name of God*; Fletcher-Louis, *Luke-Acts*, 109–215; Carrell, *Jesus and the Angels*, 53–97; Gieschen, *Angelomorphic Christology*; Sullivan, *Wrestling with Angels*. Important texts in the related question of why the earliest disciples worshipped Jesus (was it because he was God? Or did people used to worship angels? Could they have worshipped Jesus as an angel?) include: Hurtado, *One God*, 71–124; Bauckham, "Worship of Jesus," 118–49; Davis, "Divine Agents," 479–503; Stuckenbruck, *Angel Veneration*. See further Hurtado, "First Century Jewish Monotheism," 3–26; Hannah, *Michael and Christ*; Stuckenbruck, "'Angels' and 'God,'" 45–70; Wold, *Men, Women and Angels*.

as human, let alone actually took on human nature. The angels Eremiel in *Apocalypse of Zephaniah* 6, Iaoel *Apocalypse of Abraham* 11, and the angel of *Joseph and Aseneth* 14 are all of the same order, appearing as having a human form in some respects but clearly appearing as being of a different order.[3] Angels in angelophanies appear in glorious superhuman form and are not to be mistaken for human beings. Therefore, such angels provide no evidence of the line between angels and humans being crossed. In these visions the distinction between angels and humanity is maintained.

Nonetheless angels do appear as human beings elsewhere, where they are supposed to appear to be in human, rather than superhuman, form. Raphael appears as Azariah in the book of Tobit. Michael appears as a handsome young soldier in the *Testament of Abraham*. Even so the texts are at pains to point out that although the angels *appear* like normal human beings—and are mistaken for such by real human beings—they are *actually* angels. Michael is unable to eat apart from the devouring spirit which the Most High sends to make it appear to Abraham that he is eating (*T. Ab.* 4:5–11). On revealing his true identity to the family of Tobit, Raphael explains that they only saw him in a vision—he was not really a human person (Tob 12:19). Moreover, these angels appear as human solely for the duration of their mission. The only possible exception to this rule is found in the *Prayer of Joseph*. In this text, the angel Israel claims to have become the human Jacob.

> I, Jacob, who is speaking to you, am also Israel, an angel of God and a ruling spirit. 2 Abraham and Isaac were created before any work. 3 But, I, Jacob who men call Jacob but whose name is Israel am he who God called Israel which means, a man seeing God, because I am firstborn of every living thing to whom God gives life. 4 And when I was coming up from Syrian Mesopotamia, Uriel, the angel of God, came forth and said that "I [Jacob-Israel] had descended to earth and had tabernacled among men and that I had been called by the name of Jacob."

The angel Israel-Jacob becomes the human Jacob and Uriel is named as the angel with whom he wrestles. However, the text is fragmentary and so it is not clear whether Israel-Jacob only appeared human (as Raphael did when

---

3. That the angel in *Joseph and Aseneth* 14–16 eats honeycomb is no evidence that it is human. The honeycomb is procured miraculously from heaven and is the heavenly food of angels, made by the bees of Paradise (*Jos. Asen.* 16:14–15). See Sullivan, *Wrestling with Angels*, 187–88. The boundaries between angels and humanity are maintained here.

Azariah) or whether the angel actually became human. So it is possible that an angel has become human here, though not entirely certain. Generally angels only appear human rather than becoming human, and they take on human appearance only temporarily, keeping their angelic nature which they retain permanently. Again the line between humanity and angels remains pretty much unbroken.[4]

Although there is little to suggest that angels take on human nature, some scholars argue that the available evidence suggests that humans might take on angelic nature. There are texts in which they claim that human beings are angelomorphic—that is, they take on angelic form. They argue that the second temple Jewish literature and early Christian literature at points portray Adam, Abel, Seth, Enoch, Noah, Melchizedek, Jacob, Moses, David, some of the prophets, John the Baptist, Jesus, Stephen, Paul, Taxo, the High Priest (in the work of the Jewish historian Hecataeus of Abdera), and the daughters of Job in angelomorphic terms.[5]

However, the evidence is not wholly convincing. As we saw above, Jacob (in the *Prayer of Joseph*) is not a case of a human becoming angelic but of an angel appearing or possibly becoming human.[6] In the *Life of Adam and Eve*, Adam in heaven before the Fall is said to look like God, not to be an angel (*L.A.E.* 13:1–3; 14:2).[7] In the *Testament of Abraham*, the heavenly Abel *looks like* an angel (*T. Ab.* 12:4) but the angelic commander-in-chief Michael identifies him as a man (*T. Ab.* 13:2). Enoch ascends into heaven where the LORD welcomes him to live forever among the angels, clothed in robes of heavenly glory and he becomes *like* the angels rather than becoming one of them (*2 En.* 22:5–10). In the Watcher traditions, Noah does not become an angel (*1 En.* 106:2–6). Rather he looks so wonderful and radiant that Lamech suspects that Bitenosh had him by a Watcher, although this is not the case—the child belongs to Lamech and is fully human. In the ancient drama the *Exagogue* of Ezekiel the Tragedian, Moses ascends into heaven in a dream and views the armies of angels marching before him but Ezekiel does not mention him becoming angelic in any way (Ezek. Trag. 68–82).[8] In the *Testament of Job* the daughters of Job sing in the tongues

---

4. Ibid., 37–83.

5. See Gieschen, *Angelomorphic Christology*, 152–83.

6. Ibid., 159; Sullivan, *Wrestling with Angels*, 100–101.

7. The *Life of Adam and Eve* is found in the Pseudepigrapha.

8. The *Exagogue* of Ezekiel the Tragedian is found in the Pseudepigrapha.

of angels but they do not become angels (*T. Job* 48–50). Moreover the breeching of the worlds of angels and humans in the story of the Fall of the Watchers was deemed to be a great evil which implies that many ancients believed the blurring of the distinctions between angelic nature and human nature to be undesirable—and the fact that this story was well known suggests that this view was common. A careful review of the relevant literature tends to suggest that the Jewish and Christian literature in the period we are examining maintains the distinction between humanity and angels.[9]

So, human beings do not appear to become angels while they are still alive and they do not seem to become angels when they are translated into heaven permanently, like Enoch or Abel. That some human beings may be sufficiently righteous or special that they appear like angels is demonstrated by the Watcher traditions that have Noah look like this. However this story demonstrates that appearances can mislead as Noah remained wholly human.

SHINING LIKE STARS

Nevertheless some scholars argue that the literature does picture some people becoming angels when they die. The biblical book of Daniel pictures the final restoration of the righteous people of God in the following terms:

> At that time Michael, the great prince, the protector of your people, shall arise. There shall be a time of anguish, such as has never occurred since nations first came into existence. But at that time your people shall be delivered, everyone who is found written in the book. 2 Many of those who sleep in the dust of the earth shall awake, some to everlasting life, and some to shame and everlasting contempt. 3 Those who are wise shall *shine like the brightness of the sky*, and those who lead many to righteousness, *like the stars forever and ever.*

> (Dan 12:1–3)

The interpretation of the picture in the final verse is contested. The text clearly asserts that those who have died will come back to life, that they will be resurrected from the dead. However, interpreters disagree over what the life of the resurrection is actually like. Some argue that Daniel pictures the righteous living as stars in the heavens forever. Stars are identified with

9. Sullivan, *Wrestling with Angels*, 85–141.

angels in apocalyptic literature (e.g., *1 En.* 18:14).[10] In effect, Daniel says here that the righteous are to become angels.[11] Others suggest that this is imagery and that the hope here is for a resurrected body, which is pictured as very glorious. The resurrected righteous will be as shining, majestic, and glorious as stars.[12] The Hebrew text could be translated *"as* the stars" or *"like* the stars" and so either interpretation is possible.

This tradition of comparing the resurrected righteous to the angels continues in later Jewish apocalyptic literature. For example, one of the closing sections of *1 Enoch* encourages the righteous with this hope for the future: "Take courage, then; for formerly you were worn out by evils and tribulations, but now you will shine like the luminaries of heaven; you will shine and appear, and the portals of heaven will be opened for you. . . . Take courage and do not abandon your hope, for you will have great joy like the angels of heaven . . . for you will be companions of the host of heaven." (*1 En.* 104:2–6).

The second-century apocalypse of *2 Baruch* offers a similar portrait of the future hope of the resurrected righteous: "For they will live in the heights of that world and they will be like angels and equal to the stars" (*2 Bar.* 51:10). Baruch goes on to describe the glory of the resurrected state, noting that the excellence of the resurrected righteous will be more excellent than that of the angels (*2 Bar.* 51:13), implying a distinction between the righteous and the angels, which probably suggests that Baruch does not imagine that the resurrected righteous will actually *become* angels. Just as *1 Enoch* and *2 Baruch* compare the resurrected righteous to angels (rather than actually identifying them), so Philo compares humans to angels in the afterlife, without saying that human beings become angels: "God therefore having added the good doctrine, that is Abel, to the soul, took away from it evil doctrine, that is Cain: for Abraham also, leaving mortal things, 'is added to the people of God,' having received immortality, and having become equal to the angels; for the angels are the host of God, being incorporeal and happy souls. And in the same manner Jacob, the practiser of virtue, is added to the better one, because he had quitted the worse" (*Sacr.* 1:5).

None of these texts specifically state that the resurrected righteous will become stars or angels. They assert only that they will become *like* angels in

10. Collins, *Daniel*, 331–33.
11. Ibid., 393–94.
12. Wright, *Resurrection*, 109–15.

the glory that will belong to them (or more glorious in the case of 2 *Baruch*) and in that they will live with the angels in heaven.[13]

So some ancient Jewish texts do speak of the resurrected righteous being in heaven with the angels. They also compare the glorious state of the resurrected righteous to that of the angels and the stars. However, they do not speak clearly of the righteous actually becoming angels or stars in the resurrection—or, if they do, they do so sufficiently obliquely for their meaning to be easily misunderstood. However, a couple of points are certain. These texts only speak of the righteous, those who have kept the commandments of God, as being granted this glorious existence. Elsewhere the texts speak of the punishments awaiting those who disobey God. The texts also speak of the righteous attaining this state on the Day of Judgment rather than in the present. So they do not picture people generally becoming angels when they die, although they suggest that the resurrected righteous become like the angels in that they live a glorious life eternally.

ANGELS IN WAITING

The book of Acts tells the story of Peter escaping from jail as the result of the miraculous intervention of an angel (Acts 12:6–11). After being freed Peter goes to the house of Mary where many members of the church are gathered praying for him. He knocks on the door. Rhoda, the maid who comes to answer the door, recognises his voice and goes back in to tell those gathered that Peter is outside. They tell her she is mad but she insists that Peter is there. They tell her that it must be Peter's angel (Acts 12:15). Eventually somebody opens the door to Peter and he describes to them his miraculous escape (Acts 12:12–17). The use of the word "angel" here is interesting. Many commentators suggest that the church members assume that Peter is dead and if Rhoda is seeing anything at all, she sees Peter's guardian angel (the angel in heaven allotted to look after Peter personally). They suggest that the word "angel" refers to his guardian angel.[14]

---

13. For other texts that are alleged to speak of "astral immortality" see Collins, *Daniel*, 394 n. 222. For discussion of such texts suggesting that the notion of astral immortality may not best interpret them, see Angel, *Chaos and the Son of Man*, 123–24.

14. Fitzmyer, *Acts*, 489; Pervo, *Acts*, 306–7.

However, the evidence for guardian angels in this period is rather thin.[15] So David Daube offers a different interpretation of this text, which gives us another perspective on the relationship between people and angels. Daube starts with the story in Acts 23 where the Jewish sect of the Sadducees is said to not believe in the resurrection, angels, or spirits (Acts 23:8). This statement is odd as the Sadducees believed the Torah, which affirms the existence of angels from Genesis onwards. So either the text is wrong or it means something else. Daube suggests that "angel" does not refer to heavenly angels here but is used of the souls of the departed. Many first-century AD Jews believed that the souls of the departed awaited the day of resurrection in some sort of spiritual home or state—for example, certain pseudepigraphical texts depict the souls of the righteous being with the angels in heaven while the souls of the unrighteous wander in torment as both await the resurrection (1 En. 39:4–5; 4 Ezra 7:75–99).[16] On the day of resurrection they receive their new resurrection bodies. Given that soul and angel occur in the context of a debate about the resurrection, it makes sense that they both refer to the soul or spirit of the deceased person awaiting the day of resurrection.[17] So the "angel" whom the church members think Rhoda might see is the spirit of the supposedly executed Peter, now awaiting his glorious resurrection body. "Angel" here is used as a metaphor to refer to the spirit of the deceased rather than suggesting that Peter has become an angel.

The idea of contemporary folk religion, that people become angels when they die and watch over their loved ones, does not seem to be reflected in the ancient Jewish and Christian texts. Angels and humans belong to different species and the evidence that either angels become human or that humans become angels is pretty thin—and if it was ever thought to

15. We will explore this in the next chapter. See also, Daube, "Sadducees and Angels," 496.

16. Stone, *Fourth Ezra*, 234–46.

17. Daube, "Sadducees and Angels," 493–97. On the idea that the souls wait for their new bodies on the day of resurrection, see Wright, *Resurrection*, 129–206. Viviano and Taylor ("Sadducees, Angels and Resurrection," 496–98) argue the angel refers to some sort of angelic existence after death in Acts 23:8–9, citing Wis 3:1–5 as evidence of a spiritual resurrection. However, Wis 3:1–5 refers to the spirits of the deceased being kept in the hand of God before the day of resurrection when they receive new life (Wis 3:7–8; see Wright, *Resurrection*, 162–75)—precisely the scenario that Daube describes. The spiritual life after death is only temporary as the righteous soul awaits the resurrection from the dead. The Wisdom of Solomon is found in the Apocrypha.

happen, then it was thought only to happen in exceptional cases. Although a fair number of modern scholars assert the idea that the righteous become angels when they die, the literature itself does not really support this conclusion. Rather it suggests that the righteous will be as glorious as the angels, or more glorious, in their resurrection state. It also suggests that the righteous may live forever with the angels (or, in exceptional cases, may be translated into heaven to live with the angels eternally while still alive). The closest we come to the confusion of angels and human beings is a linguistic confusion, where the spirit of a deceased human awaiting the resurrection of the dead is occasionally called an angel.

8

Someone to Watch Over Me?

The teaching of some Christian churches, even where is it not their official doctrine, is that every human being has a guardian angel—that is, an
angel who guards one particular human being from the moment of their
birth to the moment of their death. Down the centuries, not least since
the Reformation, churches have disagreed over whether any angels are
appointed the permanent guardians of individual human beings. Roman
Catholic tradition interpreted the Scriptures as suggesting the existence of
guardian angels but Protestant theologians have urged, by and large, that
this either adds to or misinterprets the biblical texts. Aside from the debates
of the churches, there has been an explosion of interest in the idea of personal guardian angels in contemporary popular spirituality since the latter
years of the twentieth century.[1] This popular idea of guardian angels sent
to sort out our lives may have made inroads into modern culture, but are
they to be found in the ancient literature and how far does the modern idea
of the guardian angel (sent to sort out my crises and help me through my
difficulties) match up to the ancient idea (if there was one)?

PERSONAL GUARDIAN ANGELS

There can be no doubt that the Bible speaks of angels being sent to protect
people. In the OT, God sends angels to rescue Lot from the impending
destruction of Sodom and Gomorrah (Gen 19:1–26). The angel of the

---

1. For a discussion of guardian angels in church tradition and the renewal of interest
in them in contemporary popular spirituality, see Garrett, *No Ordinary Angel*, 139–85.

Angels

LORD comes between the army of Egypt and the army of Israel to protect the people of Israel during their flight from Egypt (Exod 14:19–20). When the king of Aram hunts down the prophet Elisha to kill him (for Elisha is reputed to tell the king of Israel, Aram's enemy, the most secret plans of the king of Aram), God sends angels to protect him (2 Kgs 6:11–19).[2] There are many other stories in the OT of God sending angels to protect individuals or individuals and their family groups. However, this is not the same as individual angels being assigned to particular human beings as their lifelong guardians and protectors.

Such stories are also found in the second temple literature.[3] The story of Tobit is a good example. Tobit and Sarah are in great trouble. God sends an angel to their rescue, who heals and restores them and their families. However, Raphael only comes to heal and rescue them from particular difficulties. As soon as his mission is complete he returns to heaven. Raphael is not the guardian angel of these families in the sense that he is permanently allotted to protect them. According to the *Genesis Apocryphon* Abram, distressed and tearful at Sarah being forcibly taken from him by Pharaoh Zoan, prays for God to deal justly with him, Sarah, and the Pharaoh (*1QapGen ar* xx 1–16a). God sends a chastising spirit upon the Pharaoh so that he is unable to approach Sarah, let alone have sexual intercourse with her, for two whole years (*1QapGen ar* xx 16–17). When Pharaoh Zoan gave Sarah back to Abram, the evil spirit ceased plaguing him (*1QapGen ar* xx 29). The spirit here, whether angelic or not, is sent only temporarily and again does not permanently guard Abram or inflict maladies on the enemies of Abram. These stories in the OT and the second temple literature certainly portray angels protecting the people of God, and afflicting their enemies, but only temporarily. Once the crisis is over, the angel returns. There is no evidence here of individual guardian angels being commanded to protect individual human beings from the cradle to the grave.

Pseudo-Philo does not provide any firm evidence of belief in the guardian angels of individuals. In his retelling the story of the spies who tell Moses that the people of the land are giants and too strong to conquer (Num 13:1—14:38), God tells Moses that he is angry that the people of Israel do not trust him and so will command the angels who watch over them to

2. Cogan and Tadmor, *II Kings*, 32, 74.

3. For a review of evidence of guardian angels in this literature, see Hannah, "Guardian Angels," 418–28.

76

cease to intercede for them, and instead will send upon the Israelites an angel of wrath (*L.A.B.* 15:5). The angels are a group who watch over the nation of Israel—not individual guardians of individual people. A group of angels watching over the nation of Israel seems to be the most natural way of reading the addition to the ninth commandment: "You shall not be a false witness against your neighbour, speaking false testimony, lest your guardians speak false testimony against you" (*L.A.B.* 11:12). If the people of Israel bear false witness against each other, the angels that protect them will report their sin to the heavenly court, which will presumably sit in judgment upon them. When David is anointed (1 Sam 16:1–13), Pseudo-Philo has him sing of the protection he receives from the angels (*L.A.B.* 59:4). David claims the help of many heavenly protectors here, not simply one guardian angel. There is evidence of angels being allotted to guard Israel generally but not of individual protectors of individual persons.

Similarly, the book of *1 Enoch* provides no evidence for individual guardian angels as such, although one verse does speak of angels being allotted to protect the righteous: "He will set a guard of the holy angels over all the righteous and holy; and they will be kept as the apple of the eye until evil and sin come to an end. And from that time, the pious will sleep a sweet sleep, and there will no longer be anyone to frighten them" (*1 En.* 100:5). However, the context of this verse is a description of the Day of Judgment. The protection of the righteous here is the protection of their souls by angels after death, as the souls of the righteous wait for the day when they will rise again from the dead with their new resurrection bodies.[4] Again, this provides no evidence of individual guardian angels for people while they are alive on earth.

The apocalypse of *3 Baruch* tells the story of angels appealing to their commander-in-chief Michael for a transfer. They do not like the people to whom they have been assigned because they never go to church or visit ministers for spiritual guidance. Also they commit murder, fornication, adultery, theft, slander, perjury, envy, drunkenness, strife, jealousy, grumbling, gossip, idolatry, divination, and all manner of sins. Therefore, the angels are suffering as a consequence through association with such people. Michael counsels them to wait while he checks the will of God (*3 Bar.* 13:1–5). While it is possible that these angels have been assigned

4. Nickelsburg, *1 Enoch 1*, 500–501.

Angels

individually to individual human beings, the text does not state this. It presents a group of angels who have been assigned to look after a mass of wicked people.

Other second temple Jewish and early Christian texts have been suggested as evidence of belief in guardian angels in early Christianity and Judaism.[5] The Christian heavenly ascent apocalypse called the *Testament of Jacob* mentions angels visiting, guarding, and strengthening Jacob in all things (*T. Jac.* 1:10).[6] Here we find angel*s* (plural), not one guardian angel, assisting Jacob. The Christian treatise known as the *Shepherd of Hermas* speaks of each person having two angels, a good one and a bad one. The good one encourages good deeds and the bad one encourages evil deeds— and the Christian disciple is to listen to the good one (Herm. *Mand.* 6.2.2). The good angel here is not a guardian angel but rather something like one's conscience, encouraging the believer to be faithful in all things.[7] Genesis 48:16 LXX speaks of the angel that delivered Jacob from trials throughout his life. However, as this angel is spoken of in parallel with God (Gen 48:15–16), Jacob most likely refers to the angel of the LORD.[8] Similarly, Philo does not speak clearly of guardian angels (*Dreams* 1:141–42; *Giants* 1:12). That the angel of the LORD protected Jacob does not imply that all people have an individual guardian angel.

Probably the nearest we come to any notion of guardian angels is *Jubilees*, where Rebecca is nervous that Esau might kill Jacob on account of his having stolen their father's blessing (which by right of primogeniture belonged to Esau). She requests that Isaac ensure the safety of Jacob. Isaac replies that she need not worry because the protector of Jacob is stronger than the protector of Esau (*Jub.* 35:17). This sounds like the two boys have guardian angels. However, the protector of Jacob is "greater and mightier and more honoured and praised" than the protector of Esau. The praising of Jacob's protector suggests that his protector is the LORD God, as God alone is to be worshipped (*Jub.* 20:8–9), which weakens the case for this text as refering to guardian angels; it seems more likely to be modeled on

5. Johnson, *Acts*, 213.

6. The *Testament of Jacob* is found in the Pseudepigrapha.

7. Osiek, *Shepherd of Hermas*, 124. Compare the spirits of truth and error who battle for the human conscience in *T. Jud.* 20:1–2, and the good and evil *yêtzers* of rabbinic teaching (e.g., *m. Ber.* 9:5), for which see Davies, *Paul and Rabbinic Judaism*, 21–23.

8. Hamilton, *Genesis 18–50*, 637–38. Similarly, Philo, *Alleg Interp.* 3:177–78.

the idea of the angels of the nations because Israel (= Jacob) did not have an angel but was protected by the LORD God.

THE ANGELS OF THE NATIONS

While neither the Bible nor the extra-biblical literature gives any clear evidence of the existence of guardian angels of individuals, both prove unequivocally the belief in angelic guardians of the *nations*. In the visionary section of the biblical book of Daniel, the interpreting angel who comes to Daniel claims to have been fighting against the prince of the kingdom of Persia and was unable to come to give further wisdom and insight until Michael came to relieve him (Dan 10:12–14). This angel strengthens Daniel before returning to fight the Prince of Persia (Dan 10:20). The consensus of scholars is that the prince against whom the angel fights is the angelic prince of Persia—in other words, an angelic guardian of that nation.[9]

The idea of angelic guardians of nations comes from Deut 32:8–9: "When the Most High apportioned the nations, when he divided humankind, he fixed the boundaries of the peoples according to the number of the gods; the LORD's own portion was his people, Jacob his allotted share." Where the Hebrew text reads "gods" above (reflecting an ancient reading found in the Dead Sea Scrolls—4QDeutj—rather than the later Masoretic text, which reads "sons of Israel"), the LXX translation reads "the angels of God." According to the text, and particularly its LXX translation, God apportioned an angel to each of the nations, or rather a human nation to each of the angels. Thus each nation has a guardian angel, except Israel whom the LORD chooses to watch over and protect.

This idea is reflected in a number of apocryphal and pseudepigraphical writings. The book of *Jubilees* offers an interesting reading of the text:

> [T]here are many nations and many people, and they all belong to him [God], but over all of them he caused spirits to rule so that they might lead them astray from following him. 32 But over Israel he did not cause any angel or spirit to rule because he alone is their ruler and he will protect them and he will seek for them at the hand of his angels and at the hand of his spirits and at the hand of all his authorities so that he might guard them and bless them and they might be his and he might be theirs henceforth and forever.

9. Collins, *Daniel*, 374–75. See further Heidt, *Angelology*, 50–59; Yates, "Angels in the Old Testament," 166.

(*Jub.* 15:31–32)

This text clearly reflects the idea of the apportioning of the nations between the angels. However, whereas Deuteronomy does not suggest that the angelic rule of the nations is either good or bad (except that Israel has the best guardian), *Jubilees* suggests that the idea of the apportioning of the nations to the angels was specifically designed to lead the nations astray. The *Animal Apocalypse* pictures the LORD summoning seventy shepherds who (with their subordinates) are to pasture the sheep given into their care (*1 En.* 89:59–60). In the language of animal imagery this text pictures God apportioning humankind (sheep) to the care of the angels (the seventy shepherds).[10] Interestingly the angels of the nations appear to have subordinate angels to help them in this task, at least according to this part of *1 Enoch*. The book of Sirach, or Wisdom of Ben Sira, also refers to this tradition (Sir 17:17).[11]

This idea appears to transmute in the early chapters of the biblical book of Revelation. There the risen Christ commands the visionary John to write messages to the angels of the churches of Ephesus, Smyrna, Pergamum, Thyatira, Sardis, Philadelphia, and Laodicea (Rev 2:1—3:22). The churches were clearly not nations. However, the idea of angelic guardianship of human *communities* was not new to Jews or, therefore, early Christians. The book of Revelation seems to develop the idea of the angelic guardianship of the nations to the angelic guardianship of Christian congregations.[12]

GUARDIANS IN THE GOSPEL?

The Gospel of Matthew contains a warning to any who might in any way despise certain "little ones" of whom Jesus speaks. The scholarly consensus is that the little ones are Jesus' disciples.[13] Jesus advises not to despise them because their angels continually see the face of God the Father in heaven (Matt 18:10). Certain traditions within the church have taken this verse to

---

10. Nickelsburg, *1 Enoch 1*, 390.

11. Skehan and Di Lella, *Ben Sira*, 283.

12. For further discussion, see Aune, *Revelation 1–5*, 108–12; Beale, *Revelation*, 217–19.

13. Davies and Allison, *Matthew*, 2:771; France, *Matthew*, 681, 685; with qualifications, Luz, *Matthew 8–20*, 440–41.

speak of guardian angels.[14] Reacting against them, the protestant reformer, John Calvin wrote in his *Harmony of the Evangelists, Matthew, Mark, and Luke* in his commentary on Matt 18:10:

> The interpretation given to this passage by some commentators, as if God assigned to each believer his own *angel*, does not rest on solid grounds. For the words of Christ do not mean that a single *angel* is continually occupied with this or the other person; such an idea is inconsistent with the whole doctrine of Scripture, which declares that *the angels encamp around* (Ps. xxxiv. 7) the godly, and not that one *angel* only, but many, have been commissioned to guard every one of the faithful.[15]

Calvin seems to be right. There is no suggestion in the text that each angel here is assigned to one particular human being for their protection throughout their lives. Given that other texts from a similar period in time have various angels occupied with the protection of the people of God (e.g., *L.A.B.* 15:5), there seems to be no good reason to interpret Matthew any differently. In another respect, the text of Matthew is interesting. The angels of Matt 18 guard the disciples of Jesus. These disciples have committed themselves to follow him and so to obey his commands. However, they struggle to live up to these standards (Matt 18:15–20) and their identity ought to be marked by their being a forgiving people just as they are a forgiven people (Matt 18:21–35). Most texts studied in this chapter have angels guard the righteous. Matthew appears to have them represent the repentant who seek righteousness.

There does not seem to be sufficiently strong evidence in either the Bible or the extra-biblical literature for the claim that there existed a belief in angels who were assigned to watch over and protect certain individuals from cradle to grave.[16] However, there are plenty of examples of authors stating that God sends angels to protect the righteous. And here there lies something of a chasm between the ancient view and the view of much contemporary spirituality. The ancient view is that God appoints angels to protect the righteous; that is, those who obey God's commandments. Contemporary spirituality tends to see guardian angels as aiding people regardless of their moral standards. Perhaps the Matthean picture

14. For modern interpreters arguing this viewpoint, see: Davies and Allison, *Matthew*, 2:769–72; Luz, *Matthew 8–20*, 440–43; Hannah, "Guardian Angels," 430

15. Calvin, *Harmony of the Evangelists*, 339.

16. So also, Williams, *Angels*, 68–80.

Angels

forms something of a bridge between the two worlds, picturing the angels as representing the repentant who seek righteousness, or maybe it presents a challenge to both.

9

And All The Angels With Him

The archangel Michael appears to Abraham as a handsome soldier (*T. Ab.* 2:4) and is referred to as the commander-in-chief of the angels in various pseudepigraphical texts (e.g., *Testament of Abraham*; *3 Baruch*). He is called upon to fight the angelic prince of Persia by another angel locked in combat with this figure (Dan 10:12–14). In the Garden of Gethsemane Jesus tells his disciples that he could ask his heavenly Father for the assistance of more than twelve legions of angels (Matt 26:53). The language used of angels in these texts is clearly military. Individual angels are pictured as soldiers and hosts of angels are pictured as regiments within the heavenly army. Most people today rarely envisage angels as soldiers, if ever. However, angels have been understood to be warriors from the earliest times in Jewish and Christian traditions.

THE DIVINE WARRIOR IN THE ANCIENT
NEAR EAST

The traditions of picturing angels as soldiers probably developed from the very ancient picture of God as a warrior. This ancient picture of the LORD as a warrior is not only embedded in the earliest Hebrew texts found in the Bible but also in ancient Near Eastern religions in general.[1] These religions tended to be polytheistic; that is to say they had many gods. They pictured their gods living in heaven where sometimes they got on well and

---

1. Cross, *Canaanite Myth*, 79–144.

sometimes they did not. Quarrels among the gods could be nipped in the bud but sometimes they developed into fully blown battles.

The Babylonian myth of the Enuma Elish tells the story of one such argument developing into a battle. The gods Tiamat (goddess of the sea) and Apsu beget many children. These younger gods make a terrible noise and cause a great deal of trouble. So Apsu suggests to Tiamat that they do away with the children. Tiamat is not impressed but Apsu plans to kill them anyway. Before he can do so, one of the children, the all-wise Ea, murders his father Apsu from whom he makes the heavens in which he dwells. There he and his wife Damkina beget the child Marduk, who turns out to be something of a wild child. Although initially unresponsive over the murder of her husband, Tiamat is encouraged to avenge his death by killing the gods. Tiamat gathers an army of terrifying monsters with her new husband Qingu. The gods send Ea and Anu to do battle against Tiamat, but both withdraw terrified before the armies even engage each other. The gods do not know what to do. Marduk, the storm-god, offers to kill Tiamat provided that the gods make him their king. Without any other option, the gods agree to this deal. Marduk goes into battle against Tiamat and her monstrous army. After a great struggle and with the aid of his storm winds, Marduk kills Tiamat and Qingu, and disposes of their army. Marduk splits Tiamat in two and creates the world out of her carcass. Humanity is created from the blood of Qingu. Marduk is crowned king of the gods and Babylon is built as his sanctuary. The story ends with the praises of Marduk being sung.[2]

The myths of the ancient city-state of Ugarit tell a very similar story. It opens with the high god 'Ilu declaring the sea god Yammu to have royal status and instructing the craftsman god Kôṯaru-wa-Ḥasīsu to build Yammu a palace. Yammu sends messengers to the council of the gods to demand that Ba'lu surrenders to him. Ba'lu reacts violently to the suggestion and is restrained. Nonetheless, Ba'lu is incensed and decides to fight Yammu. Aware of how powerful Yammu is, Ba'lu procures the services of Kôṯaru-wa-Ḥasīsu to provide him with powerful maces for the battle, with which Ba'lu defeats Yammu after a struggle. There is a feast in honor of Ba'lu.

2. For the text of this myth, see "Epic of Creation," translated by Benjamin R. Foster (COS 1:111:390–402). For a discussion of the myth and its historical background, see Jacobsen, *Treasures of Darkness*, 167–91; and for an introduction and translation, see Foster, *From Distant Days*, 9–51.

Ba'lu's consort 'Anatu promises Ba'lu that she will demand that 'Ilu builds him a temple. 'Anatu goes to the court of 'Ilu, and demands, with menacing threats, that 'Ilu build Ba'lu a palace. 'Anatu and Ba'lu persuade 'Aṭiratu (the mother of the gods and the wife of 'Ilu) to represent their case before 'Ilu—which she does. 'Ilu listens to her request and Kôṯaru-wa-Ḫasīsu is commissioned to build Ba'lu a temple. The temple is built in seven days and a banquet is held in celebration.[3]

The storyline of these two myths is almost identical. Although the reasons for the quarrel differ, the story begins with an argument amongst the gods. The argument escalates into a battle. The fight takes place between the storm god (Ba'lu, Marduk) and the god of the sea (Yammu, Tiamat). The storm god wins. This victory ensures that the storm god gains some sort of ascendancy among the gods. Scholars debate the meaning and purpose of these myths, but our concern here is merely to demonstrate that the storm god in these ancient Near Eastern myths is pictured as a warrior.[4]

The ancient Hebrew Scriptures allude to a very similar story. Nowhere does the OT tell the story in full; it only uses fragments of a story that looks remarkably similar.[5] The fullest account of the story in the OT is probably found in Ps 18. The psalmist tells of a distressing situation which was probably life threatening, and from which he called out to the LORD for help (Ps 18:4–6). God responds, emerging from the heavens like this:

> Then the earth reeled and rocked; the foundations also of the mountains trembled and quaked, because he was angry. 8 Smoke went up from his nostrils, and devouring fire from his mouth; glowing coals flamed forth from him. 9 He bowed the heavens, and came down; thick darkness was under his feet. 10 He rode on a cherub, and flew; he came swiftly upon the wings of the wind. 11 He made darkness his covering around him, his canopy thick clouds dark with water.

> (Ps 18:7–11)

---

3. For the text of this myth, see Wyatt, *Religious Texts from Ugarit*, 39–146. For a discussion of this myth and its historical background, see Smith, *Ugaritic Baal Cycle*, 58–114.

4. For discussion of the various versions of this myth in the ancient Near East and its meaning or purpose, see Green, *Storm-God*. For a briefer and more accessible account, see Longman and Reid, *God is a Warrior*.

5. The classic study of these fragments of myth in the OT is Gunkel, *Creation and Chaos*. For two key texts that are more recent, see Cross, *Canaanite Myth*; Day, *God's Conflict*.

The psalmist pictures God as the god of the storm. As God emerges from heaven the earth convulses. He is clothed in clouds and rides on the wind. The storm imagery becomes clearer as the psalmist describes the battle:

> Out of the brightness before him there broke through his clouds hailstones and coals of fire. 13 The LORD also thundered in the heavens, and the Most High uttered his voice. 14 And he sent out his arrows, and scattered them; he flashed forth lightnings, and routed them. 15 Then the channels of the sea were seen, and the foundations of the world were laid bare at your rebuke, O LORD, at the blast of the breath of your nostrils.
>
> (Ps 18:12–15)

The LORD battles the sea, which is laid bare (i.e., dried up) and defeated. The weapons that the LORD uses are hailstones and coals of fire, thunder, and lightnings—which lightnings are compared to arrows. With the obvious exception of coals of fire these weapons are all elements of the storm.[6] The LORD rescues the psalmist from the mighty waters and brings him into a broad or good place (Ps 18:16–19). The reference to the enemies of the psalmist in Ps 18:17 suggests that the rescue the LORD actually performed was one of delivering the psalmist from human enemies and that the language of the fight against the mighty and powerful sea is metaphorical.[7]

Although Ps 18 uses the language of the LORD defeating the sea metaphorically to speak about the LORD defeating the enemies of the psalmist, the resemblances between this episode in the psalm and the stories from Babylon and Ugarit are more than passing. There is a battle. The victor in the battle is the storm god. The defeated foe is the god of the sea. The OT has its own version of this ancient Near Eastern myth. Fragments of this myth can be found all over the OT.[8]

Various texts speak of an animal called Leviathan. Older commentators on Job identified Leviathan (Job 41:1–34) as a crocodile, an identification

---

6. Although note the interesting speculation of Cross (*Canaanite Myth*, 169) that the origin of such imagery to describe the action of God was probably the experience of storms in the mountains in which explosions of smoke and fire result from lightning hitting trees near the timber line, which might well account for such things as "coals of fire."

7. Craigie, *Psalms 1–50*, 173.

8. For a good survey, see Day, *God's Conflict*. For a brief and readable introduction to the ancient Near Eastern background to the story of the battle between God and the forces of chaos, see Boyd, *God at War*, 73–113.

that can still be found in some English Bibles. However, this is most unlikely as Leviathan breathes fire (Job 41:18–21) and has many heads (Ps
74:14). More probable is that Leviathan is a dragon, as suggested by the
parallelism in Ps 74:13–14: "You divided the sea by your might; you broke
the heads of the dragons in the waters. You crushed the heads of Leviathan;
you gave him as food for the creatures of the wilderness." The heads of
the dragons and the heads of Leviathan appear in parallel. This suggests
that Leviathan is one of the dragons. Given that this creature breathes fire
and is many-headed, this identification makes sense. The Ugaritic myths
have a similar defeated monster with a similar name, *Lôtan* (*KTU* 1:3 iii
38–42). Psalm 74:13 puts the dragons, including Leviathan, in parallel with
the sea—all being defeated by God. The sea, the dragons, and Leviathan are
all identified as the monstrous enemies of God, the divine warrior.[9]

Elsewhere in the OT, the LORD fights a dragon called Rahab (not
to be confused with the prostitute of that name in Josh 2:1–21; 5:17). A
prophecy to the Jews in exile in Babylon announces:

> 9 Awake, awake, put on strength, O arm of the LORD! Awake, as in
> days of old, the generations of long ago! Was it not you who cut Rahab
> in pieces, who pierced the dragon? 10 Was it not you who dried up the
> sea, the waters of the great deep; who made the depths of the sea a way
> for the redeemed to cross over? 11 So the ransomed of the LORD shall
> return, and come to Zion with singing; everlasting joy shall be upon
> their heads; they shall obtain joy and gladness, and sorrow and sighing
> shall flee away.
>
> (Isa 51:9–11)

Here Rahab is identified as the dragon that the LORD cuts in pieces. This
defeat of the dragon Rahab parallels the drying up or defeat of the sea, so
the text seems to be working with the same mythical fragment—God the
divine warrior defeating the sea of chaos and evil and the monstrous foe.
The chaos sea in turn is identified with the drying up of the Red Sea and
so the mythical battle with the monster and the sea is identified with the
ancient victory over Egypt at the Red Sea. The prophecy then declares that
just as God the warrior has won these battles in the past, so God will liberate
the people from the exile in Babylon and bring them back to homeland.[10]

9. On Leviathan, see Day, *God's Conflict*, 62–75.

10. Blenkinsopp, *Isaiah 40–55*, 330–33.

Angels

The OT uses this language of God the divine warrior, of God saving
and delivering the people of Israel. Therefore, in some ways the language
is treated as metaphorical or as imagery. The real earthly events of which
this language of defeating dragons and mythical chaos waters speaks are
events in which God saves the children of Israel and defeats their enemies.
It is also used of the creation of the world (e.g., Pss 33:6–7; 74:12–17).[11]
However, it would be a mistake to draw the conclusion that the OT does
not picture God as really being like a warrior with real angelic armies. It
does. Even the name of God, the "LORD of *Hosts*," reflects this—the "hosts"
of which it speaks are the armies of angels.[12]

Moreover, there are stories of angels appearing as warriors. When
Elijah ascends into heaven, his friend and prophetic successor Elisha cries
out as he sees Elijah ascend to heaven in a chariot of fire accompanied by
horses of fire. Chariots and horsemen are military figures, suggesting that
Elisha is taken into heaven by warrior angels.[13] When the king of Aram
hunts down Elisha to kill him, he sends a great army to surround the city
where he finds Elisha (2 Kgs 6:11–14). The LORD surrounds the horses
and chariots of Aram with horses and chariots of fire. These are the angelic
warriors of the heavenly army.[14] At first Elisha's servant could not see the
heavenly host that had come to protect them. Only after Elisha prayed that
his eyes would be opened could he see them (2 Kgs 6:17). These angels
are invisible to normal sight and can only be seen as in a vision when one
is permitted or enabled to see them, much as is the case in the story of
Balaam, where Balaam could not see the angel with his sword drawn at first
(Num 22:23–31). Nonetheless, this demonstrates that OT narratives did
portray warrior angels as beings that were believed to exist.[15]

ANGELIC WARRIORS IN THE POST-EXILIC PERIOD

The tradition continued in the post-exilic era (the era after the exile of the
Jews in Babylon, from the late sixth century BC onwards). The books of

11. Day, *God's Conflict*, 21–25, 56.

12. Cross, *Canaanite Myth*, 94, 99, 105.

13. Cogan and Tadmor, *II Kings*, 32.

14. Ibid., 32, 74.

15. On the background to angels as warriors in the Bible, see also Noll, *Angels of
Light*, 154–76.

the Maccabees tell stories of warrior angels. When Heliodorus attempts to misappropriate money from the temple, three warrior angels prevent him from carrying out his plan. One of these is described as having armor and weapons of gold (2 Macc 3:25–27).[16] When an enemy of the Jewish people, named Timothy, brings a formidable army against Judea, the Jewish army goes out to meet him under the leadership of Judas Maccabeus. In the thick of the battle, five resplendent warriors on horseback appear from heaven and lead the Jewish forces in full view of their enemies. Two of them guard Maccabeus, shielding him with their own armor to prevent him from coming to any harm. These angelic warriors shower thunderbolts on the enemy in order to decimate their army (2 Macc 10:24–31).[17] When Lysias invades Judea all the people implore God to deliver them. As Maccabeus again takes up arms an angelic horseman dressed in white with weapons of gold appears, encourages them, and appears to accompany them in battle. They win a resounding victory over the forces of Lysias (2 Macc 11:6–12).[18] On another occasion King Ptolemy Philopator of Egypt imprisons the Jews in the hippodrome in Schedia and decides to massacre them by setting stampeding elephants and soldiers upon them. A prominent Jewish priest cries out to God for mercy. When the elephants and soldiers are sent upon them, God opens the gates of heaven and sends out two glorious angels who appear terrifying. They fight the enemy, putting both soldiers and elephants to flight and saving the Jews (3 Macc 6:16–21). God sends out angelic warriors to deliver his people from danger.

Although Jonathan Goldstein tries to explain it away as a mirage caused by strong atmospheric temperature inversion projecting images of a distant but advancing army into the air above Jerusalem, there seems to be another vision of angelic armies fighting in 2 Maccabees.[19] When the Greek king Antiochus IV Epiphanes invades Egypt for the second time, for forty days people saw cavalry in golden armor charging through the air with lances and swords drawn over the city of Jerusalem. They saw spears and missiles hurled, shields held up in defense, and all kinds of armor (2 Macc 5:2–4). The book of 2 Maccabees describes this as an apparition. Josephus reports a similar apparition of warrior angels charging through

16. Goldstein, *2 Maccabees*, 212–13.

17. Ibid., 391–94.

18. Ibid., 405–6.

19. Ibid., 247.

the sky above Jerusalem shortly before another invading army besieges the city (*War* 6.5.3§297–300):

> 297 a certain prodigious and incredible phenomenon appeared: I suppose the account of it would seem to be a fable, were it not related by those who saw it, 298 and were not the events that followed it of so considerable a nature as to deserve such signals; for, before sun setting, chariots and troops of soldiers in their armor were seen 299 running about among the clouds, and surrounding the cities. Moreover, at that feast which we call Pentecost, as the priests were going by night into the inner court of the temple, as their custom was, to perform their sacred ministrations, they said that, in the first place, they felt a quaking, and heard a great noise, 300 and after that they heard a sound as of a great multitude, saying, "We are departing from here."

Josephus admits that he would have found the account incredible were it not for the credibility of the testimony of his sources. The angelic armies appear to have been surrounding the cities of Judah. Very likely it is the angelic hosts who are leaving the temple before the Roman invasion. This seems to be Josephus' interpretation of the event given that he follows it with the story of Jesus son of Ananus, who prophesies the doom of Jerusalem and the temple.

These stories (and that of Elisha and the armies of Aram in 2 Kgs 6) bear an interesting resemblance to two stories Billy Graham relates of angels. The first concerns the Revd. John G. Paton, a missionary in the New Hebrides:

> Hostile natives surrounded his mission headquarters one night intent on burning the Patons out and killing them. John Paton and his wife prayed all during that terror-filled night that God would deliver them. When daylight came they were amazed to see the attackers unaccountably leave. They thanked God for delivering them. A year later, the chief of the tribe was converted to Jesus Christ, and Mr. Paton, remembering what had happened, asked the chief what had kept him and his men from burning down the house and killing them. The chief replied in surprise, "Who were all those men you had with you there?" The missionary answered, "There were no men there; just my wife and I." The chief argued that they had seen many men standing guard—hundreds of big men in shining garments with drawn swords in their hands. They seemed to circle the mission station so that the natives were afraid to

attack. Only then did Mr. Paton realize that God had sent His angels to protect them. The chief agreed that there was no other explanation.[20]

Although Graham focuses on the miraculous nature of the deliverance rather than the military nature of the angels, the depiction of angels as warriors guarding the righteous resembles the appearances of angels examined above.

Graham relates another story of angels appearing as warriors: "A Persian colporteur was accosted by a man who asked him if he had a right to sell Bibles. 'Why, yes,' he answered, 'we are allowed to sell these books anywhere in the country!' The man looked puzzled, and asked, 'How is it, then, that you are always surrounded by soldiers? I planned three times to attack you, and each time, seeing the soldiers, I left you alone. Now I no longer want to harm you.'"[21] The more obvious modern comparison with this picture of heavenly warriors aiding those on earth is the alleged appearance of an army of angels at Mons. Much as the appearance of angels at this battle has been widely disparaged, the accounts abound. Heathcote-James offers the report of a lady she interviewed who tells of her father's experience at Mons:[22]

> My father won a military medal during that battle—how he won it I'll never know, because he said it was too terrible to talk about. There were about sixty thousand who went out to fight this battle and he [told me] "We were down to about thirty odd thousand . . . I cannot give you the exact figures but . . . we were more than half left and the battle was getting impossible because the Germans had bigger and better equipment than [us]." He said he'd never experienced anything like it—they were dropping down like flies and all of a sudden, [there] was an eerie sound and there was a white light across the hill and they saw these crowds on horses riding across the top of the hill. The Germans kept firing for a while but all of a sudden gave up. He said they'd never seen anybody run as fast as these Germans over the hill and he [told me], "We were all awe-inspired and we looked up and said someone was doing some work." He said to me, "Always be a Christian and believe in the Lord, because he saved us that day through the angels."

20. Graham, *Angels*, 14–15.

21. Ibid., 15.

22. Heathcote James, *Seeing Angels*, 70–71.

Much as many discredit the reports of the experience, this account from the daughter of a soldier at Mons bears fascinating similarities to the accounts of heavenly cavalry that we find in 2 Macc 10.

The Dead Sea scrolls also bear witness to warrior angels and their involvement in divine warfare on behalf of the people of God. The War Scroll depicts a war between the forces of light and the forces of darkness (1QM 1 1:10–15). The forces of light are led by Michael (1QM 17:5–8) or the Prince of Light (1QM 13:10) (the two figures are probably to be identified).[23] The forces of darkness are led by Belial (1QM 13:2). The end of the battle will be the eternal destruction of Belial and the spirits of his lot and the salvation of the people of God (1QM 1:5–7). Again the battles between the holy angels and their chaotic or demonic counterparts concern and bring about the deliverance of the people of God from evil.[24]

The picture of the battle between forces of light and forces of darkness has led some to suggest that the mythology of Zoroastrianism (a religion from Persia) has influenced the traditions of divine warfare in Israel. Zoroastrianism pictures Ahura Mazda (the good God) and his angels locked in battle against Ahriman (the prince of evil) and his angels. Supposing that the OT does not possess a picture of two heavenly armies lined up against one another in this way, some scholars see Persian influence as the simplest explanation for the sudden appearance of this tradition in the Jewish traditions we find in the Dead Sea scrolls.[25] However, the Persian texts in which this aspect of Zoroastrianism is found are considerably later in date than the Dead Sea scrolls, and this casts doubt on the theory of Zoroastrian influence on the Jewish tradition here.[26] Moreover, as we have seen, the OT does speak of the angelic warriors and armies of the LORD—not least in the title "the LORD of Hosts." The idea of an evil foe with an army of helpers is also found. God has defeated Rahab and her band of helpers (Job 9:13).[27]

23. Davidson, *Angels at Qumran*, 225–27.

24. On angelic warfare in the War Scroll, see further Davidson, *Angels at Qumran*, 212–34; Wassen, "Angels," 508–11.

25. Langton, *Satan, A Portrait*, 21–25; Kobelski, *Melchizedek and Melchiresa*, 84–98; more recently, Collins, *Apocalyptic Imagination*, 20, 29–33.

26. The Pahlavi writings, our main source of Persian apocalyptic, can only be dated as far back as the ninth century AD. The relative dates of texts make Persian influence on Jewish texts unlikely.

27. This is probably a Hebrew version of the demonic helpers of Tiamat in the Babylonian myth; so Day, *God's Conflict*, 41.

God has conquered Leviathan and all the other dragons (Ps 74:13–14). The LORD fights and defeats the forces of chaos in the form of the sea and the dragons or chaos monsters. All the elements of the myth as we have it in the War Scroll are present in the early Hebrew and Jewish traditions.[28]

However, unlike the earlier and some contemporary divine warrior traditions, the language of the warfare of the heavenly forces of good against the spiritual forces of evil is not used metaphorically of the deliverance by God of the righteous. Instead this language is used realistically. The War Scroll envisages the armies of the Qumran sect as fighting alongside the armies of the angels (1QM 12:7–18):

> 7 You, God, are awesome in the splendor of your majesty, and the congregation of your holy ones is amongst us for everlasting assistance. We will treat kings with contempt, with jeers 8 and mockery the warriors, for the Lord is holy and the King of Glory is with us, the nation of his holy ones are our warriors, and the army of his angels is enlisted with us; 9 the war hero is in our congregation; the army of his spirits is with our steps. Our horsemen are like clouds and fogs of dew that cover the earth, 10 like torrential rain that sheds justice on all its sprouts. Get up, Warrior; take your prisoners, Man of Glory; 11 collect your spoil, Performer of Valiance! Place your hand on the neck of your enemies and your foot on the piles of slain! Strike the peoples, your foes, and may your sword 12 consume guilty flesh . . . !
>
> (1QM 12:7–12)

The leader of the armies of light here is the LORD God rather than the archangel Michael or Prince of Light. However, the text is clearly a war cry encouraging the LORD, the King of Glory, to lead the forces of good into battle against their enemies. God the war hero, or man of war, is present in the congregation of the author. The congregation of the holy ones assists the congregation of the Qumran community. This congregation or nation of holy ones is identified as the armies of angels, which army marches into battle with the forces of the Qumran community. Just as the community at Qumran envisaged itself worshipping with the angels, so the community imagined that it would march into battle against its enemies alongside the warrior angels of God.[29]

---

28. For the language of divine warfare in the War Scroll as developing from earlier Hebrew traditions, see Cross, *Canaanite Myth*, 111, 326–46.

29. Davidson, *Angels at Qumran*, 229–30.

Angels

Just as the angelic warriors of the heavenly hosts are expected to fight alongside the armies of the Qumran community, so the armies of an earthly people called the Kittim are thought to fight alongside the demonic hordes of Belial: "All those who are ready for the war shall go and camp opposite the king of the Kittim and opposite all the army of Belial, assembled with him for the day of vengeance by God's sword" (1QM 15:2–3). In the Dead Sea scrolls the Kittim is a codename for the Romans who had, in effect, ruled Palestine since 63 BC, through local kings and Roman governors.[30] The Qumran community hoped that in this battle against the forces of evil and the armies of Rome God the mighty warrior and the heavenly hosts would help their own armies to victory. In the event, during the Jewish War of 66–70 AD, the Romans won.

Despite the fact that the eventual outcome was not that which the community at Qumran hoped for, many texts that the community cherished envisage this war. There are a series of psalms, the *Hodayot*, which picture the battle between the forces of light and the forces of darkness in graphic detail:

> When all the arrows of the pit fly without return and are shot without hope. When the measuring line falls upon judgment, and the lot of anger [28] on the forsaken and the outpouring of wrath against the hypocrites, and the period of anger against any Belial, and the ropes of death enclose with no escape, [29] then the torrents of Belial will go out against all the armies of heaven like a devouring fire in all their watering channels, destroying every tree, green [30] or dry, from their canals. It roams with flames of fire until none of those who drink are left. It consumes the foundations of clay [31] and the tract of dry land; the bases of the mountains does he burn and converts the roots of flint rock into streams of lava. It consumes right to the great deep. [32] The torrents of Belial break into Abaddon. The schemers of the deep roar with the din of those stirring up mud. The earth [33] cries out at the calamity that overtakes the world, and its schemers scream, and all who are upon it go crazy, [34] and melt away in the great calamity. But God will thunder with the roar of his strength, and his holy residence echoes with the truth of [35] his glory, and the host of the heavens adds to their noise, and the eternal foundations melt and shake, and the battle of the warriors of heaven [36] goes over the earth, and it does not return until it is finished, as decreed for eternity and there is nothing like it.

(1QH 11:27–36)

---

30. Baker, "Kittim," 93.

The text is clearly poetic and its images stark.[31] Nonetheless, for all the wild images the battle between the good and the evil can be discerned. Belial and the schemers of the deep create chaos upon earth as they fight the armies of heaven. However, God the divine warrior thunders from heaven and wins the victory over Belial and his hordes with the help of the hosts of heaven. In less graphic terms, the Dead Sea scroll *11QMelchizedek* describes the war against Belial as the moment when the people of God experience their long awaited liberty.[32] In the meantime the community at Qumran rely on God to enable them to live according to the Law:

> But we are the remnant of your people. Blessed be your name, God of mercies, who guards the covenant with our fathers, and during 9 all our generations you have wondrously bestowed your mercies to the remnant of your inheritance during the empire of Belial. With all the mysteries of his enmity, they have not separated us 10 from your covenant. You have chased away from us his spirits of destruction. When men of his dominion acted wickedly you protected the soul of your redeemed one. You raised 11 the fallen with your strength.
>
> (1QM 14:8–11)

The author thanks God for helping them in what may be described as a moral battle against Belial: resisting the temptation to do evil, whatever the provocation. The righteous are tempted to fall into error and so become trapped by Belial but God promises to give them rest from the temptations of Belial (4Q174 1 i 7–9). Aspects of this battle against Belial can be found all over the Dead Sea Scrolls.[33]

The biblical book of Revelation draws on this imagery of the divine warfare in which God, or the archangel Michael, fights and defeats the forces of evil: from the four angelic horsemen who conquer and destroy (Rev 6:1–8) to the victory of the rider of the white horse over the nations (Rev 19:11–21).[34] And right at the centre of the book, John sees the dragon fighting Michael:

31. For a brief but detailed analysis of the text, see Angel, *Chaos and the Son of Man*, 50–54.

32. On heavenly warfare in *11QMelchizedek*, see Kobelski, *Melchizedek and Melchiresa*, 49–83.

33. For a brief survey of the battle between God and the forces of chaos from Ugaritic mythology, through the early religion of Israel, and to the community at Qumran, see Davila, "Melchizedek," 259–72.

34. The classic study of this motif in Revelation is Gunkel, *Creation and Chaos*. See

Angels

> And war broke out in heaven; Michael and his angels fought against
> the dragon. The dragon and his angels fought back, 8 but they were de-
> feated, and there was no longer any place for them in heaven. 9 The great
> dragon was thrown down, that ancient serpent, who is called the Devil
> and Satan, the deceiver of the whole world—he was thrown down to the
> earth, and his angels were thrown down with him. 10 Then I heard a
> loud voice in heaven, proclaiming, "Now have come the salvation and
> the power and the kingdom of our God and the authority of his Messiah,
> for the accuser of our comrades has been thrown down, who accuses
> them day and night before our God."

(Rev 12:7–10)

Michael leads the armies of the angels against the dragon and his armies. The image of heavenly warfare here is similar to that found at Qumran. The dragon is most likely Leviathan—having seven heads just as the biblical Leviathan has multiple heads (Ps 74:14) and the Ugaritic *Lôtan*, upon whom Leviathan may be modeled, has seven heads (*KTU* 1:5 i 1–3).[35] John now identifies the dragon Leviathan as the devil, Satan, and the deceiver of the whole world. Michael and the heavenly hosts defeat the devil and his hordes, at which point salvation is said to come for the people of God.[36]

However, the war breaks out in heaven (Rev 12:7). The result is that the dragon and his minions are banished to earth (Rev 12:9, 13). And on earth the battle will continue, when the kings of the earth will rise up against the Lamb (Jesus) who is the Lord of Lords and King of Kings (Rev 17:13–14). When the battle does continue, the kings of the earth and their armies are allied to the beast—one of the arch henchmen of the dragon (see Rev 13)—and his army (Rev 19:19). They are lined up against the rider on the white horse (identified as the Word of God, and King of Kings and Lord of Lords, and so Jesus the Lamb) and the armies of the heavenly angels, also on white horses (Rev 19:11–14). The outcome is that Christ and the angelic armies defeat the beast and his minions (Rev 19:20–21).

Noticeable by their absence from the battlefield are the people of God. The covenanters at Qumran believed they were called to fight both a moral and a military battle. Unlike the community at Qumran, the Christian disciples of Revelation are not to fight a military battle. They are called to

also, Collins, *Combat Myth*.

35. Day, *God's Conflict*, 162.

36. Beale, *Revelation*, 650–58; Osborne, *Revelation*, 467–80.

endure the persecution that they believe is coming upon them, even to the point of dying for their commitment to Christ (Rev 12:17; 13:9–10). They must live out the life of holiness and righteousness to which they have been called, and of which they have been reminded, by Christ (Rev 2–3). They are encouraged to remain holy in order that they might inherit the kingdom of God when Christ comes again (Rev 22:12–15).[37] The same kind of exhortation to fight the battle for righteousness and holiness can be found in the writings of Paul (Rom 13:11–14).[38] There is no military battle for the saints in the book of Revelation. Their battle is of a very different order—against sin, the flesh, and the devil in order to remains righteous and holy until the coming of Christ.

ON CLOUDS AND WITH A MIGHTY ARMY

The Gospels also picture Jesus as the divine warrior heading up the heavenly army in the context of judgment. In the garden of Gethsemane Jesus declares to his disciples that they do not need to fight on his behalf because he could request twelve legions of angels to command in the fight against his enemies (Matt 26:53). However, Jesus does not plan to fight those come to arrest him in the same way that the Qumran community hoped to fight with the angels against Rome and Belial. Hence he instructs the disciple who drew a sword to fight to put it away (Matt 26:52).

According to the evangelist Mark, Jesus prophesied the following:

> But in those days, after that suffering, the sun will be darkened, and the moon will not give its light, 25 and the stars will be falling from heaven, and the powers in the heavens will be shaken. 26 Then they will see the Son of Man coming in clouds *with a great army* and glory. 27 Then he will send out the angels, and gather his elect from the four winds, from the ends of the earth to the ends of heaven
>
> (Mark 13:24–27)

The translation here differs from that in most Bibles. The phrase which is normally rendered "with great power" is here translated "with a mighty army." The reason for this is that the Greek phrase in Mark (*meta dunameōs pollēs*) occurs in the LXX eight times where it always means "with a large army" (Isa 36:2; 1 Macc 7:10, 11; 9:60; 11:63; 12:24, 42; 13:12). So it seems

37. Ibid., 787–91.
38. Jewett, *Romans*, 822–24.

best to translate it as "with a large army" here. Jesus comes with clouds, just as God the divine warrior travels on clouds. Jesus leads the army of the heavenly hosts and clearly acts as their commander as he sends them out to gather in the elect from the ends of the earth.[39] Mark has Jesus speak as the commander-in-chief of the heavenly forces just as Michael is elsewhere in Jewish traditions of a similar period.[40] The text pictures Christ coming to rescue his disciples at the time when he judges the earth, and it is the angels who gather in the disciples for whatever reward awaits them.

The picture of Jesus coming as Son of Man with the angels in order to judge humanity is found elsewhere in the Gospel tradition: "For the Son of Man is to come with his angels in the glory of his Father, and then he will repay everyone for what has been done. Truly I tell you, there are some standing here who will not taste death before they see the Son of Man coming in his kingdom" (Matt 16:27-28). These sayings and their parallels (Matt 24:29—31; Mark 8:38—9:1) suggest that Christ was to come as Son of Man in glory before the generation of Jesus' audience passed away (see Matt 24:34–5; Mark 13:30). There has been some discussion recently as to whether these pictures of Christ coming with the angels to judge refer to the second coming of Christ or whether they refer to Christ judging the Jewish nation in the first century AD by sending the Roman army to destroy the temple (just as God had sent the Babylonians to destroy an earlier temple to punish the sins of the people in the sixth century BC). Tradition tends to suggest that these texts refer to the second coming in which case Jesus may have been mistaken as that did not happen in the lifetime of the followers of Jesus.[41] Some recent scholars have argued that the language of Jesus coming as the divine warrior refers metaphorically to the destruction of the temple in AD 70, partly because the coming of the Son of Man seems to be the only answer given in the text to the question that sparked the discourse: when will the temple be destroyed? On this reading Jesus and the early Christians were not mistaken.[42]

39. See further Angel, *Chaos and the Son of Man*, 125–34.

40. For a study of similarities in Michael and Christ traditions, see Hannah, *Michael and Christ*.

41. Allison, *Jesus of Nazareth*, 152–69; Allison, "Victory of Apocalyptic," 126–41.

42. Wright, *Victory of God*, 339–68; in response to the criticisms of Dale Allison, see Wright, "In Grateful Dialogue," 264–68.

However this debate is resolved, there is one picture of Jesus as Son of Man coming to judge that clearly has nothing to do with the destruction of the temple, is generally thought refer to the second coming, and is subject to no time-frame that might invalidate the prophecy: "When the Son of Man comes in his glory, and all the angels with him, then he will sit on the throne of his glory. All the nations will be gathered before him, and he will separate people one from another as a shepherd separates the sheep from the goats, and he will put the sheep at his right hand and the goats at the left" (Matt 25:31–46). The opening lines of this passage picture Christ coming with all the angels in order to judge all nations. This text speaks starkly of judgment, noting that those who have not cared for the "little ones" of Jesus will depart into the "fire prepared for the devil and all his angels" (Matt 25:41). There is something of a parallel with the myth of the Watchers here as it too speaks of the fiery abyss into which Shemihazah and all the fallen Watchers are thrown forever (*1 En.* 10:11–13). However, Matthew lacks the shocking descriptive force of the scene as portrayed in *1 Enoch* and other roughly contemporary judgment scenes. It seems odd to say it given the modern distaste for the judgment of God, but the judgment scene in Matthew appears more compassionate compared to those of his contemporaries.[43]

Another difference between this scene and other judgment scenes is the fact that Matthew has no specific role for the angels here. The book of the Watchers has the Most High pronounce judgment and command the four archangels (Michael, Sariel, Raphael, and Gabriel) to carry it out (*1 En.* 9:1—11:2). The Animal Apocalypse simply has the angels enact the judgment (*1 En.* 88:1–3). The details of the judgments in the book of the Watchers verge on the grotesque. For example, Raphael is commanded to bind Asael hand and foot, throw him into the wilderness of Doudael, cover him with sharp and jagged stones, cover his face so he sees no light, before taking him into the burning conflagration on the Day of Judgment (*1 En.* 10:4–6). Michael is told to bind Shemihazah and his associates, make them watch their offspring (the giants) kill each other off, then leave them bound in the depths of the earth before leading them off to the fiery abyss on the Day of Judgment.

---

43. Davies and Allison, *Matthew*, 3:432.

Angels

Elsewhere in his Gospel, Matthew does have angels play a part in the final judgment of humanity. Jesus tells two parables of judgment that refer to the part that angels play. In the first a farmer sows a field and an enemy comes along afterwards by night and sows weeds in the same field. The farmer leaves the weeds in the ground for fear of uprooting the wheat along with the weeds. When harvest came the two were separated and the wheat stored while the weeds were burned (Matt 13:24–30). In the second, fishermen catch all sorts of fish in a net. When they pull it ashore, they put the food fish into baskets and throw away the bad fish (Matt 13:47). The parables refer to the same role of the angels in the judgment, that of separating out from the kingdom of God all evildoers and everything that causes people to sin, and throwing them into "the furnace of fire" (Matt 13:41–42, 49–50).

A related text in the Gospel of Luke pictures the tribunal at which judgment is meted out very much in the mould of the divine council: "And I tell you, everyone who acknowledges me before others, the Son of Man also will acknowledge before the angels of God; but whoever denies me before others will be denied before the angels of God" (Luke 12:8–9). The Son of Man here acknowledges or refuses to acknowledge people according to whether they publicly confess Jesus. The scene portrays the Son of Man, presumably Jesus, surrounded by angels as they deliberate in judgment upon people.[44]

So the Gospels take up the picture of the final battle in which the commander-in-chief of the angels and the heavenly hosts defeat the Belial, the dragon, or Satan and his demonic hordes. Christ becomes the commander-in-chief of the hosts of warrior angels, defeating Satan and the armies of demons and earthly leaders opposed to his rule. Christ judges humanity, Satan, and the demons meeting out justice to all. The warrior angels of heaven assist in carrying out the judgment.

Angels have been warriors since the earliest times in Jewish and Christian traditions. Their role has been to fight alongside God, pictured as the warrior who engages in a war against injustice and evil. God also fights on behalf of the people of God in order to deliver them from their enemies. As the tradition progresses, this language of divine warfare speaks not only of the deliverance of God's people from evils in this world but

44. Fitzmyer, *Luke X–XXIV*, 958–61.

also of a final deliverance of God's people from all evil at the end of time. Those who perpetrate injustice on others stand to be judged. Within this tradition the language is used in visionary literature where seers are given a glimpse of what is happening in heaven. However, angelic warriors are also thought to be real beings that influence events on earth. Some groups even expected the angelic warriors to fight alongside them against their enemies. The language is also used to refer to the battle against thinking and doing evil, which takes place in the human soul. Within the NT the language transmutes and the only battle that Christian disciples are to fight is this battle against sin. God will judge and punish others with the help of the holy angels—Christians are only to love others. Although the motif of warrior angels and divine warfare may not be to the taste of people today, what it refers to in the NT is surely worthy of consideration: the establishment of justice; the battle against selfishness to love others; and the judgment that ensures that those who have done good will get their reward.

10

Is Satan Misunderstood?

During the last couple of decades a wind of reconciliation has been blowing through certain parts of the scholarly world. At one time, talking with terrorists was deemed completely unacceptable behaviour but the public debate was had and politicians decided to try it. Some recent scholarship has taken this a step further. It appears that Satan has been badly misunderstood and other people are responsible for the crimes attributed to him. Where his character has been maligned, Satan has only been doing his job as a loyal angel of the LORD God. To make things worse, he never got on with his father as his father rejected him in favour of another child. Satan has been mistreated, unfairly criticised, and unloved. Perhaps people should take the time to understand him. From the point of view of traditional Christianity, these ideas are at the very least interesting and so worth examining to see if these scholars have a point.

THE EARLY HISTORY OF SATAN

The arguments start with a reassessment of the early history of Satan. Satan figures little in the OT and where Satan does appear, he is not pictured as the prince of demons. The picture of Satan in the OT is quite different and in order to understand Satan one has to examine the biography of the figure as it develops throughout the OT and into the second temple period.

Before becoming the name of a particular figure in the divine council, *śāṭān* was simply a Hebrew word, the basic meaning of which is "adversary." Sometimes the term refers to a military adversary. So, for example, when David appears among the Philistines as an ally of the Philistine king, Achish, the other Philistine kings naturally query his presence—as David was previously an enemy and they suspect his motives for entering the ranks of the Philistine army. They suggest that in battle he may become their *śāṭ ān* or adversary and suggest that Achish sends David away (1 Sam 29:4). The word is used of military adversaries elsewhere in the OT: Solomon is said to be without an *adversary* (1 Kgs 5:4); king Hadad of Edom becomes Solomon's *adversary* (1 Kgs 11:14) as does king Rezon of Syria (1 Kgs 11:23, 25). The term may be used in a vaguely similar sense to this of the angel of the LORD who appears with a drawn sword to block the way of Balaam, a military looking angel who opposes the journey of the prophet (Num 22:22, 32).

Most of the remaining uses of the term in the OT describe an angel in the heavenly council. All but one of these use the term with the definite article (*haśśāṭān*), meaning "the satan." The fact that the term occurs with the article, "*the* satan," suggests that the figure referred to is fulfilling a particular role, that of the adversary. This seems to be what we find in the first two chapters of the biblical book of Job. Job is a righteous man and God has blessed him with great prosperity (Job 1:1–5). The heavenly beings present themselves to the LORD one day and the satan comes with them (Job 1:6). The LORD enquires where the satan has been and the satan answers that he has been walking around the earth. God asks the satan if he has noticed the righteousness of Job. The satan immediately accuses Job of self-centredness, fearing God for the material blessings he receives from God. The LORD permits the satan to test Job's righteousness by removing his family and wealth but Job still praises God (Job 1:7–22). Later the satan enters heaven again and the conversation continues. The satan accuses Job of blessing God because he still has his health. God permits the satan to test Job further by sending him ill-health but Job refuses to curse God (Job 2:1–10).[1]

A similar picture of the satan appears in the biblical book of Zechariah. In a vision Zechariah sees the Jewish high priest Joshua standing in front of the LORD in the divine council. The satan is standing nearby to accuse Joshua. The LORD rebukes the satan and vindicates Joshua (Zech 3:1–5). The nature of the accusation is not explicitly mentioned but the role of the

---

1. Clines, *Job 1–20*, 18–23.

satan is clear enough. The satan is accusing Joshua of something of which the LORD acquits him.[2] Both Job 1–2 and Zech 3 picture the satan as an accuser in the heavenly council. Other ancient Near Eastern religions had members of the divine councils who acted as the prosecution, or legal accuser, and it appears that the satan performs a similar role in the Hebrew divine council.[3]

The single instance in the OT of *śāṭān* being used of a heavenly being without the presence of the definite article is found in 1 Chr 21. David is incited to take a census of the people, an action for which the LORD punishes him. 1 Chronicles has Satan, or "*a* satan" (no article) incite David to perform this act (1 Chr 21:1). Given that there is no article, some commentators suggest that *śāṭān* ought to be written with a capital "S," as the accuser figure in heaven has taken the name of his role as his personal name. No longer is he simply "the accuser," or the satan (*haśśāṭān*) but he has taken the name, Satan (a little like whichever blacksmith[s] first adopted Smith as a surname).[4] Given that God incites David to take the same census in the parallel story in 1 Sam 24, some theologians have suggested that Satan is the dark or angry side of God.[5] However, others scholars have suggested that the simplest way of taking the article-less *śāṭān* in 1 Chr 21:1 is the same way it is taken in the rest of the OT, simply as "an adversary."[6]

At some point, and certainly by the time of the writing of *Jubilees* sometime in the second century BC, Satan *does* appear to have become the name of a heavenly adversary: "And all of their days they will be complete and live in peace and rejoicing and there will be no Satan and no evil one who will destroy because all of their days will be days of blessing and healing" (*Jub.* 23:29). Satan is identified as the evil one who will destroy. This bears more resemblance to the demonic figure who seeks to destroy humanity than to a heavenly accuser who demands that justice be done to the unrighteous or that righteous people be tested to see if they are truly as good as they appear.

---

2. Meyers and Meyers, *Haggai, Zechariah 1–8*, 182–94.

3. See further Day, *Adversary in Heaven*.

4. For example, Braun, *1 Chronicles*, 216–17.

5. Wink, *Unmasking the Powers*, 30–38.

6. Day, *Adversary in Heaven*, 127–45; Bentjes, "Satan, God and the Angel(s)," 139–54; Knoppers, *1 Chronicles 10–29*, 743–44.

In the following centuries, the understanding of the character of Satan develops in different ways in differing religious traditions. In rabbinic Judaism Satan remains the servant of God accusing sinners, especially in Israel, although the rabbis discuss amongst themselves whether to pity Satan for the role God assigns him or to attribute to him some kind of malicious intent (*b. B. Bat.* 16a). In Christianity Satan is understood to be an evil power opposing God until the time when God defeats him and his power to accuse the people of God is broken (Rev 12:7–12). In Islam Satan is called Iblis, who is punished for refusing to worship Adam and so swears revenge on him. Iblis disobeys God, although he is unable to rebel against God.[7]

SATAN IN REHAB

Working partly against this background of the early history of Satan, Kirsten Nielsen argues for understanding Satan differently from traditional Christianity. Her starting point is family relationships, which are often dysfunctional. Noting the popularity of stories about fathers and sons in the Bible, Nielsen suggests that the story of God and Satan should be read as a father and son story.[8]

Nielsen takes the parable of the prodigal son (Luke 15:11–32) as a paradigm, or pattern, according to which to read the story of God and Satan. In this parable the father has two sons, one of which seems to win the favour of the father despite his wild behaviour. Indeed some readers of the parable might feel that the father rewards the son for his irresponsible extravagance. The other son is loyal and faithful and yet never receives the rewards that the other son gains. The parable might be read as a dysfunctional family in which the extravagant love of the father marginalizes the loyal and honest son who understandably feels aggrieved.[9]

In a similar manner, God marginalizes Satan in Job. God approaches Satan with questioning that might be read as suggesting suspicion and

---

7. For a study of Satan in these three religious traditions, see Jung, *Fallen Angels*.

8. Nielsen, *Satan: The Prodigal Son*.

9. For my own part, I would distance myself from such a reading of the parable. Extravagant love for sinners is something from which I have benefitted and continue to benefit and much as I believe in personal responsibility, I would not want to begrudge anybody such extravagant love.

disapproval (Job 1:7). God proceeds to sing the praises of Job, whom God portrays as blameless and perfect in every way (Job 1:8). Therefore, it ought not to come as a surprise that Satan feels jilted and so turns on Job in his response to God, finding reasons to criticize his earthly brother out of motives of jealousy (Job 1:9–11). Satan has a negative reaction to God, which is rooted in the lack of love and approval he receives from God.[10]

On this reading Satan is not a demon, let alone the prince of demons. Nor does Satan qualify as the dark or angry side of God. Far from it, Satan is the son that God fails to appreciate. Perhaps the dark or angry side of God has helped to mould Satan into who he is in Job but Satan is his own person and not simply an aspect of his father. Nor may Satan simply be read as a member of the divine council with a certain role to play, seeking out and sorting out unrighteousness in humanity.[11]

Satan appears again as the rejected brother in the NT. The Matthean temptation narrative is read as presenting Jesus and Satan as two sons of God (Matt 4:1–11). The temptations of Jesus by Satan are read as a case of sibling rivalry over who is truly God's heir.[12] The parable of the prodigal son is examined within the framework of reading Jesus as the younger son and Satan as the elder brother. Jesus may not have sinned when he left his heavenly glory but like the younger son he did not always follow the Torah. The elder brother demands justice and equity just like Satan who, as heavenly accuser, demands that justice is done. In flaunting Torah Jesus is less than loyal to the father and in demanding justice Satan shows himself firmly loyal to Torah—and yet the Father favors Jesus.[13]

Nielsen concludes her study with a plea that the church returns to its own text, the Bible, and examines exactly what it does say about Satan rather than simply repeating what orthodoxy dictates. Family life is difficult and it may be that God has more than one son. Christian spirituality needs to be open to other readings of Scripture than those provided by the tradition and to be informed and shaped by them.

Nielsen offers an interesting reading of the texts but Satan probably cannot be rehabilitated quite so easily. Reading God as having two sons, Job and Satan, is difficult. The text of Job never identifies Job and Satan as

10. See further Nielsen, *Satan: The Prodigal Son*, 17–27, 59–105.

11. Ibid., 52–58.

12. Ibid., 106–28.

13. Ibid., 129–55.

particular sons of God let alone the relationship between Job and Satan as one of sibling rivalry. This counts strongly against the argument. Moreover, interpreting the Matthean temptation narrative as a case of sibling rivalry reads into the text things that are simply not there (i.e., Jesus and Satan as sons of God and sibling rivalry between them). Given the importance of the theme of Jesus as the Son of God in Matthew, one might reasonably expect Matthew to make the sonship of Satan and the sibling rivalry more obvious, had this been his intention.[14] The interpretation of the prodigal son is also strained. The prodigal son sins and Jesus does not. This makes the parallel very weak, not least when much historical scholarship sees Jesus as a Torah-abiding Jew.[15] The father tries to persuade the elder brother to join the party (Luke 15:25–32) whereas Luke has Satan cast out of heaven (Luke 10:18). All told, the interpretations of the text required to support this thesis are too weak to hold water. This kind of rehabilitation will not work for Satan.

DEMONIZING SATAN

In an amusing (if provocative and at times flippant) work, Henry Ansgar Kelly also attempts to rehabilitate Satan. Kelly seeks to demonstrate that Satan ought not to be read primarily as the arch demon who fell from heaven and since his fall has been waging a cosmic war on God. Nor does the Bible connect Satan with the Fall of Adam and Eve in Gen 2–3. The day the early Christian fathers turned Satan into the prince of demons, waging cosmic war on God, which involved bringing about the fall of humanity from grace, was "A BAD DAY" for Christianity and has had many unforeseen evil consequences.[16]

In the OT, a *śāṭān* is merely an accuser or adversary. The angel of the LORD in Num 22 is one such adversary. The satan in Job is an angelic member of the divine council who has the responsibility for keeping an eye out for bad behavior and reporting it to "High Command." The same is true of the satan in Zech 3. In the LXX, the *śāṭān* is translated as *ho diabolos* ("the devil") and here Kelly suggests the idea of Satan is born. Nonetheless

---

14. For a brief introduction to the importance of the title Son of God for Matthew, see Davies and Allison, *Matthew*, 1:339–40.

15. See chiefly Meier, *Law and Love*; Casey, *Jewish Prophet*, 58–64.

16. Kelly, *Satan: A Biography*, 191–298.

Angels

there is no mention of Satan in the Dead Sea scrolls or in the stories of the
Fall of the Watchers in *1 Enoch*. The diabolical figure of Mastema in *Jubilees*
is responsible for punishing or disciplining humankind—a role not so far
removed from that of "the satan" in the OT. There is no Satan figure in the
Dead Sea scrolls if by that we mean an active personification of evil. There
are only metaphorical figures, which are largely passive, such as Belial.[17]

By and large, in the NT Satan retains his role of testing the righteous
and meeting out justice on wrongdoers. So he tests the faith of new believers (1 Thess 3:5), punishes an errant believer (1 Cor 5:5), and tests the
faith of those who are lacking self-control (1 Cor 7:5). Satan even tests Paul
himself (2 Cor 12:7). Additionally Satan sows seeds of strife in Christian
communities (2 Cor 2:10–11) but Paul assures his readers that Satan will be
crushed (Rom 16:20). In the Gospels Satan retains his position as the tester,
as witnessed by his role in the temptation narratives (e.g., Mark 1:12–13)
and his testing of those who hear the word preached by Jesus (Mark 4:15).
Satan tests the resolve of Jesus through Peter's denial of the necessity of
the crucifixion (Mark 8:33). Kelly reads other NT texts as basically demonstrating the same pattern, that Satan remains the tester until we get to
the book of Revelation, where Satan is called the accuser (Rev 12:10), but
he has become many other things as well; as Kelly puts it, "he's a bad 'un."
Although in John Satan has become the ruler of this world, in Hebrews he
has the power of death and in Revelation he is defeated, nowhere in the NT
(including 2 Cor 11:14) is Satan connected with the fall of humanity.[18]

Kelly then outlines how the Satan was connected with the fall of humankind in the work of the early church fathers, including Justin Martyr,
Tertullian, and Cyprian. He goes on to demonstrate how Origen interpreted Isa 14 (originally an oracle about the defeat of the king of Babylon)
as being about the fall of Satan himself from heaven. And at this point the
story of the fall of Satan and his role in the fall of Adam and Eve is complete. As they say, the rest is history. This story becomes the official line of
the church and becomes foundational to later developments in theology
as well as the justification of some shameful practices, such as the ways
in which the Spanish Inquisition treated sorcerers. In reviewing the way
in which the church has re-written the biography and role of Satan, Kelly
urges Christians to go back to their own Scriptures and study what they say

17. Ibid., 13–52.
18. Ibid., 53–172.

108

about Satan. He recommends that they peel off the Zoroastrian accretions of Satan as the demonic opponent of God in the cosmic battle for spiritual supremacy, and the stories of the fall of Satan and Satan having a role in the fall of humanity, and that they look at what the Bible *really* says. By rehabilitating Satan as the heavenly accuser, people can forget the idea that Satan is the ultimate cause of evil and they can concentrate on discovering the "real causes of evil actions that people actually commit."[19]

Kelly overplays his hand. He does make some valid criticisms of the way in which the traditional biography of Satan is read out of the Bible. It is true that in Gen 3 a talking snake, which is never explicitly identified as Satan, tempts Eve to disobey God. Neither does Paul explicitly state that his reference to Satan disguising himself as an angel of light (2 Cor 11:14) recalls Jewish legends built around Genesis 3 in which Satan does disguise himself as an angel of light to tempt Eve a second time (*L.A.E.* 9:1–5).[20] However, the idea that Satan is not the diabolical leader of the armies of demons in a cosmic struggle against the LORD of hosts and the warrior angels in the NT (as paralleled in the second temple literature) is mistaken.

The figure of Belial or the Prince of Darkness heads up an army of devils in many of the Dead Sea Scrolls, and the *War Scroll* and the *Hodayot* outline the battle between the angelic armies of the Most High and the demonic hordes of Belial. Although not entirely consistent in their portrayal of Belial, the scrolls do portray him as much more than a passive metaphorical figure of the sort that Kelly imagines Belial to be. While Belial remains in some way subordinate to God (as does Satan in Christian tradition), he tries to tempt the members of the Qumran community to do evil (1QS 12:2). So great is the concern of being led astray by Belial, the community curses him at their covenant ceremony in order to protect community members (CD 16:4–5). At the same time, God uses Belial as an instrument of judgment (CD 8:2), much the same as God uses Satan in Paul's writing (1 Cor 5:5). The figure of Belial is a diabolical adversary to God in the cosmic battle for supremacy and Belial plays a role similar to that of Satan in the NT and Christian tradition.[21]

19. Ibid., 175–328.

20. Thrall, *Second Corinthians*, 2:695–96.

21. See further on Belial in the Dead Sea Scrolls, Steudel, "God and Belial," 332–40; Martone, "Evil or Devil?" 117–27.

Angels

Similarly, *Jubilees* identifies Mastema as the prince of the evil spirits (*Jub.* 10:7–8). Although playing the role of the accuser (*Jub.* 48:15), his actions cannot all be explained as testing righteousness or seeking the punishment of sin. Mastema encourages the Egyptians to pursue the Israelites as they leave Egypt. The children of Israel have done nothing wrong and there is no suggestion in the text that Mastema is testing their righteousness (unlike the satan in the Book of Job). The fact that the angels deliver Israel from the hand of Mastema (*Jub.* 48:13) suggests that he was seeking to destroy them. Throughout *Jub.* 48 the angels bind and release Mastema to perform his evil deeds such that they might continue the unfolding of the heavenly plan. Although the actions of Mastema enable the continuance of the divine plan, this is not through his willingness to cooperate with God so much as through divine control of his evil and destructive tendencies. *Jubilees* paints a similar picture of Satan (*Jub.* 23:29).

The Gospels also identify Satan as the ruler of demons and his activity with the demonic activities traditionally attributed to him. The evangelist Mark reports a debate between Jesus and the scribes:

> And the scribes who came down from Jerusalem said, "He has Beelzebul, and by the ruler of the demons he casts out demons." 23 And he called them to him, and spoke to them in parables, "How can Satan cast out Satan? 24 If a kingdom is divided against itself, that kingdom cannot stand. 25 And if a house is divided against itself, that house will not be able to stand. 26 And if Satan has risen up against himself and is divided, he cannot stand, but his end has come."
>
> (Mark 3:22–26)

The scribes suggest that Jesus casts out demons by Beelzebul, the ruler of demons.[22] Jesus retorts that Satan cannot cast out Satan. His response only makes sense if he understands "Satan" to be another name for "Beelzebul" and as the ruler of demons. Jesus identifies Satan as the *ruler of the demons* and not simply as the prosecuting attorney of the divine council. Jesus' ministry of exorcism constitutes a form of divine warfare—casting out demons prevents them from influencing people and so destroys the grip that they have on humanity.[23]

---

22. On Beelzebul, see Day, *Yahweh and the Gods*, 77–81.

23. See further, Twelftree, *Jesus the Exorcist*; Evans, "Inaugurating the Kingdom," 49–75. Specifically on Mark 3:22–26, see Marcus, *Mark 1–8*, 269.

Something similar lies behind the following conversation between Jesus and his disciples: "The seventy returned with joy, saying, 'Lord, in your name even the demons submit to us!' He said to them, 'I watched Satan fall from heaven like a flash of lightning'" (Luke 10:17–18). The disciples have returned from a mission upon which Jesus sent them and they are amazed at their authority over the demons. They have been exercising a ministry of exorcism. Their delight at the effectiveness of their exorcistic ministry leads Jesus to exclaim that he saw Satan fall from heaven. The effective exercise of exorcistic ministry is identified with the fall of Satan from heaven. It is very difficult to read this text with the idea that Satan is primarily the heavenly prosecuting attorney rather than the leader of the armies of demons.[24]

The book of Revelation does the same thing, only more bluntly, identifying Satan as the devil, the dragon, the ancient serpent, and the deceiver of the whole world:

> 9 The great dragon was thrown down, that ancient serpent, who is called the Devil and Satan, the deceiver of the whole world—he was thrown down to the earth, and his angels were thrown down with him.
>
> (Rev 12:9)

> 2 He seized the dragon, that ancient serpent, who is the Devil and Satan, and bound him for a thousand years . . .
>
> (Rev 20:2)

The dragon, being seven-headed like the multi-headed Leviathan and the seven-headed *Lôtan*, is best identified as Leviathan. The ancient serpent is slightly more difficult. It is possible that the ancient serpent refers to Leviathan also, as Leviathan is described as a fleeing and twisting serpent in Isaiah, though not as an *ancient* serpent (Isa 27:1). However, nothing in the Greek wording suggests this. The majority of commentators identify the ancient serpent as the serpent in the Garden of Eden who tempts Eve.[25] This being the case, the NT does provide some evidence of the serpent of the garden of Eden being identified as Satan, contrary to

24. Ibid., 273–74, 280–82.

25. For example, Caird, *Revelation*, 156; Harrington, *Revelation*, 132; Mounce, *Revelation*, 237; Aune, *Revelation 6–16*, 696–97; Beale, *Revelation*, 665–66; Osborne, *Revelation*, 471–73.

what Kelly would have us believe. Moreover this interpretation of Gen 3 is not original to Revelation as it can be found in the Wisdom of Solomon, which was likely written slightly earlier (Wis 2:24).[26] Likewise the most likely background to the Pauline affirmation that "Satan will soon be crushed under your feet" (Rom 16:20) is the crushing of the serpent's head by Adam's foot (Gen 3:15). Such an allusion would demonstrate that Paul read the serpent of Gen 3 as Satan also.[27] Given that the dragon Leviathan is the cosmic enemy who opposes God with the other dragons, Satan is also identified as the arch demon who opposes the armies of heaven (which is obvious from the context of Rev 12 anyway where Satan opposes Michael and the armies of angels).

The NT also portrays Satan as opposing the growth of Christian disciples in holiness. Paul talks of Satan preventing him from visiting his converts in the church at Thessalonica (1 Thess 2:18). Paul is very concerned for them as he believes that they are rather young in the faith and that the persecutions they experience might shake their faith and he feels he needs to be there for them to encourage them (1 Thess 2:9—3:5). Satan blocks Paul's way and so opposes the growth and development of the gospel of God. This is more an act of warfare against the churches than the action of the counsel for the heavenly prosecution. Satan is described as using many kinds of wicked deception to prevent people from converting to Christ (2 Thess 2:9). Again, this seems more like warfare against the gospel than the actions of a responsible celestial lawyer or a tester of righteousness. The biblical book of Ephesians pictures the devil using anger to cause difficulties among Christian disciples (Eph 4:27) and given that "the devil" is the standard LXX translation for the satan or Satan, we seem to have Satan trying to create dissension among Christians. The picture we have in the

---

26. Winston, *Wisdom of Solomon*, 121–22. The fact that English translations have "the devil" does not nullify the identification of the serpent as Satan as the LXX translation of the Hebrew "*śāṭān*" is always "*ho diabolos*" ("the devil"), and Wis 2:24 has the Greek "*ho diabolos.*" On the date of the Wisdom of Solomon, see Winston, *Wisdom of Solomon*, 20–25. On the date of Revelation, see Beale, *Revelation*, 4–27.

27. Fitzmyer, *Romans*, 746; cautiously Moo, *Romans*, 932–33; Jewett, *Romans*, 994 although note that Jewett lists a number of other possible backgrounds to the use of this phrase that would suggest that Paul does not necessarily have Gen 3:15 in mind. It is difficult to make a strong case for the allusion as the two texts do not have sufficient vocabulary in common to warrant claiming a verbal allusion.

epistles suggests that Satan has become the *enemy* of the churches and not simply the accuser of the unrighteous.

Kelly is correct to point out that the NT continues to portray Satan as the heavenly accuser. However, the NT also depicts Satan as the prince of the demons, the diabolical head of the demonic hordes that oppose the armies of the heavenly hosts and ultimately God. This image of Satan as the enemy in the divine warfare is prevalent in second temple literature and present in the texts of the NT. The identification of Satan as the serpent in the garden of Eden is also present both in the second temple Jewish literature and in the book of Revelation. Although it may not be the most prominent theme in the literature, it is by no means absent from it either. While any reasonable person would have to agree with Kelly that discerning the true causes of evil actions may well result in enabling good to flourish, they may also have to dissent from his opinions on Satan's role in the biblical texts. Satan is the cosmic adversary in divine warfare and he does appear to have tempted Eve in the garden of Eden—or that, at least, is what many Jews and Christians thought in the second temple period.[28]

DEMONIZING OTHER PEOPLE

In a similar vein Elaine Pagels writes what she calls a social history of Satan. This is not like the history of religions biography of Satan in which texts are studies in chronological order to discover how the beliefs of people about Satan developed.[29] A social history of Satan traces how the idea of Satan and the way in which people identify others with Satan or as followers of Satan—i.e., how they demonize them—develops over time. Pagels traces her social history of Satan through the biblical texts to the writings of the early church fathers.

In the OT Satan is a member of the divine council who acts as the heavenly prosecuting attorney (Job 1–2; Zech 3). At some point in the second temple period Satan becomes identified as the enemy of God in the cosmic battle between the spiritual forces of good and the spiritual forces of evil. Satan (or Mastema, Beliar, or Belial—these are all names for the

---

28. See further on Satan in the biblical texts Page, *Powers of Evil*.

29. This she believes has been done well by Neil Forsyth, *The Old Enemy*.

same figure) is the father of the reprobates, those among the people of God, Israel, who do evil.[30]

The Gospel of Mark continues in this trend. Rather than admit that the Romans crucified Jesus as a terrorist and blame Pontius Pilate, the Roman governor, for his death, Mark blames the Sanhedrin (the council of leading Jews) for his death (Mark 14:53–65; 15:1). However, Mark does not portray the crucifixion of Jesus as a failure but as part of the cosmic battle of the forces of good against the forces of evil. The opening scene of the Gospel has Satan attack Jesus in the temptation (Mark 1:12–13). Then Jesus launches a counterattack through his ministry of exorcism. Jesus calls twelve disciples around himself as the nucleus of a new Israel. The Jews who do not follow him are identified as his enemies, in league with Satan. Pilate is cleared of responsibility for the crucifixion and the Sanhedrin is blamed. Mark distorts history in order to demonize Jews who chose not to follow Jesus.

Matthew, Luke, and John are said to follow the outline Mark laid down before them, and each in his own way accentuates the demonization of the Jews. Pagels prefers the Gnostic *Gospel of Thomas* as a source for reconstructing the life of Jesus historically, suggesting that Jesus was really a philosopher.[31] The early fathers continued the trend and extended it by demonizing the pagan culture of the Roman world. Finally the church turned on its own people by demonizing those whose beliefs were not deemed orthodox enough by branding them heretics; for example, the Gnostics.[32] Pagels concludes her study with a comment to the effect that the combat myth (the picture of divine or spiritual warfare) has led Christians to fight evils over the centuries but it has also led Christians to demonize other people. She urges the reader to combat evils but not to demonize others.[33]

Pagels makes a point with which many would sympathize—demonizing people does not demonstrate the love that Christians are called to show to both their friends and their enemies. However, her social history of Satan rests on insecure foundations. Much as scholars furiously debate who Jesus was historically and why he was crucified, it is very unlikely that Pagels' reconstruction of events is true. Any reconstruction of the life

30. Pagels, *Origin of Satan*, 35–62.

31. Ibid., 63–111.

32. Ibid., 112–48.

33. Ibid., 148–78.

of Jesus must explain how he got crucified. His crucifixion is one the basic facts of his life. The Romans were not in the habit of crucifying harmless philosophers and if this is all Jesus was then it is most unlikely that they would have crucified him as a terrorist. It is also very unlikely that he was a terrorist (and that the Gospels have hidden the fact well) because those who rebelled against Rome were crucified along with their followers and nobody attempted to crucify Jesus' disciples along with him.[34] Mark cannot be accused of re-writing history in the way that Pagels suggests and it may well be that certain Jewish figures or groups did plot to get Jesus crucified by the Romans.[35] As Pagels' thesis either stands or falls with this reading of events, her thesis must be viewed as profoundly insecure. Moreover, the *Gospel of Thomas* is unlikely to be more historically reliable than Matthew, Mark, or Luke. It is almost certainly much later than the canonical Gospels and less historically reliable.[36] Ironically Pagels' social history of Satan runs the risk of committing the very act she is so keen that we all avoid—demonizing others; in this case the evangelists of the canonical Gospels. Perhaps we ought to admit that in social conflict situations (whether they lead to physical violence or not), we do brand those with whom we disagree as wrong and if we hold to a particular religious view of the world, we may see them as in some way inspired by Satan. Jews and Christians of the second temple period certainly did. However, at the same time, we ought to ask how we are called to treat those whom we perceive to be our enemies—and the unequivocal answer of the NT is to love them and pray that God will bless them (Matt 5:43–48; Rom 12:14–21).

SATAN RETURNS?

Reconciliation works for good when it rests on the firm foundations of truth, the honest recognition of guilt, and the wholehearted rejection of

---

34. Sanders, *Jesus and Judaism*, 294–95.

35. For plausible historical reconstructions of events along these lines, see Wright, *Victory of God*, 540–611; Sanders, *Jesus and Judaism*, 294–318.

36. The Coptic text of the *Gospel of Thomas* is dated to around AD 400. Two fragments of what look like earlier versions of sayings found in the *Gospel of Thomas* are found in the Oxyrynchus Papyri 1, 654 and 655 which may be dated to the second century AD. On the reliability of the Synoptic Gospel traditions about Jesus, see Gerhardssohn, *Reliability of the Gospel Tradition*.

partisanship in favor of genuine open relationship. While the attempts at rehabilitating Satan demonstrate motives of seeking better functioning relationships, they appear to rest on rather insecure foundations when it comes to truth and the recognition of all the salient facts. Perhaps part of the motivation for rehabilitating Satan comes from the desire of modern people to make sense of what seems an outmoded mythological character with which Christianity is uncomfortably saddled on account of his appearance in the canonical Scriptures. Another earlier biographer of Satan saw things differently. Edward Langton covered very much the same ground as Nielsen, Kelly, and Pagels in his *Satan, A Portrait: A Study of the Character of Satan through all the Ages*. However, his conclusions were very different from theirs. Working as a historian of religion within a scholarly world that was more interested in the history of religious ideas than their reality, he ends his study surprisingly with the question of whether Satan really exists. He was researching and writing his book during the Second World War and found the evil with which the world was confronted inexplicable in terms of normal human badness. The monstrous cruelty of the twentieth century to that point, particularly the persecutions of the Jews, led him to question whether in fact there was an evil spiritual power at large in the world. The "god of this world" and "prince of the air" seeking to destroy humanity (in both its senses of humankind and humane compassion) seemed a rather plausible explanation.[37] Food for thought.

37. Langton, *Satan, A Portrait*, 118–19.

11

Principalities and Powers

Politics or Pentecost?

The atrocities committed by the Nazis prior to and during the Second World War shook the theological world. There were some who assumed that just as animal species evolved physically through natural selection, so humanity was evolving morally. The world was gradually becoming a better place as enlightened Western civilization spread throughout the globe. The complacency of those who saw the world as gradually getting better through some kind of moral evolution was undermined by the facts of what human beings in enlightened and civilized nations were capable of doing to others. Radical modern theology had developed a tendency in the nineteenth and early part of the twentieth century to dispense with the old fashioned ideas of the ancient world enshrined in the Scriptures in favour of finding new ways of expressing spiritual ideas that fitted better a modern scientific worldview. The atrocities of the Nazis led some theologians to question whether there was more wisdom in the ancient ideas than they had perhaps admitted recently.

PRINCIPALITIES AND POWERS

One of the aspects of the ancient worldview that theologians had tried to interpret for the modern mind was the language of the principalities and powers. This language may be found in the writings of Saint Paul. Scattered throughout the correspondence he had with the churches for which he was responsible, we find Paul using the following terms: *archai* or "principalities" (Rom 8:38; 1 Cor 15:24; Eph 1:21; 3:10; 6:10; Col 1:16; 2:10, 15); *exousiai* or "authorities" (1 Cor 15:24; Eph 1:21; 3:10; 6:12; Col 1:16; 2:10, 15); *dunameis* or "powers" (Rom 8:38; 1 Cor 15:24; Eph 1:21); *kuriotētes* or "dominions" (Eph 1:21; Col 1:16); *thronoi* or "thrones" (Col 1:16); *kosmokratores tou skotous toutou* or "cosmic rulers of this darkness" (Eph 6:12); *angeloi* or "angels" (Rom 8:38); and *stoicheia tou kosmou* or "elemental spirits of the universe" (Gal 4:3, 9; Col 2:8). The general consensus is that these terms refer to spiritual powers.[1]

The key to understanding these terms comes from their use in certain pseudepigraphical texts. For example, the later first-century AD text of *2 Enoch* uses certain of these terms to refer to spiritual powers: "And I saw there [in the seventh heaven] an exceptionally great light, and all the fiery armies of the great archangels, and the incorporeal forces and the dominions and the origins and the authorities, the cherubim and the seraphim and the many-eyed thrones" (*2 En.* 20:1). This text is roughly contemporary with the Pauline epistles and refers to "authorities," "dominions," and "thrones." The fact that they are mentioned alongside the armies of archangels, cherubim, and seraphim in what appears to be a list of spiritual powers in the heavens strongly suggests that these powers are to be understood as some sort of spiritual powers or angels. *1 Enoch* refers to "powers" alongside angels (*1 En.* 41:9) and to the "angels of power" and the "angels of the principalities" alongside the cherubim, seraphim, and ophanim (*1 En.* 61:10). The context in both these texts bears witness to these terms being used of angels. The *Testament of Levi* refers to thrones and authorities in the context of angels: "In the heaven below them are the messengers who carry the responses to the angels of the Lord's presence. There with him

---

1. Within the following discussion, I assume the Pauline authorship of Ephesians and Colossians, although I realize that this is controversial. For discussions of the authorship of Ephesians, see Best, *Ephesians*, 6–44; Hoehner, *Ephesians*, 2–61. For discussions of the authorship of Colossians, see O'Brien, *Colossians, Philemon*, xli–xlix; Wilson, *Colossians and Philemon*, 9–19. However, whether one accepts the pauline or deutero-pauline authorship of these epistles makes very little difference to the ideas of principalities and powers in the NT documents. Some would add *archontes* or "rulers" (1 Cor 2:6–8) to this list, see Walter Wink, *Naming the Powers*, 40–45. Similarly, Thiselton, *First Corinthians*, 233–39. In favor of this reading is the use of *archōn* to refer to the devil in Eph 2:2. However, the context of 1 Cor 2 suggests the interpretation of earthly powers, and the evidence for *archōn* being used of demonic powers in the relevant Jewish and Christian literature is lacking; see Fee, *First Corinthians*, 103–4 ; Fitzmyer, *First Corinthians*, 175–76.

are thrones and authorities; there praises to God are offered eternally" (*T. Levi* 3:7–8). These pseudepigraphical texts use the terms we find in Paul of spiritual powers or angels. Reading the terms as angelic powers in Paul makes sense as Paul uses these terms alongside the term "angel" also (Rom 8:38).[2] The LXX also throws light on these terms as it translates the Hebrew for "the LORD of hosts" as *ho kurios tōn dunameōn* or "the LORD of the powers." The powers (*dunameis*) here are the heavenly armies of the angels.

There has been some debate over whether the "elemental spirits of the universe" (*stoicheia tou kosmou*; Gal 4:3, 9; Col 2:8) ought to be included in this group. Do they refer to spiritual powers or to something else, such as the elements of the physical universe (earth, air, fire, and water—according to some of the ancients) or to the basic principles of religion?[3] There is some evidence that the *stoicheia tou kosmou* ought to be read as referring to spiritual powers:

> They [seven demons that appeared before Solomon] replied: "We are heavenly bodies [*stoicheia*], rulers of this world of darkness."
>
> (*T. Sol.* 8:2)

2. For a fuller discussion of the identification of these terms as referring to spiritual or angelic principalities or powers, see Wink, *Naming the Powers*, 39–96. This identification has been questioned recently by Forbes, "Paul's Principalities and Powers," 61–88, and Forbes, "Pauline Demonology," 51–73. Forbes argues that the evidence for the concept is weak in account of its being either in documents that are later than Paul or in documents in which the relevant terms are not found in Greek. He suggests the terms come from Middle Platonist philosophy. However, he only accounts for the terms *archē*, *dunamis*, and *stoicheia* and not the full complement of terms for which the prevailing theory of angelic powers does account. Also his theory fails to account for the way in which these terms are used in the context of divine warfare in Paul (e.g., 1 Cor 15:24), for which the prevailing theory does account. Therefore, the prevailing theory is to be preferred.

3. See the discussions in Bruce, *Galatians*, 193–94; Dunn, *Colossians and Philemon*, 148–51. Wink, (*Naming the Powers*, 67–77) concludes that the *stoicheia* function like gods in Paul. Bandstra (*The Law and the Elements*) argues against reading the *stoicheia* as personalized cosmological powers who control aspects of the universe by demonstrating that it refers to teaching in Heb 5:10 and the elements of the universe in 2 Pet 3:10–12, rather than controlling spirits in the universe. On this basis he argues for not reading controlling spirits in Gal 4:3, 9 and Col 2:8, 20. However, if one begins the definition of the word with Colossians and Galatians, one is less likely to come to the same conclusion as the exegesis of Hebrews and 2 Peter no longer controls the readings of these texts. Moreover, if Hebrews uses the term of the elements of religious faith and 2 Peter of the elements of the universe, why cannot Colossians and Galatians use *stoicheia* in another, different sense, i.e., that of controlling spirits? Admittedly the evidence for such a reading is quite likely late.

Angels

> Then I [Solomon] commanded another demon to appear before me.
> There came to me thirty-six heavenly bodies, their heads like formless
> dogs. But there were among them those who were in the form of hu-
> mans, or of bulls, or of dragons, with faces like the birds, or the beasts,
> or the sphinx. 2 When I, Solomon, saw these beings, I asked them, say-
> ing, "Well, who are you?" All at once, with one voice, they said, "We are
> thirty-six heavenly bodies [*stoicheia*], the world rulers of the darkness
> of this age."

> (*T. Sol.* 18:1–2)

Without any doubt the *Testament of Solomon* identifies the *stoicheia* as
demons in both citations. The second quotation identifies the thirty-six
stoicheia as "world rulers of the darkness of this age." The term used is the
kosmokratores tou skotous, which Ephesians uses of the demonic spirits
that set out to undermine the faith of Christian disciples (Eph 6:12). The
Testament of Solomon also refers to these demonic powers as "principalities" and "authorities" (*T. Sol.* 20:15). However, the validity of the evidence
of the *Testament of Solomon* is open to question as the text has been dated
anywhere between the first and fourth century AD.[4] If the text is dated
early, then this is clear evidence of first-century Jews using these terms in
this way. If the text is dated in the fourth century, then the ground upon
which the identification rests for early Christian texts becomes a little
shaky. Regardless of the exact identification of the *stoicheia tou kosmou*,
there is sufficient evidence elsewhere to establish that these terms generally
refer in the Pauline epistles to angelic powers.

IDENTIFYING THE POWERS

The principalities, rulers, authorities, powers, dominions, thrones, cosmic
rulers of this darkness, and probably the elemental spirits of the universe
are spiritual powers or angels. But what kind of angels are they? Taken
together, the Pauline letters present the following picture of the principalities and powers. They are part of creation and were created by Christ (Col
1:16). However, they now present themselves as spiritual forces of evil (Eph
6:12). God defeats the powers through Jesus' death on the cross (Col 2:15).
Although humanity has been subject to the powers of these elemental spirits (Gal 4:3, 8), Jesus Christ the Son of God has come to set humanity free

4. For the date of the *Testament of Solomon*, see McCown, *Testament of Solomon*,
105–8.

from their influence (Gal 4:3–10). Like the god of this age (2 Cor 4:4), the elemental spirits enslave humanity in hollow and empty worldviews. These worldviews imprison humanity in religious rituals and the moral demands of religion, preventing people from finding freedom and salvation in Christ (Gal 4:3–10; Col 2:8, 16–23). Primarily Paul refers to the worldviews of his Jewish contemporaries who have not accepted Christ.[5] However, Christ is stronger than these spiritual powers and so those who believe in Christ may be freed from the influence of the powers and discover the love of God in Christ (Rom 8:38–39). Followers of Christ need not be imprisoned in the worldviews imposed by the powers or act in the ways they prescribe (Gal 4:3–11; Col 2:8–23). Christian disciples are called upon to resist the influence of the powers and live instead the life to which Christ has called them (Eph 6:10–17; Col 2:8–23). At the end of time the powers will finally be defeated (1 Cor 15:24–26). So the powers are angels who have turned aside from following God and now oppose God. They hold human beings imprisoned within beliefs and legal demands that prevent them from living the good life that God intended people to live. At the end of time, Christ will defeat these angels.[6]

This language of the principalities and powers in Paul is most probably partly rooted in the traditions of the guardian angels of the nations where the LORD God divides responsibility for the nations among the angels. The earliest text of the Hebrew OT has God divide responsibility for the nations among the gods (Deut 32:8–9) and the LXX translation interprets this as the responsibility for the nations being divided up between the angels of God (Deut 32:8–9 LXX). The second temple literature continues this tradition of God putting angels in charge of nations (*Jub.* 15:31–32; *1 En.* 89:59–60; Sir 17:17). So each nation on the earth has an angelic representative on the divine council, except for Israel, which is represented by the LORD himself (Deut 32:8–9).

The LORD God of Israel presides over the divine council and so over the angels of the nations. The OT does not always picture the angels of the nations as performing their tasks competently:

5. On Gal 4:3–10, see Bruce, *Galatians*, 194; Martyn, *Galatians*, 393–406. On Col 2:8, 16–23, see Wilson, *Colossians and Philemon*, 226–27.

6. On the pauline understanding of the powers, see further Arnold, *Powers of Darkness*, 87–165.

Angels

> God has taken his place in the divine council; in the midst of the gods he
> holds judgment: 2 "How long will you judge unjustly and show partiality
> to the wicked? 3 Give justice to the weak and the orphan; maintain the
> right of the lowly and the destitute. 4 Rescue the weak and the needy; de-
> liver them from the hand of the wicked." 5 They have neither knowledge
> nor understanding, they walk around in darkness; all the foundations of
> the earth are shaken. 6 I say, "You are gods, children of the Most High, all
> of you; 7 nevertheless, you shall die like mortals, and fall like any prince."
>
> (Ps 82:1–7)

God presides over the divine council and berates the angels of the nations
for failing in their task to establish justice and protection for the weak and
needy upon earth (Ps 82:2–4). Therefore, he addresses the gods or angels of
the council and tells them that they will be destroyed for their failures (Ps
82:6–7). In the final verse of the psalm, the psalmist calls upon the LORD
to establish the justice on earth that the angelic guardians have manifestly
failed to maintain.[7]

The picture of the judgment of disobedient or incompetent angels
persists in the second temple literature. An apocalyptic vision in 1 *Enoch*
portrays the division of responsibility for the nations, pictured as sheep,
among the angels of the nations, pictured as seventy shepherds (1 *En.*
89:59–60). These shepherds are given authority to judge and punish the
sheep. However, the shepherds exceed the number of sheep they are permitted to kill and destroy and they abandon the sheep to wild animals,
which attack and devour the sheep (1 *En.* 89:65–9). However, the Lord
of the sheep (the LORD God) has an angel keep a record of the abuses
of the shepherds and this record is presented to the Lord of the sheep (1
En. 89:61–64, 70–71). The Lord of the sheep takes his place on throne of
judgment in the divine council (here pictured as in the land of Israel) and
pronounces judgment on the seventy shepherds for killing and destroying
more sheep than they were instructed. The shepherds are consigned to the
fiery abyss (1 *En.* 90:20–25). This story presents part of the history of Israel
in mythological form, referring to the way in which the angelic representa-
tives abused their powers at the fall of Jerusalem to Babylon in 586 BC.
God decided to judge Judah for the sins of the people. However, the angels
of the nations allowed the destruction to become far worse than God had

7. Similarly, Hossfeld and Zenger, *Psalms 2,* 328–37.

ordained.[8] The result is the judgment of these angels for the failure to carry out the commands of God and the resulting injustice that this disobedience or incompetence caused. This vision in *1 Enoch* pictures the angels of the nations being given responsibility for administering justice and being punished for their failure to carry out this task.

Paul uses the language of principalities and powers to describe angels. The kinds of angels he describes have been created by God (Col 1:16)— as are all angels in second temple Jewish and early Christian literature, whether they are fallen (like the Watchers) or they remain loyal to the Most High. The angels Paul describes are responsible for aspects of human cultures, although not nations as such (Col 2:8–23; Gal 4:3, 9). In both these texts Torah observance is primarily in view although Gal 4:8–9 implies that the elemental spirits (or *stoicheia*) may be identified with aspects of pagan cultures and beliefs.[9] These angels are not doing the will of the LORD God as they are imposing worldviews, values, and regulations that prevent people from finding freedom in Christ (Col 2:8–23; Gal 4:1–11). At the final judgment Christ will destroy these angels (1 Cor 15:24–26). The parallels between the origins, functions, and final destiny of angels of the nations in Jewish tradition and the origins, functions, and final destiny of the principalities and powers in Paul are sufficient to suggest that the pauline picture of the principalities and powers is best understood against the background of the ancient Jewish beliefs about the angels of the nations, though the pauline picture is not necessarily identical with the traditions upon which it draws.

Another ancient Jewish motif that recurs in the pauline depiction of the principalities and powers is that of divine warfare. Paul writes of Christ destroying every ruler, authority, and power in the same context as putting all his enemies under his feet (1 Cor 15:24–26). The language Paul uses here has a markedly military flavor. Colossians uses the picture of disarming the rulers and authorities and leading them in a triumphal procession. Victorious ancient Roman generals used to lead their troops in victory processions through Rome in which some of their defeated enemies (particularly their nobles or leaders) were paraded in front of the chariot of the victorious general and the spoils of war displayed for all to see. Colossians

8. Nickelsburg, *1 Enoch 1*, 393–94.

9. Martyn, *Galatians*, 410.

pictures the cross as achieving such a victory, and the angelic powers are paraded as a defeated foe (Col 2:14–15).[10] The language of defeat and victory, and the image of the triumphal procession here strongly suggest that the pauline picture of the principalities and powers draws on the ancient motif of divine warfare.

This would explain the way in which the language is developed in Ephesians. The final chapter particularly pictures the principalities and powers as being engaged in warfare against the Christian disciples. Disciples are to put on the amour of God (Eph 6:11) with which God fights the cosmic enemy (Isa 59:15b–19; Wis 5:17–23).[11] Their fight is described as being against cosmic powers rather than earthly enemies (Eph 6:12). This sounds rather like the way in which the divine warfare motif is developed in the book of Revelation where Christian disciples are not to do battle on the battlefield (as were the community at Qumran) but rather in living out the life of holiness and righteousness to which they are called. The enemies are described as authorities, cosmic rulers of the present darkness, and spiritual forces of evil in the heavenly places (Eph 6:12). Their opponents are the principalities and powers. Here they are clearly the enemies of Christian disciples and ultimately of God the divine warrior, whose armour the disciples don.[12]

So the pauline epistles paint a picture of the principalities and powers as angels who are possibly incompetent in that they impose beliefs and practices (particularly Torah observance on Gentiles) that prevent people finding freedom in Christ. Whether they are incompetent or not, they are certainly malevolent, attacking the church and trying to prevent Christians from growing in freedom, peace, and justice in Christ. These angels were defeated by Christ on the cross and will be defeated by Christ on the Day of Judgment when their rule will finally end. The battle motif describes the way in which Christian disciples are to resist the attempts of such spiritual

10. Wilson, *Colossians and Philemon*, 212–23.

11. On the picture of the armour of God being rooted in OT traditions of God the divine warrior battling the forces of chaos (particularly in Isa 59:15b–19 and Wis 5:17–23), see Angel, *Chaos and the Son of Man*, 89–95. For a detailed study, see Yoder Neufeld, *Put on the Armour of God*.

12. The cluster of divine warfare motifs surrounding the principalities and powers here renders most unlikely the thesis of Wesley Carr that the angels and principalities are good angels rather than demonic powers opposed to God; see Carr, *Angels and Principalities*, 93–114. Against Carr, see particularly Wink, *Naming the Powers*, 84–89.

powers to make them conform to any beliefs or practices that contradict the life of holiness to which Christians are called or the truths of the gospel.

INTERPRETING THE POWERS

Before the Second World War, there was a movement in theology to demy-thologize the Scriptures for modern believers. The task of theology had become the identification of the essence of the faith, stripping off the ancient views of the world in which it was clothed in the Scriptures, and re-clothing it in modern dress. This involved extracting the essence of the gospel out of texts that spoke of angels and demons and cosmic battles as modern people were thought to have grown out of such ancient and old-fashioned ways of looking at the world.[13] We cannot take that kind of stuff literally any longer.

After the war, the Dutch NT scholar Hendrik Berkhof responded to this program of demythologization in a study of the principalities and powers in Paul. His study constitutes a direct challenge to those who assume that the pauline language of principalities and powers is irrelevant in the modern era. Accepting the picture of angels painted in the second temple Jewish apocalyptic literature, Berkhof asserts that the powers are personal spiritual beings that administrate the universe and so influence events on earth both within human society and nature. Berkhof asserts that Paul himself partly demythologizes the language of the powers and principalities, using them to describe the bondage under which humanity without Christ labors.[14]

The powers were created good (Col 1:16). However, they are part of the fallen creation. The powers are identified with human governments, and so in the twentieth century might be identified with the government of Adolf Hitler. The powers are supposed to conserve order (Gal 4:1–11), which is not negative in itself although such world orders are all superseded in Christ. Jesus Christ triumphs over these powers on the cross (Col 2:13–15)

---

13. For example, see Bultmann, "New Testament and Mythology," 1–43.

14. Berkhof, *Christ and the Powers*, 7–20. The Dutch original of this work appeared in 1953. In support of the alleged partial demythologization of the language of principalities and powers in Paul, Berkhof notes that the powers are rarely described as angels. However, the identification is made in Rom 8:38, which counts against Berkhof's contention.

and will ultimately defeat them at the end of time (1 Cor 15:24–26). In the interim Christ limits the powers.[15]

In this time between the defeat of the powers on the cross and their ultimate defeat at the end of time, the church is called to live outside the sway of the powers and to demonstrate the wisdom of God to the powers (Eph 3:10). This involves the attempt to Christianize the powers, to instill into human cultures and societies the values of Christ so that they might not succumb to the powers of sin and death, as they had done in recent decades with devastating results. The church is tasked with preaching and teaching the values of Christ to each new generation so that the world might not sink into the power of the principalities and powers.[16]

Heinrich Schlier wrote similarly. On his analysis the powers are present in the theology of the NT and of the Apostolic Fathers. The powers are *personal*, rather than being spiritual forces or even partly demythologized social or cultural forces, though they are not always individual (so for example, the demons called "Legion" in Mark 5:1–14 act as a group). The powers manifest themselves as demons in the stories of the Gospels of Matthew, Mark, and Luke. The powers exercise influence over humanity, nature, and history. They even influence Christianity in the form of the growth of heresies. They are invisible and their nature is autonomous self-centeredness. They interpret the world as a world of death and a universe of temptation and act according to their understanding.[17]

The NT pictures Christ defeating the powers. On the cross Christ won a decisive victory over the powers and they are, in effect, a defeated foe. However, they are still at large and their full and final defeat will take place at the second coming of Christ. In the meantime the church is called to live the life of victory in Christ against the principalities and powers and their influence for sin and death. Although the powers attack the church, the church will overcome. Reading this language against the atrocities of the Nazis, Schlier affirms that this language speaks right to the heart of the mission of the church to live for justice and truth, to resist the temptations to succumb to the spirits of the age, and to pray unceasingly for the work of God to be done in the world.[18] Against the background of the chaos of the

---

15. Ibid., 21–37.

16. Ibid., 39–54.

17. Schlier, *Principalities and Powers*.

18. Ibid., 53–68.

first half of the twentieth century, the language of principalities and powers seemed to speak into the situation in which the church found itself.[19]

REDEFINING THE POWERS

In an influential trilogy of books, Walter Wink has developed this kind of interpretation of the principalities and powers in the NT. The foundation of his interpretation of the principalities and powers is an analysis of the terms used for the powers (*archē* and *archōn*, or "ruler"; *exousia*, or "authority"; *dunamis*, or "power"; *thronos*, or "throne"; *kuriotēs*, or "lordship"; *onoma*, or "name"; angels; fallen angels and demons; and the angels of the nations).[20] This is followed by a thoroughgoing exegesis of the power language of relevant NT texts where the use of power terms is disputed (1 Cor 2:6–8; 15:24–27a; Rom 8:38–39; 13:1–3; Col 1:16; 2:9–10; 2:13–15; Eph 1:20–23; 2:1–2; 3:10; 6:12).[21] The conclusion of his investigation is that the language of power pervades the NT. Although he finds the language of power in the NT imprecise, he claims that there are certain patterns to the ways in which the language of power is deployed in the NT. This language describes powers that are "earthly and heavenly, divine and human, spiritual and political, invisible and structural." He also notes that these powers are both good and evil.[22] Wink expresses reservations about demythologizing if this means stripping belief in the powers away with belief in angels and demons that are out there somewhere. However, he follows Berkhof in suggesting that Paul had already started to demythologize the Jewish apocalyptic notions of the principalities and powers and suggests that we follow Paul's lead here. The powers are best understood not as separate and individual heavenly beings (the "real" angels and demons of Jewish apocalyptic) but as the "*inner aspect of material or tangible manifestations of power.*"[23]

Wink unpacks this thesis in a study of Satan, demons, the angels of the churches, the angels of the nations, the gods, the elements of the universe,

---

19. Other important works written around the same time and on the same subject include MacGregor, "Principalities and Powers", 17–28; Caird, *Principalities and Powers*.

20. Wink, *Naming the Powers*, 13–35.

21. Ibid., 39–96.

22. Ibid., 6–12, 99–102.

23. Ibid., 103–48, esp. 104–5.

and the angels of nature.[24] Assuming that 1 Chr 21:1 refers to Satan rather than an adversary, Satan becomes the dark or angry side of God. Satan serves God as the heavenly accuser. This role of *agent provocateur* overspills into the role of destructive persecutor and so Satan becomes the evil one of Christian apocalyptic literature. Wink draws parallels with the clandestine activities of the FBI and CIA sinking as morally low as the evils these organizations seek to prevent. In this sense Satan becomes the dark side of human personalities and institutions and can only be redeemed by being recognized and held in check.[25] Demon possession takes three forms: the acting out of the dysfunctional nature of society by an individual who has become the scapegoat for society; the infection of a whole society by evil values; psychological problems caused by failing to love and accept aspects of people's personalities which they find difficult to own. The way to gain control over the demons is to recognize them, accept their existence, and so hold them in check.[26] The angels of the churches (Rev 2–3) are the interior or invisible structures of the visible and physical congregations (Wink declines to answer the question as to whether these angels have any real individual existence). The way to minister to an angel of a church is to discern the nature of the angel (or structure of the church) and where it falls short of fulfilling its vocation, and to re-orientate the church towards its true vocation.[27] The angels of the nations are the inner personality of the nation, which is fallen, and the role of the Christian in relationship to the angels of the nations is to love them and encourage them to fulfill their heavenly vocation (as an angel of a nation that turns its back on its vocation becomes demonic, like Nazi Germany). Ministering to the angel of a nation involves discerning how that nation falls short of its vocation and speaking into this situation to demand that it becomes a more just society.[28] In repressing the gods of paganism Christianity turned them into demons that burst into the individual and collective conscious with destructive power, most notably in the case of the resurgence of the cult of the Norse God Wotan in Nazism. People must recognize the power of the gods and

24. Walter Wink, *Unmasking the Powers*.

25. Ibid., 9–40.

26. Ibid., 41–53.

27. Ibid., 69–73.

28. Ibid., 87–107, esp. 87–88.

through worship subordinate them to the one true God.[29] The elements of the universe have become idols in contemporary societies that assume that material things are of ultimate value. So the elements have become demonic as people see the darker side of their own spirituality in nature as a consequence of not recognizing and dealing with their spiritual dark side. People must recognize that matter can reveal something of the glory of its creator so that matter might reveal good to us instead of acting as a mirror of our own evil.[30] Recognition of the angels of nature might lead people to take a less mechanistic view of the natural world, to treat the creation with more respect, and so to act more ecologically.[31] As Wink interprets these different kinds of angels, he is keen to illustrate how recognition of the powers enables us to overcome their influence to the good of humanity and the environment. Throughout his work, Wink draws extensively on the psychotherapeutic models and methods of Carl Gustav Jung in his recommendations for how to overcome the influence of the powers.

In the third and final volume of the trilogy, Wink addresses how Christians might address the principalities and powers in practice.[32] He begins by outlining the myth of the *Enuma Elish* and the defeat of Tiamat by Marduk. This combat myth enshrines an axiom of most human cultures— that power and might are necessary to destroy evil and that those in power control evil in order to create peace and security. Wink labels this belief and the systems of control that flow from it "the domination system." He argues that far from bringing peace and security, the domination system oppresses people and prevents them from finding freedom. The domination system is present at all levels of society, from the large-scale military programs and resources of nations to the plots of children's television programs (which use their own versions of the combat myth).[33] The domination system even perverts religion, being present in the political hopes of the dominion of the people of God in texts like Daniel 7, and in the social teaching of the early churches where men are granted authority over women and so dominate and oppress them.[34] The domination system is identified with the

29. Ibid., 108–27.
30. Ibid., 128–52.
31. Ibid., 153–71.
32. Wink, *Engaging the Powers.*
33. Ibid., 13–31.
34. Ibid., 43–46.

powers, specifically the elements of the world (Col 2:8), which hold people in place, preventing them from finding freedom in Christ.[35] Interpreting Col 1:15–20, Wink asserts that the powers were created good, that the powers are fallen, and that the powers will be redeemed. The task of the church is to redeem the powers.[36] To illustrate this he tells the story of a conversation with a Chilean Roman Catholic charismatic woman:

> A devout Roman Catholic charismatic in Chile attempted to persuade me that Christians have no business trying to change structures, that we are simply called to change individuals, and that as a consequence of changed individuals, the structures will automatically change. Jesus himself, she asserted, did not try to reform the structures of first-century society. He was not a revolutionary, nor did he propose alternative institutions. Political science is a field of great complexity requiring specialist knowledge. Christians have no business telling politicians what to do or how to do it. The church's task is to nurture persons who feel called to politics and are steeped in Christian values.[37]

Wink asserts that such perspectives only reinforce the status quo and leave social evils unchallenged and unchanged. He states that the then Chilean dictator Augusto Pinochet had nothing to fear from her.[38] By contrast, Jesus' proclamation of the kingdom (Mark 1:14–15) inaugurated a new world-order that defied the domination system (particularly in politics, male authority over women and children, and ethnocentrism/racism) in favor of an egalitarian community marked by its nonviolent methods of demanding change. Christians must participate in bringing down the powers in these ways if they are to live out their Christian vocation.[39] In order to achieve these goals, Christians must unmask the values and spirit of the

---

35. Ibid., 51–63, esp. 63.

36. Ibid., 65–85.

37. Ibid., 73–74, for her gender, see the personal pronoun "her" on p. 82.

38. Ibid., 82. It is slightly disturbing that Wink chooses to tell this story. He is white, from the USA, protestant, male, and right. She is non-white (we are not told what kind of Chilean, whether Hispanic, Mapuche or from another ethnic group), from Chile (then a "developing" country), Roman Catholic, female, and wrong. This could be described as a manifestation of the domination system he alleges corrupts society. Even for those of us who do not subscribe to his theory of the domination system, the choice of this example raises an eyebrow.

39. Ibid., 109–37.

domination system (the powers that constitute its interior).[40] Then they are to engage in non-violent resistance to all forms of the domination system.[41]

ACKNOWLEDGING THE POWERS

Despite its influence, the work of Walter Wink has not gone unchallenged. Clinton Arnold criticizes Wink for demythologizing in that Wink does not acknowledge the existence of evil powers as a reality *distinct from human institutions* (a point on which he prefers to remain agnostic), preferring to reduce them to something akin to psychological and social forces. Arnold argues that there are good reasons to take seriously the idea of the actual existence of evil spirits. The natural sciences possess no method for demonstrating the existence or non-existence of evil powers and so the fact that their existence cannot be demonstrate is irrelevant to the question of whether they exist or not. Naturalistic explanations of the facts of alleged experiences of evil powers do not explain all the aspects of these phenomena. Most people in history have believed in the existence of evil powers and most contemporary cultures believe in evil spiritual powers. Even in "enlightened" Western cultures, many people believe in the spiritual forces of evil and this trend is increasing in the West.[42] If knowledge is what is publicly believed to be true, then Arnold has a point.

Peter Williams criticizes Wink for similar reasons. If the spiritual world is identified as the interior or inner reality of the material world, then there is no reality outside the world. Traditionally Christianity has asserted as a fundamental doctrine that God is transcendent; in other words, God is higher than or outside and certainly not confined by the world. God is contained by neither the physical nor spiritual aspects of the world. Therefore Wink is not interpreting Christianity in a reliable or orthodox manner when he investigates the language of principalities and powers in the NT. In more technical language Wink is a panentheist rather than a theist. Nonetheless these arguments may not trouble those who do not subscribe to Christian orthodoxy. However, Williams argues further that if there is nothing beyond the world, then there is no absolute or perfect standard. All standards are simply those that are created by the human imagination. This

40. Ibid., 87–104.

41. Ibid., 169–317.

42. Arnold, *Powers of Darkness*, 167–82.

means that ideas of right and wrong are simply asserted by people rather than given absolutely by God or existing as absolute standards apart from the world. Therefore, when Wink talks of good and evil he is merely stating his own preferences rather than speaking about objectively real good and evil and moral codes that apply to everybody, as no such things exist. If cogent this criticism is highly damaging to Wink's project as its whole point is to move from theology to the promotion of (what he believes to be objectively) the good and the redemption of the evil powers through social action and inner healing. Finally Williams suggests that the Bible does not portray angels as interior states of material phenomena but as real individual beings.[43]

This final point highlights a more fundamental criticism, that Wink does not interpret the NT texts fairly. He begins his interpretation of the power language of the NT with the observation that Paul partly demythologizes power language and this line of interpretation is one to follow.[44] However, Paul identifies the powers with angels (Rom 8:38). The NT understands angels to be real individual spiritual beings. This fact is beautifully illustrated by the picture of Peter pinching himself as he realizes that the angel who led him out of prison he saw *in person* and not in a vision (Acts 12:9–11). Besides which, those to whom Paul wrote believed in a whole variety of spiritual powers and so there was no reason for Paul to demythologize this language.[45] In order to maintain that Paul uses the language of the powers simultaneously of human institutions and angelic beings, Wink relies on 1 Cor 2:6–8 and Rom 13:1–3, which texts scholars generally assume refer only to human institutions and not at all to angelic powers.[46] Apart from these two texts there is *no* evidence that Paul uses this language of powers to refer to human institutions.[47] In fact, Paul uses the language to refer only to spiritual powers as distinct from human institu-

43. Williams, *Case for Angels*, 66–67.

44. Wink, *Naming the Powers*, 104.

45. Arnold, *Ephesians: Power and Magic*, 48–51.

46. Wink, *Naming the Powers*, 40–47. On 1 Cor 2:6–8, see Fitzmyer, *First Corinthians*, 175–76. On Rom 3:1–3, see Fitzmyer, *Romans*, 666–67.

47. I suspect that the reason for beginning his study with an examination of 1 Cor 2:6–8 and Rom 13:1–3 was to establish the link between the angelic powers and earthly authorities (against the background of the angels of the nations ideas in the OT and second temple Jewish literature) in order that all the other NT texts would be read through the same lens. Take away this lens and the texts only speak of spiritual powers.

tions in stating that spiritual warfare is not against flesh and blood (other human beings) but against the spiritual powers (Eph 6:12). The central plank of the thesis is rotten. Indeed the NT as a whole does not use the language of the angels of the nations in the same way as, for example, *1 En.* 89–90 does. These angels appear in transmuted form as angels of churches but the NT authors present no evidence of a future hope of the destruction, let alone the redemption, of the fallen angels of the nations. When Jude and 2 Peter use the Watcher myth, they do so to illustrate that the wages of sin is a grizzly end. They do not predict the abysmal destiny of the fallen angels. The question as to why the NT authors do not use the language of the defeat of the angels of the nations is fascinating, and I suspect that it is rooted in Jesus' rejection of Zionist visions of Jerusalem restored and Judah governing all the land within the borders of Israel, and the early churches' adoption of his vision that the kingdom of God was about the defeat of sin, death, and the devil rather than the gentile nations. (Indeed, the concern of the NT authors is the conversion rather than the conquest of the gentile nations.) This would explain why the NT authors were concerned about the defeat of the spiritual powers but not the angels of the gentile nations. Whether or not this speculation holds any water, the fact remains that the NT authors show little interest in developing a theology of the angels of the nations. In sum, there is no real evidence that Paul or any other NT author regarded the principalities and powers as the angels of the nations or the spirits of any other secular institution. The evidence that angels are the interior or inner aspect of such institutional realities is wholly lacking, and with this the greater part of Wink's project collapses.[48]

The only institutions that have angels in the NT are the seven churches of Asia Minor addressed in Rev 2–3. However, this text provides little evidence for the idea that angels are the interior or inner spiritual reality of the churches as Wink suggests.[49] The angels of the nations in apocalyptic Judaism were understood to be real spiritual beings. The angels of the churches developed out of the idea of the angels of the nations.[50] Therefore these angels of the churches were also most likely thought to be real spiritual beings. Wink asserts that the reason John does not address members of the congregations in these letters is because the angels are the inner spiri-

48. See further Arnold, *Powers of Darkness*, 194–209.

49. Wink, *Unmasking the Powers*, 70.

50. So also Wink, *Unmasking the Powers*, 70.

tual reality of the congregations; in other words, in addressing the angels, John addresses the congregations.[51] However, there is no need to explain John addressing the angels as if it were an oddity.[52] It is not really an oddity in second temple Jewish or Christian apocalyptic literature. The human being Enoch prophesies to the angels in the books of the Watchers (1 En. 12:1—13:3). Indeed, Enoch acts as mediator between the angels and the Lord of heaven (1 En. 13:4–10). Admittedly the LORD instructs Enoch to include this in the admonition of the Watchers: "Go and say to the watchers of heaven, who sent you to petition in their behalf, 'You should petition on behalf of humans and not humans in behalf of you. Why have you forsaken the high heaven, the eternal sanctuary; and lain with women, and defiled yourselves with the daughters of men; and taken for yourselves wives, and done as the sons of the earth; and begotten for yourselves sons, giants?'" (1 En. 15:2–3). There is an irony in Enoch petitioning on behalf of the angels, for part of the role of angels is to petition on behalf of humans. However, this role-reversal does not prevent the LORD from using Enoch to pronounce the coming judgment on these wicked angels. So although it may seem strange to many modern minds, there is nothing odd about human beings prophesying to angels in apocalyptic literature. The angels of the churches are clearly closely related to the communities over which they are guardians. However, there is no reason to reduce the angels to being nothing more than the inner spirituality of the churches. They are addressed as separate persons.

Although Wink does not directly deny the reality of angels, his reluctance to pronounce upon their existence in favor of a functional analysis of angels leads him into a practical reduction of angels to social and psychological forces.[53] This is most obvious in the recommendations for how to deal with the demonic or re-orientate the angels of churches and nations towards their God-given vocations. For example, to discern the spirituality of a church Wink recommends analysis of its physical structures, power structures, liturgies, ability to handle conflict, and the economic, racial, and educational backgrounds of its members.[54] To re-orientate the angel of a church, the church needs to analyze its "angel" and address the dysfunction-

51. Ibid., 70.
52. Ibid., 81.
53. Ibid., 71.
54. Ibid., 73–77.

al behaviors of its members.[55] Now such basic management techniques may be useful in enabling congregations to overcome some of their problems. However, they are quite far removed from the ministry envisaged in Rev 2–3. There the congregations receive a prophecy from the risen Christ, via the angel of their churches, and are called to act on this prophecy. The NT attests this phenomenon of the spiritual gift of prophecy elsewhere. For instance, Paul refers to a "word from the Lord" or prophecy that had been given to the congregation at Thessalonica (1 Thess 4:15).[56] Paul discusses the proper use of this gift of prophecy in communal worship at length in 1 Cor 12–14. The prophetic ministry of the early church, including to the angels of the churches, was far closer to the charismatic spirituality of Wink's Chilean conversation partner than to the social-scientific analyses of institutions that Wink recommends, however prayerful they may be.

At the heart of Wink's work lies an unexamined thesis—that the principalities and powers can be identified in the domination system and that the domination system reveals itself in social institutions that Wink uniformly identifies as right-wing governments, multi-national institutions, traditional family values and lifestyles, and charismatic and Pentecostal spirituality, which on his reading silently collude with all the above.[57] The spirituality, or "angel," of the trilogy is nicely summarized in the following statement: "It is all so clear. We are simply to proclaim to IBM and Gulf + Western and the current political administration and the pettifogging bureaucrat that they do not exist as ends in themselves, but for the humanizing purposes of God as revealed in Jesus."[58] Given that he argues for reading the language of principalities and powers as providing the church with the theological grounding for critiquing corrupt social institutions, the reader leaves his work asking why he only really critiques institutions that are arguably or identifiably right wing. His critique might be extended to organizations that are arguably on the other side of the political spec-

55. Ibid., 78–86.

56. Malherbe, *Letters to the Thessalonians*, 267–69.

57. For examples of this see the lists of the manifestations of the domination system in Wink, *Engaging the Powers*, 9, 17, 46–49, 95–96. Typical of this tendency is his frequent critique of Chile (under Pinochet), El Salvador, and South Africa (under apartheid), see e.g., Wink, *Engaging the Powers*, 27. By contrast his critique of human rights abuses under the communist regime in China is infrequent and his critique of such abuses in North Korea is pretty much lacking.

58. Ibid., 167.

trum. For example, my experience over the last twenty years is that much charity fundraising for "world development" and projects to help "the marginalized" (at least in the UK, where I live) works increasingly on the basis of guilt manipulation. The campaigning for many such enterprises increasingly works from the basis of the promulgation of anger against the status quo. The guilt manipulation scapegoats me—I am told that I am responsible for the death or continued poor quality of life for the people concerned if I do not give to this cause. The encouragement of anger asks me to scapegoat "the system" and to add my voice to those who are already scapegoating "the system." If there is such a thing as the domination system, such activities are surely part of it. And yet these activities escape criticism. Wink never gives any indication of where the left-wing program he proposes is found in the writings of Paul on the powers. The truth is that there is no evidence in Paul that the powers are to be identified with right-wing political agendas or large economic organizations. One suspects that this rather dominating aspect of Wink's thesis finds its justification in Wink's own political viewpoint rather than in anything Scripture says about the principalities and powers.[59] (Incidentally there are some excellent exceptions to the trend in charity fundraising that I have described above.)

Wink offers an interesting reading of the principalities and powers, and one that has been theologically influential. However, he founds his project on readings of texts in Paul (1 Cor 2:6–8; Rom 13:1–3) that are without evidence or proof. The political agenda he builds on this misreading of Paul finds no basis in the writings of Paul. He uses this project to persuade thinking Christians to subscribe to his particular left-wing agenda. Given the weaknesses of Wink's argumentation and the unexamined assumptions he makes, I believe that those Christians who have subscribed to his agenda are under an obligation to re-think their ideas quite carefully.

RETHINKING THE POWERS

The identification of principalities and powers with gentile nations works well for interpreting some second temple Jewish texts but not those of the New Testament. The principalities and powers may be loosely

59. Though, to be fair, Wink does admit that his understanding of how to discern the activities of the powers may be colored by his own experiences; see Wink, *Naming the Powers*, 106.

connected with pagan beliefs and moral codes and with Torah observance in Galatians and Colossians but Paul never identifies them as the
angels, let alone interiority, of pagan nations. The pauline principalities
and powers are not to be identified as angels of the nations and we ought
not to use them as a basis for constructing any political theology. To use
these texts as the basis of a theological justification for social critique is
to abuse these texts because, if anything, they de-politicize the OT and
second temple use of such language.

However, the language of the principalities and powers and the angels
of the churches may yet speak. Revelation does not use this language for
critique of the angels of the nations. John of Patmos does not speak to those
outside the covenant community of how they must make their societies
more just. He prophesies to the angels of the churches and their congregations, warning them to lead holy lives of faithfulness and obedience to
God. In a similar vein Paul uses the language of the elemental spirits to
encourage those Gentile believers in the Galatian and Colossian churches
to live out their Christian faith without observing Torah, which Paul identifies with moving back to paganism. Instead Paul recommends that they live
out the life of the Spirit. Paul and John of Patmos use this language of the
powers to critique churches where they do not hold fast to the Jesus tradition and fully live out their faith in Christ. Where churches today fail to live
according to the teachings of Jesus and the gospel of salvation in Christ, the
use Paul and John make of this language may well apply again.

Interestingly, both John and Paul use the language and ideas of the
principalities and powers and angels of the churches in contexts that assume that the charismatic gifts experienced by early Christians (and many
today) enable them to lead a life of Christian freedom and holiness. John of
Patmos speaks prophetic words to the seven churches of Asia Minor (Rev
2–3). The churches are enabled to live the life of holiness to which they are
called if they listen to the voice of the risen Christ speaking by the prophet.
Paul contrasts the life of Torah (subject to the elemental spirits) with the
life lived in the Spirit, which is marked by miraculous occurrences (Gal
3:1–5). Far from lending theological support to those who would question
the use of spiritual gifts, the NT authors who use this language encourage Christians in the use of charismata in order to experience freedom in
Christ, which is no longer subject to the principalities and powers.

Angels

The aftermath of the Second World War saw a rejuvenation of interest in the language of the principalities and powers in the pauline epistles. Theologians have found new relevance in these texts, interpreting them as using the ancient Jewish idea of the angels of the nations to refer to the conquest of corrupt governments and societies by Christ on the cross. The atrocities of the Nazis have lent an urgency and relevance to such interpretations of this language. Walter Wink has developed such readings of this language in the NT into a theology of resistance and development that calls the church to resist power structures in society, particularly as associated with right-wing governments and multi-national companies. However, his exegesis of NT texts is flawed and so the basis upon which he rests this theology is precarious. No good reasons could be found for identifying the principalities and powers with right-wing organizations either. And no good reason could be found for building a left wing political theology (or any other political theology) on the basis of the NT language of principalities and powers and angels of churches. Rather the early Christians transformed the prophetic critique of this language. Instead of addressing the nations oppressing the covenant people, they prophesied to the covenant people upbraiding them for not keeping the covenant with God in Jesus in holiness and obedience. Any modern theology of the principalities and powers or the angels of the churches must take this as its starting point.

12

Bewitched

A question was posed through the discussion in the last chapter, the ques-tion of whether evil spiritual powers are objectively real. The growth in interest in the occult in the Western world during the second half of the twentieth century suggests that even enlightened, modern people are not ready to lay to rest the idea of powers of evil. Despite the protests of certain ancient philosophers that the gods were not real, many of the ancients were equally reluctant to subscribe to the idea that evil powers were nothing more than characters in ghoulish tales. This was nowhere more evident than in ancient ideas surrounding and practice of magic.

Magic was widespread in the ancient world.[1] Insights into ancient magical practices can be gained from the study of a group of papyri from Egypt, dated between the first and seventh centuries AD.[2] Essentially magic concerned the manipulation of the spiritual powers for the purposes of the magician or the person who was paying the magician to procure something on their behalf. The spiritual powers were believed to have the ability to effect changes in the physical world. Therefore they could bring harm to people or prosper them. They could harm a person's enemy on their behalf or fulfill their deepest desires. There were many situations in which magic might be used. Magic might be apotropaic or protective; that is, it could be used to protect people from harm. Magic could be aggressive or malevo-lent, used in order to bring harm to another or others. Magic might be used

1. For the following description of magic in the ancient world, see Arnold, *Powers of Darkness*, 21–34; Arnold, *Colossian Syncretism*, 11–31

2. See the introduction in Betz, *Greek Magical Papyri*.

Angels

to gain power or influence over another human being. Lastly, magic might be used to gain revelation of heavenly secrets.

In all these kinds of magic angels might be invoked as spiritual beings to come to the aid of the magician. So, for example, the following spell addresses the Egyptian god Helios and his angels to protect the person using the spell: "Stand facing east and speak thus: "I call upon you, lord Helios, and all your holy angels on this day, in this very hour: Preserve me, NAME, for I am THĒNŌR, and you are holy angels, guardians of the ARDIMALECHA" (PGM IV.1930–40). The spell continues with some magic language (sounds and reads like gibberish to the uninitiated) and then a request for power over the soul of a deceased person to protect the one casting the spell. Here angels are invoked to effect protective magic. Angels might also be invoked to bring prosperity:

And sing the same spell when you get up in the morning before you open your shop [there follows a spell in magical language]. "Give me all favor, all success, for the angel bringing good, who stands beside the goddess Tyche, is with you. Accordingly, give profit and success to this house. Please, Aion, ruler of hope, giver of wealth, O holy Agathos Daimon, bring to fulfillment all favors and your divine oracles." Then open your establishment and you will marvel at the unsurpassed holy power.

(PGM IV.3155–70)

This spell is designed to help the shop owner to harness the cosmic powers of the universe in order to grow their business. Angels might also be invoked to ensure that harm is done to an enemy, as the following spell illustrates:

Take a lead lamella and inscribe with a bronze stylus the following names and the figure, and after smearing it with the blood from a bat, roll up the lamella in the usual fashion. Cut open the frog and put it into its stomach. After stitching it up with Anubian thread and a bronze needle, hang it up on a reed from your property by means of hairs from the tip of the tail of a black ox at the east of the property near the rising of the sun [there follows magic language and a picture to copy]. "Supreme angels, just as this frog drips with blood and dries up, so also will the body of NAME whom NAME bore, because I conjure you, who are in command of fire MASKELLI MASKELLŌ"

(PGM XXXVI.231–55)

This gruesome ritual was clearly designed to bring about the demise of the person upon whom the spell was cast. It is an example of malevolent or aggressive magic.

Another spell prescribes the drowning and burial of a cat in order that its angel might prevent certain charioteers from winning in the races: "I conjure you, the powerful and mighty angel of the animal in this place; rouse yourself for me and perform the NN [deed] both on this day and in every hour and day; rouse yourself for me against my enemies, NN, and perform NN deed" (add the usual), "for I conjure you by IAŌ SABAŌTH ADŌNAI ABRASAX, and by the great god, IAEŌ" [there follows magical language] (PGM III.1–164, here 70–80). Although particularly efficacious in determining that your favorite will win the chariot races, this spell is advertised as being something of a multipurpose incantation, ending with the note: "This is the ritual of the cat, suitable for every ritual purpose: a charm to restrain charioteers in a race, a charm for sending dreams, a binding love charm, and a charm to cause separation and enmity" (PGM III.163–64).

Angels were also invoked to reveal heavenly secrets. Another spell (PGM I.293–327) invokes "god" by many names, including the Greek gods Apollo, first angel of Zeus, whom the magician also called ABRASAX, PAKERBĒTH and ADŌNAIOS. After the invocation is over, the god will reveal to the magician whatever heavenly secrets he wishes to discover, whether they concern the art of prophecy, divination through the use of epic poems, sending dreams, getting revelations from dreams, causing illnesses, or any other kind of magic. There is a fascinating reversal of the scheme of heavenly ascent here. Where in the heavenly ascent God calls the seer to travel through the heavens to the throne room in the highest heaven, here the magician calls God (or a god or the revealing angel or a syncretistic mixture of the lot) down to earth. Where in the heavenly ascent God privileges the seer with the knowledge of heavenly secrets, here the magician demands such knowledge or acquires it by manipulating divine beings. There is a reversal in the mode of acquiring heavenly knowledge. In place of righteousness, humble obedience, and honest prayerfulness magic recommends the acquisition of knowledge through prioritization of personal goals, manipulation of the heavenly powers through ritual techniques, and demand. In heavenly ascents God takes centre stage, in magic the magician does.

Angels

The angels invoked in this kind of magic were not simply the gods of paganism. Spells can be found that invoke the God and angels of Judaism alongside the pagan gods and angels. The spell which calls upon Apollo to descend also invokes the archangel Gabriel, the archangel Michael, and ADŌNAI or "the LORD" (PGM I.300–305). This syncretism (mixing of religious traditions) was not necessarily a superficial matter of borrowing words and names without any regard to their meaning or the religious tradition from which they were borrowed, as the following spell illustrates:

> Love spell of attraction, fire divination over unburnt sulfur, thus: Taken seven lumps of unburnt sulfur and make an altar fire from vine wood. Say this spell over the lumps one by one and throw them into the fire. This is the spell: "The heavens of heavens opened, and the angels of God descended and overturned the five cities of Sodom and Gomorrah, Admah, Zeboiim, and Segor. A woman who heard the voice became a pillar of salt. You are the sulfur that God rained down on the middle of Sodom and Gomorrah, Admah and Zeboiim and Segor; you are the sulfur that served God—so also serve me, NAME, in regards to her, NAME, and do not allow her to go to bed or to find sleep until she comes and fulfils the mystery rite of Aphrodite." As you throw the lumps into the fire, say: "If I throw you into the fire, I adjure you by the great PAP TAPHEIAŌ SABAŌTH ARBATHIAŌ ZAGOURĒ PAGOURĒ, and by the great MICHAEL ZOURIĒL GABRIĒL SESENGENBARPHARANGĒS ISTRAĒL ABRAAM, attract her, NAME, to NAME."
>
> (PGM XXXVI.295–311)

The story of the destruction of the cities of the plain, the flight of the family of Lot, and his wife turning to a pillar of salt all come from Gen 19. The names of the angels Michael and Gabriel are present as names of the power evoked alongside the name Abram—again all drawn from Judaism. Whoever wrote this spell had a knowledge of the stories of the Torah (at least of Abraham and Sodom and Gomorrah) and of Jewish traditions about angels, even if their theology was unlike the more traditional and orthodox theology of the rabbinic Judaism that existed in the fourth century to which this text may be dated. Another spell that identifies itself as Hebraic (PGM IV.3007–86) calls upon the God who rescued Osrael from Pharaoh and who drew back the Jordan River and the Red Sea. The text also refers to this god of the Hebrews as Jesus (PGM IV.3019). Pagan magical,

Hebrew, and Christian epithets for God are all mixed in this "Hebraic" spell. The syncretism is obvious.[3]

For all the questions they raise, these spells settle one question. Those who wrote and used them did not demythologize the language of angels, powers, and principalities. The direct address to the angels or angel/gods of these spells demonstrates that those who wrote and used them believed in their existence. The fact that the spells concern requests that these spiritual powers manipulate the natural world to the advantage of the person chanting the spell demonstrates the belief that these angels had the power to effect changes within the natural world (or at the very least that they might have this power) or there would be no point to invoking the aid of these angels. Given that magic was widespread in the ancient world, there must have been widespread belief among the ancients that spiritual powers objectively exist.

This may form the background to the interpretation of the books of Ephesians and Colossians. Although the *Greek Magical Papyri* are from Egypt and many are later than the first century AD, Clinton Arnold argues that these texts give us an insight into the magical practices that existed in the cities of Asia Minor in the first century AD, including Ephesus and Colossae.[4] The reconstruction seems plausible, although tentative given the date and provenance of much (although not all) of the evidence. However, in favor of his reconstruction is the picture in Acts of the widespread nature of magic in Ephesus (Acts 19:11–20). The magical texts attest angels being invoked in magical incantations to manipulate events in the natural world on behalf of those practising magic. Given the tradition in Judaism that magical practices were banned (e.g., Lev 19:26; 2 Macc 12:32–45), and that Paul himself rejected such practices (note the prohibition of sorcery in Gal 5:20), we can say that Paul would have regarded the spiritual powers addressed in such practices as *evil* powers.

Arnold argues that Paul's prayer for the Ephesians (Eph 1:17–23, esp. vv. 19–22) and the prayer and doxology at the centre of the book (Eph 3:16–21) use disproportionate amounts of power language. Ephesians makes more reference to the principalities and powers than any other

3. On the depiction of angels in the magical papyri, see further Kraus, "Angels in the Magical Papyri," 611–27.

4. Arnold, *Ephesians: Power and Magic*, 5–69; Arnold, *Colossian Syncretism*, 19–102. See also, Sheppard, "Pagan Cults in Roman Asia Minor," 77–101.

epistle. These facts taken together establish power as the key theme of the epistle. Paul desires that the Ephesians know the power of the risen Christ at work in their midst.[5] The power language climaxes in Eph 6:10–20 where Paul speaks of the spiritual war which believers must fight against the principalities and powers.[6] Given the popularity of magic in Ephesus, the rallying call to fight the principalities and powers is understandable. Given the nature of some of the aggressive and malevolent spells, Paul is eager for the Ephesians to understand that these powers have been conquered by Christ and that this same Christ has become the head of the church (Eph 1:21–23). Therefore, the Ephesians ought not to fear the use of this form of magic. Indeed the Ephesians themselves have access to the power of God by which God achieves the victory over the spiritual powers, hence they are told to put on the armor of God and be strong in the power of God (Eph 6:10–11).[7]

Arnold interprets Colossians against the background of the magic practices of Asia Minor also.[8] The epistle is written to provide assurance to the Christians in Colossae who are likely to have been concerned about magical practices, which were probably rife in their part of the world. The hymn assures that the powers that are invoked in magical rituals were created by Christ as were all spiritual powers. Apart from the power of Christ, they could not exist. Therefore, it is clear that Christ has power over these thrones dominions, rulers, and powers (Col 1:16–17). Moreover Christ defeated the powers on the cross (Col 2:15) and so Paul prays that the Colossians might be strengthened in the power of God and affirms them in the belief that Christ has rescued them from the grip of these powers of darkness (Col 1:11–13). The message is similar to that of Ephesians— Christ has the power to deliver you from the influence of these evil powers as he has already conquered them.[9]

Should these interpretations of Ephesians and Colossians be accepted (which in turn depends partly on whether one accepts Arnold's

5. Arnold, *Ephesians: Power and Magic*, 70–102.

6. Ibid., 103–22.

7. Ibid., 167–72.

8. I do not accept his interpretation of the Colossian heresy in all its details, as outlined in chapter 3. Nonetheless, the interpretation of the Colossian hymn that follows seems very plausible.

9. Arnold, *Colossian Syncretism*, 246–70, 277–87.

reconstruction of magical practices in Asia Minor in the first century AD), then another question is answered. The early Christians (at least Paul and those in the churches of Asia Minor) believed in the existence of real evil spiritual powers. They did not demythologize the principalities and powers.[10] Working from these interpretations of Ephesians and Colossians, Arnold argues that the church today must recognize both the reality of evil spirits and the ministry of exorcism.[11]

The reality of evil spirits and the validity of the ministry of exorcism have been increasingly recognized in recent decades.[12] This may be illustrated anecdotally by the following account in which David Instone-Brewer recalls an experience from his work in psychiatry which persuaded him that reductionist psychological explanations cannot explain all seeming manifestations of demon possession:

> I once went to interview a patient but found that he was asleep. He was lying on his bed, facing the wall, and he did not turn round or respond when I walked in. I sat in his room for a while thinking that he might wake up, and after a while I thought I might pray for him. I started to pray silently for him but I was immediately interrupted because he sat bolt upright, looked at me fiercely and said in a voice which was not characteristic of him: "Leave him alone—he belongs to us."
>
> Startled, I wasn't sure how to respond, so we just sat and stared at each other for a while. Then I remembered my fundamentalist past and decided to pray silently against what appeared to be an evil spirit. I prayed silently because I was aware that an hysterical disorder could mimic demon possession. If the person felt that I was treating them as if they were possessed, this would exacerbate the condition and confirm in his mind that he really was possessed. I also prayed silently in case I was making a fool of myself. I can't remember exactly what I prayed but probably rebuked the spirit in the name of Jesus. Immediately I did so, I got another very hostile outburst along the same line, but much more abusive. I realised that I was in very deep water and continued to pray, though still silently.
>
> An onlooker would have seen a kind of one-sided conversation. I prayed silently and the person retorted very loudly and emphatically. Eventually (I can't remember what was said or what I prayed) the person cried out with a scream and collapsed on his bed. He woke up a little later, unaware of what had happened. I was still trying to act the role of

10. Arnold, *Powers of Darkness*, 169–82.

11. Ibid., 167–217.

12. E.g., Suenens, *Renewal*, 115–17; Perry, *Time*, 167–81.

a medic, so I did not tell him anything about what had happened. His behaviour after waking was quite striking in its normality. He no longer heard any of the oppressive voices which had been making him feel cut off and depressed, and his suicidal urges had gone.[13]

The result of this experience was a renewed acceptance of the reality of evil spirits alongside a genuine appreciation of the insights of modern psychology. This worked out in both the practice of psychology and exorcism in practical ministry.

This chapter began with the question of whether evil spiritual powers exist. The ancient world had its sceptics just as the world today does. Ancient documents bear witness to a fascination with occult powers amongst many people just as contemporary culture does. Whatever our answer to this question might be, it is fascinating how the culture facing the earliest Christians seems remarkably similar to the culture beginning to face the contemporary Church. People of faith would do well to think through their response to these developments in the world around us.

13. Instone-Brewer, "Jesus and the Psychiatrists," 140.

13
Why Angels?

Ancient Jewish and Christian texts have a great deal to offer on the subject of angels. This whistle-stop tour of the subject has not been unlike a heavenly ascent in that in the space of a few chapters a great deal of information has been shared about many and varied topics. The figure of the interpreting angel has also been present in the form of scholarly examinations and explanations of texts, although at points the interpreting angels have not agreed with each other and they have argued in front of us during the tour. At times I have argued with the interpreting angels. Here we come to the end of the tour. Traditionally this is the point at which the great revelation takes place and the heavenly secrets we so desire to know are disclosed. No such luck today, I'm afraid. Even though our heavenly ascent might not be a complete success in terms of finding the absolute truth about angels at the end of the tour, there are some questions of angels that it might be profitable to ponder.

SUFFICIENTLY HEAVENLY MINDED?

One question that concerns the professionally religious (priests, theologians, and others of that ilk) is whether they need to come to terms with angels as objectively real spiritual beings once again. For some time now many Western university departments of theology and churches have tended to sideline (if not ignore) the subject of angels. Angels have been an embarrassment to the modern mind.

Angels

The best that many modern theologians and ministers could do with angels has been to attempt to accommodate them to the modern world. Walter Wink provides us with an excellent example of this approach to angels. He makes the assumption that we may not accept the objective existence of angels, on the basis that such an assumption does not sit easily within the modern Western mindset. He then re-reads the texts concerning angels to discover whether angels can have any use in a contemporary theology. With some creative interpretation of biblical and other ancient texts he finds that biblical texts about angels speak directly into political and social situations that are facing people today with a social and political agenda of which he approves. This theology of social reconciliation, which moderns find useful and appealing, guarantees that angels have a place in contemporary theology after all.

However, we found that the relevant texts did not support the reduction of angels to social or political forces. Indeed the texts assumed that angels were living spiritual beings (e.g., Acts 12:6–11). And approaching the texts with a *practical* reductionism (i.e., not knowing whether angels do or do not exist and so shelving the question) does not take them seriously either, because the ancient texts clearly assume the reality of angels, and thus such an approach guarantees some disparity between text and interpretation.

The texts bear witness to an understanding of reality that most Western modernists and postmodernists do not hold and we simply have to acknowledge this. The ancient texts stand as a witness against modernist and postmodernist worldviews. Majority world theologians are more open to explore how they might explain reality than are many Westerners.[1] Nonetheless, some Western theologians are willing to explore how the realities of the biblical texts may explain human experience more fully than modernist and postmodernist theories. As the Prefect of the Congregation for the Doctrine of the Faith, Pope Benedict XVI wrote, "Whilst a rationalist and reductionist theology is explaining away the Devil and the world of evil spirits as a mere label for everything that threatens man . . . a new, concrete awareness of the Powers of Evil and their cunning, which threaten man, is growing in the context of Renewal."[2] Particularly in the light of charismatic renewal within the churches, some theologians are willing to

1. For example Fernando, "Screwtape Revisited," 103–32.
2. Ratzinger, "Foreword," ix.

accept that the spiritual realities of which biblical texts speak may need more acknowledgment and less (reductionist) explanation.

If the question of the existence of angels is taken seriously, then ministers and theologians must recognize the importance of examining the subject of angels as a serious part of theological and spiritual enquiry rather than a medieval embarrassment to be explained away with the aid of the social sciences. This does not only apply to biblical and doctrinal studies but also to practical theology.

I cannot be the only Christian minister who has entered houses where people have their angel chart up on the wall explaining which angel they need to invoke for which particular problem they have. There has been a cultural shift in certain parts of modern Western societies, which have moved beyond the assumption that there must be a pill or psychological technique for every problem towards the assumption that there may be more effective spiritual remedies for life's difficulties. Surely the Christian churches have the responsibility in this new cultural setting to explore their own texts and traditions in order to understand better their own theological heritage and then draw on it in their practical ministry.

Taking seriously the question of the existence of angels might impact on another aspect of the work of religious professionals. The practical reductionism of those like Wink enables the minister to maintain control. Following his lead in keeping the existence of angels under debate enables the minister to reduce spiritual explanations of reality to social and spiritual forces that the minister then works with the community to examine, bring under control, and reshape. Control of the ministry resides with the minister.

Moving beyond practical reductionism involves admitting that while self-control, forgiveness, and reconciliation are important parts of Christian ministry alongside the appropriate deployment of pastoral skills learned from the social sciences, sometimes human beings are powerless in the face of sin and evil. Similarly it involves the recognition that sometimes the arsenal of pastoral techniques may be counterproductive or unhelpful if not used with uncommon wisdom and insight. The admission of spiritual realities that ministers may not be able to control or access through human means requires the minister to draw on spiritual resources such as prayer and prophecy. At times the ministry of exorcism may be appropriate. The minister has to acknowledge that only God has authority over all spiritual forces and that all ministry is nothing more or less than participation in the work of God through the enabling power of God. The minister has to relinquish control and accept and employ only the authority she or he has been granted. The minister has to acknowledge that the living God resides at the heart of every spiritual encounter.

Asking questions of angels might encourage religious profession-als to move beyond modernist and postmodernist reductionism in their understanding of the faith and their practice of ministry. Such questions might encourage a greater openness to spiritual realities and to depen-dence on God within practical ministry. Angels may help ministers and theologians to recover aspects of faith and ministry that may have lain dormant or neglected.

FOOLS RUSH IN?

Another question worth pondering concerns the growth in the public interest in angels. Since the 1980s, the Western world has experienced a resurgence of belief in angels. In some ways surprisingly, this resurgence initially took place largely outside of mainstream religions.[3] However, this is not to say that the resurgence has not taken place within religious tradi-tions—it has done.[4] A few theologians, having brushed angels aside as an embarrassing part of an outmoded worldview, have begun to return to the topic with interest.[5] Certain philosophers too are renewing their interest in angels. This interest in angels is not limited to those branded religious nuts and flaky new-agers. What sparks the resurgence of interest in angels?

This resurgence of interest is mirrored by the growth of interest in angels in the second temple Judaism. Angels are not particularly prevalent in the OT; various popular stories in the first seven books of the Christian Bible (especially in Genesis, Exodus, Numbers, and Judges) involve angels, but after this angels all but disappear from the text. There are relatively few references to angels in the Psalms and fewer still in the book of Job.

3. For evidence of this, note the enormous popularity of Sophie Burnham's *A Book of Angels*.

4. Witness the expressed need of Terry Law (*Truth about Angels*) to help Christians to understand what angels really are and what they really do.

5. The Deuterocanonical and Cognate Literature Yearbook of 2007 was given over to the subject of angels for precisely this reason, see Reiterer et al., *Angels*, v.

Ecclesiastes, Song of Songs, and Proverbs do not use the word "angel." The prophetic books have very little to say about angels until we get to Zechariah and Daniel, where angels begin to flourish. By the time we get to some of the earlier second temple literature like parts of *1 Enoch* and *Jubilees* angels are everywhere. The apocalyptic texts of this period particularly make reference to myriads of angels.

This phenomenon, both in the ancient and the modern world, raises the question of where this growth in interest came from. Saul Olyan reviews the various scholarly explanations for the explosion of interest in angels in second temple Judaism. Perhaps it resulted from the influence of foreign religious traditions, and particularly the Zoroastrianism of the Persians who governed Judea for much of the early part of this period; although a difficulty with this view is that the apocalyptic literature in which the phenomenon is most prevalent was precisely that used by the Jewish groups which were most hostile to any foreign interference in their religious beliefs and practices. Possibly angels became the heavenly intermediaries between humanity and the divine as God felt more remote to people. However, the psalmist of the Qumran *Hodayot*, who writes extensively of angelic warfare, has no difficulty in addressing praises directly to God or writing of direct divine intervention in his life. Similarly the seers of the heavenly ascent tradition, who describe in such detail the tasks of the heavenly angels, bear witness to *meeting God in person*—a very rare occurrence in the OT. The growth in magical traditions might account for the developing interest in angels, but the evidence for the magical traditions largely occurs towards the end of the period. The religious movement known as Gnosticism may account for the phenomenon but again Gnosticism appears towards the end of the period in question.[6] Olyan prefers the explanation that new classes of angels were developed through the detailed study and interpretation of biblical texts.[7] Nonetheless Olyan notes that many scholars have simply found it a baffling phenomenon.[8]

The phenomenon of increasing interest in angels in societies that in many ways are becoming more secular is equally baffling. Of course, the reasons for the current interest in angels may be completely different from

6. See further Olyan, *A Thousand Thousands*, 1–13. On the date of Gnosticism, see Yamauchi, *Pre-Christian Gnosticism*.

7. Olyan, *A Thousand Thousands*.

8. Ibid., 3.

the reasons for the ancient interest. However, it is always worth asking the question of whether the past helps to explain the present and so it is probably a good idea to see if any of the explanations of growing interest in angels in the ancient world help to explain the similar phenomenon in the modern world. Given the scholarly disputes of the origins and nature of Gnosticism (or whether such Gnosticism, as such, really existed), comparisons between contemporary interest and Gnostic interest in angels are unlikely to prove immediately illuminating. So we will leave this aside for the moment. There seems to be little to no evidence that the contemporary interest in angels results from the close study of biblical texts. It is most unlikely to be the result of God seeming remote, as within these prevalently secular societies it would be more accurate to say that humanity has become increasingly remote from God. Why should people who have dispensed with God seek God through intermediaries? Despite the growth of religious plurality in secular Western societies, it hardly explains the increased interest in angels as the growth in interest in angels is not matched by an increase in interest or participation in these religious traditions. That leaves magic and to this I will return below.

Returning to the modern world, the social scientific study of religion is rarely short of a proponent of the thesis that the growth of religion may be attributed to social or psychological dysfunctions. Something is wrong with the world and this worries individuals or groups of people. The result is that they feel insecure. To counter this insecurity people reach for the old certainties as they provide a measure of comfort in the face of whatever is wrong with the world. This helps people to face the perceived threat and function more effectively as human beings and human societies. However, this explanation simply will not do in the face of the current resurgence of belief in angels. People are not reaching for the old certainties. They continue to reject the authority of traditional religion, which either continues in decline or at least fails to revive substantially. The resurgence of angel experiences is more marked in contemporary spirituality and in the newer movements within Christianity, which are further away from the traditional centers of authority and church hierarchies. That people enjoy the experiences of angels seems true enough but not in the form of the old religious traditions. People are not reaching for the old certainties. They are searching for new experiences.

THERE MUST BE AN ANGEL?

Before discussing this further, it would be wise to put this renewal of interest in context. That people are generally more interested in angels does not mean that all contemporary people are interested in angels or are open to the possibility of their existence. There are always those who regard religion as spurious or simply a mythical version of earthly events, and the ancients also had their own philosophers who took such views.

Even among the religious, however, there are a wide variety of attitudes towards angels, which variety of ideas substantially mirrors that of ancient Judaism and early Christianity. There are those who are willing to assent to the belief that angelic encounters happened in the past, as reported in Scriptures (given their prior commitment to religious faith), but who feel uneasy with the idea that angels might intrude on the present—which is generally a little more sophisticated and less open to primitive religious ideas. This appears to be the view of the ancient Jewish historian Josephus who tends to downplay the presence of angels overall in his re-writing of OT accounts and rarely allows angels to intrude into recent history.[9] In preferring not to include accounts of angel experiences in his telling of recent history, Josephus differs markedly from the author of 2 Maccabees who positively relishes including such material. Nonetheless, Josephus is not a skeptic. Where there are grounds from eyewitness testimony to take such a story seriously (as in the case of the chariots flying across the sky before the destruction of the temple in AD 70; *War* 6:5.3§297–300), Josephus does so, although he would assume the story was a complete fabrication apart from the reliability of the people who told him of the event.

Some will assent to the doctrine and officially believe in the reality of angels. However, their actual religious interests lie elsewhere and they only engage with angels spiritually, where their real interests lie. In ancient Judaism this can be seen in Philo's discussion of the Watchers. Philo may accept the reality of angels (*Giants* 1:7–8) but in discussing the Watcher myth, he is keen to use the story as a means to teaching the importance of leaving aside base passions and attending to the development of the soul (*Giants* 1:16–19). The nineteenth-century English preacher Charles

9. On Josephus and angels, see Begg, "Angels in the Work of Flavius Josephus," 525–36.

H. Spurgeon treats the theme of angels similarly in his sermons on angels. Each of these sermons moves from the story of the angels that occurs in the text upon which he preaches to an ethical exhortation. He does not dwell on the reality or nature of angels, and even less on the possibility of angel experiences among his contemporaries.[10]

Others become wholehearted about the experience of angels. They engage in excited and extravagant mystical explorations, such as those seers who engaged in heavenly ascents. (I am personally not convinced that all heavenly ascents were written from scratch according to a blueprint for ascent visions, as some scholars seem to suggest and as some romantic novels are written today. I think it more likely that actual *religious experience* inspired the form of literature and sustained the tradition.) They participated, via religious experiences, in the worship of the angels, which they found so much more glorious than the worship of the faithful on earth. They also sought out such experiences when they heard of the angelic encounters of others, like some in the church at Colossae. Every age has its spiritual enthusiasts and ours is no exception. Both inside and outside the churches there are people who seek experience of angels.

Still others experience angel encounters but are cautious about making too much of them. We can see this in Paul. Although he experienced a heavenly ascent, he wanted to communicate to the spiritual enthusiasts of his day that the work of Christ in his broken life was far more important than exciting mystical experiences. He preferred to speak of Christ strengthening him in his weakness than of the heavenly secrets that were revealed to him in his own experience of ascent. The same humility can be found among many today who have had remarkable spiritual experiences but prefer to speak humbly of the work of Christ in their lives.

LOVING ANGELS INSTEAD

One feature of the renewal of interest in angels cannot be stressed enough however. The excitement about angels does not necessarily indicate renewal of interest in religion or even in God. The reality seems to be that people are loving angels *instead*. Perhaps angels are becoming more popular than God. The focus of contemporary spirituality on finding one's angel guardian and communicating with one's angel seems to put angels very much

10. Spurgeon, *Sermons on Angels*.

in the foreground and God in the background. One might well ask what a biblical or extra-biblical second temple Jewish or early Christian angel would make of this. The answer would most likely be that they would feel rather uncomfortable. The evidence is in the angelophany. Angelophanies begin with the (often very glorious) appearance of the angel to a human being. This human person is shocked by the appearance of the strange visitor. Generally they fall to their knees, as if to worship the heavenly (divine?) visitor. The angel strictly instructs the poor bewildered human *not* to worship him. *Ancient angels do not want to become the focus.* They come to focus human beings on *God*; on how God heals or plans to heal them, and on how God plans to heal creation.

So how do we reach the situation in which these good God-fearing angels are in danger of becoming more popular than God? I think the answer lies in contemporary attitudes to authority.[11] Nowadays most Westerners do not enjoy being subjected to the exercise of authority. They prefer to share authority (although I personally suspect that many enjoy wielding authority, for all the protested reaction against authority). This preference for shared authority affects the religious preferences of modern people and explains the predilection for angels.

God sits at the head of the divine council. God rules. God exercises authority over all things in heaven and on earth, whether visible or invisible. God is the ultimate authority figure. For many people today, this picture of God does not simply suggest that God is authoritative but that God is also authoritarian. People react against authority being exercised over them and so prefer not to relate to God. They very much dislike authoritarianism and so those who perceive God as authoritarian will wholeheartedly reject God.

However, it is different with angels. Angels do not preside over the divine council. Angels are part of the community of heaven. Although some traditions have angels work within hierarchies, angels do not set the rules. As angels traditionally carry out the wishes of their LORD God, they do not wield personal authority. Angels are more like most of us. Angels do not characterize or embody the authoritarianism or even the authority with which so many contemporary people are uncomfortable. Angels perform the tasks of revealing heavenly secrets and bringing healing into the lives

11. The following ideas come largely out of conversations. In particular I am grateful to Joanne Keane for honest conversations about angels and authority from our different spiritual perspectives.

of ordinary people. Therefore, angels are able to bring about the benefits of belief in God without the unpalatable acceptance of authority. Angels are our companions.

Many of those who wish to bring people to faith in Christ find the phenomenon of contemporary spirituality greatly encouraging. They imagine that this signifies a turn in the spiritual tide. The Western world is turning its back on the secular experiment it began in the Enlightenment (the movement beginning in the seventeenth century AD that promoted the view that reason and education can do a better job of making the world a better place than religion and the churches) and, like the prodigal son, is returning to spirituality. I am not convinced by this analysis of the situation. It seems to me that the rejection of religion and the churches is continuing in the new spirituality. People mistrust the churches. The churches are seen as authoritarian, and any authority they seek to exercise is weakened (even among those who might respect it) by the much-publicized failings of church authorities. As a friend once put it to me, she loves the spiritual side of life but cannot accept religion as it is tied up in human institutions and thus becomes muddied and corrupt. Contemporary spirituality, on the other hand, is free from human institutions and so remains pure and beautiful. If the baby has been thrown out with the bathwater, then it is the bathwater (plus healing essential oils) that has gone back into the tub.

This is the point at which we come back to magic. I do not imagine that there are many people today who invoke angels while performing distasteful ritual practices involving cats in order to ensure that their favored horse or car wins the race and has them laughing all the way back to the bookies. However, I think that there may be an underlying similarity between ancient magic and contemporary angel spirituality. This similarity lies in the fact that these spiritualities empower the participant to exercise a measure of control in their communications with the realms of the divine. By contrast religion (at least in its Christian form) demands complete surrender of the self to God. Those who want to save their lives will lose them and those who lose their lives for Christ will save them. The expectation is that the religious person will live according to the agenda God sets every day of their lives. The loss of control that meeting this challenge demands is unappealing to many people. Magic does not demand this. Magic offers access to the spiritual world, and a measure of power to invoke angels and get them to work towards our self-fulfillment and the fulfillment of our desires.

Contemporary spirituality offers the same kind of power of access to the angels for the same goal of self-fulfillment. Like ancient magic, contemporary spirituality offers spirituality with the freedom to set our own agenda.

But this paints a subtly different picture of angels from the angels we find in the ancient sources we studied. The angels in the vast majority of the ancient sources are ministering spirits who do the will of the Almighty. The book of Hebrews sums it up nicely (Heb 1:14). Put negatively (though I would not put it this way myself), the angels collude with what some modern people perceive to be the authoritarianism of God by carrying out God's every command. Perhaps those so inclined might find refuge in the stories of the fallen Watchers. After all, Shemihazah and Asael came to earth to teach humanity the secrets of heaven (*1 En.* 8:1–3). But this resulted in godlessness and death (*1 En.* 8:2, 4). The angel marriages resulted in chaos and the near destruction of humanity by the giants. It is only the texts on the religious periphery, the magical texts, that present a different picture—one in which human control of the spiritual world is offered and the achievement of personal desires is advertised. As with so many things in life, it comes down to trust and choice.

A variety of different views on angels is on offer, as indeed it was in the world of ancient Judaism and early Christianity. Take the role of angels in the war of Judea against Rome as an example. The community at Qumran envisaged itself fighting alongside the angels in the war against Rome and the demonic hordes of Belial. Their religious literature predicted victory and yet the Romans won. Josephus who seems rather wary of angel encounter stories links the vision of warrior angels leaving the temple to a prediction of the destruction of the temple, tentatively suggesting that Rome might win this war (a view he claims to have taken as a result of a vision, *War* 3:8.3§351). Jesus used the language of the divine warrior and angels to predict the destruction of the temple by Rome. All these ancient Jews used the same language of the same event but predicting different outcomes with different degrees of certainty. They could not all be right. Different views present choices. Just as these different views among ancient Jews present choices to their hearers and readers so differing views on angels present choices to people today.

WHERE ANGELS FEAR TO TREAD

At this point we return to the theme of embarrassment as I put my own cards down on the table. I am not going to offer an argument for my point of view. I believe in the importance of offering arguments to establish truth. However, my experience of talking theology to date is that presenting most people with too many arguments about complex issues produces spiritual fatigue. As the welter of ideas grows ever thicker in our minds and spins around more and more slowly until they all finally congeal, we simply lose interest. I am not keen to lose the interest of anyone who has got this far. So what I write below is simply the personal testimony of where I currently stand in relation to the question of angels.

I believe in angels. I accept the reality of angels as spiritual beings that objectively exist. I confess that I am not wholly persuaded by the example of out of body experiences that minds can exist outside of bodies. Without doing more research into the area, part of me remains open to the idea that these experiences may have a perfectly plausible physical explanation. However, I do believe in God (for many reasons, which I shall not outline here) and so cannot say that the idea of minds without bodies is incredible, as I clearly already accept the existence of the one transcendent God, who among other things is surely Mind without body. Thus I think that angels are certainly conceptually possible; there is nothing incoherent about the idea.

As a Christian who takes the Bible as authoritative for faith, and given that angels regularly appear in the Bible, I ought to address the question of what I make of angels. To be very honest, until I wrote this book I held two rather contradictory views on angels. The Bible speaks about them as real beings and so, as a faithful believer, I supposed they existed. As someone who has read some theology and is interested in the sociology of knowledge, I reckoned angels belonged to ancient worldviews that used mythological language to speak of events in this world. Angels were metaphors, at least in divine warfare language. The two views may be slightly contradictory but they are not very difficult to hold in tension—I did so for over twenty years. My understanding has moved a little towards ascribing some kind of visionary reality to the angels of apocalyptic. However, I confess that I hardly begin to understand how to describe this visionary reality in which angels can appear in addition to "normal" reality (for the distinction, revisit Acts 12:6–11) and that I am still more interested in what the interpreting angel says it all means about events on earth. Nonetheless, as is obvious from my interaction with the work of Walter Wink above, I am not persuaded that any biblical writer demythologized the language of angels. Nor am I persuaded that we need to interpret the reality of angels in the Bible in a new way for a modern generation that does not believe in angels. They do not believe in God either, but this does not persuade me to interpret the Christian faith such that belief in God is not required. I find such theology dishonest. It is much more honest to abandon the faith altogether as belonging to an outmoded worldview, but I have no desire to do that. So I shall stick with angels and see where the growth in knowledge that comes with prayer, study, and conversation leads me.

Besides which, I have personal religious experience that leads me to question the tidiness of social (or even pseudo) scientific explanations for everything religious or mystical. I enjoyed the call of Luke Timothy Johnson to NT scholars to do the work of theology within the messy context of religious experience.[12] However, I disagree with his statement that speech in tongues or *glossolalia* does not involve speaking a real language but rather the patterning of sounds.[13] In the early months of 1986 I was present in a youth worship meeting in Lima, Peru. During the course of the meeting a young lady spoke in tongues—in English. She was a Spanish-speaking Peruvian who spoke literally just a few words of English (I can vouch for this) and during this meeting spoke a prophetic word to the church in a number of paragraphs of English. The grammar was not perfect but the English flowed and the message was clear enough (in summary, get out of this self-indulgent middle-class worship meeting and take my love to the broken who are literally lying on the streets of this city). She may have spoken with the tongues of mortals rather than those of angels but the experience is not easy to account for on the normal psychological explanations of tongues. A woman who could not speak English suddenly comes out with pretty fluent English. A few months later, I was in Bolivia travelling in a bus high up in the Andes. There was a spectrum sunrise and I found myself in prayer asking for healing from a traumatic experience in my early teenage years. I felt an astounding sense of release. There is nothing particularly odd in that—many people

12. Johnson, *Religious Experience*.
13. Ibid., 112.

have similar experiences. However, on my return to England three or four months later I discovered something slightly more difficult to explain. My grandmother had been praying, as was her custom, on her sofa in the drawing room one morning and saw a vision of me inside a cage. The door was opened and I stepped out. A wise old woman, she noted the picture, the date, and time. A skeptical youth, I refused to explain the picture until I discovered the day and hour she saw it. Accounting for time differences, she saw the vision at *exactly* the same time as I was praying. This would seem strange and slightly spooky if other people I know and trust had not had sufficient experiences of a similar nature to lead me to accept that such religious experiences really happen. I am no longer inclined to write them off without first giving them due consideration.

These experiences have also contributed to my understanding of the love of God. For all the hideous evils in the world (and I have encountered a few), my experience is that God works to heal people and communities today. I cannot explain why evil exists or why God heals some people and situations but has not yet healed others. However, I am not inclined to deny the reality of the healing work of Christ that I have encountered in my own experience and that of others I know. In fact, it is precisely at this point that I prefer the traditional Christianity that many spiritual people are rejecting in favor of angels. Given the choice I would prefer that God came in person and experienced human life with all its beauty and suffering than that he simply sent angels (who have no experience of what it is like to be human) to comfort and guide me. I prefer to worship a God who has worked out in practice how to live as a human person than to seek the company of angels who only appear human when they turn up to help me. I can listen more easily to the advice of such a God than I can to any words of a heavenly visitor who will never experience my reality. The God of Christianity is precisely this kind of deity. God became human in Jesus and experienced life as we experience it. God comes alongside us and from personal experience teaches us how to live our lives the best way we can. So I will not be loving angels instead. I prefer to recommend the Christian God as not only the LORD of heaven and earth (with all the authority that entails) but also as the most loving, trustworthy, and faithful friend anyone will ever have.

Nonetheless, I remain devoid of angel experiences. So I take what the Christian Scriptures say about angels on *trust*. Consequently, I do not hanker after angel encounters either. If I have understood Paul at all well, the focus of the Christian pilgrimage is growth in Christ. There may be extraordinary experiences along the way but they are not the focus. My desire ought to be to grow deeper into the love of Christ. As I grow in this love, so my own love for others should grow and I hope increasingly to lead a life of generosity and hospitality towards others. And who knows who I may entertain unawares.

Appendix

This book refers to texts that can be found in the Christian Bible and other second temple Jewish and early Christian literature. Below I give brief introductions to this literature and also bibliographic details of the translations of these works that I have quoted. These may be of use for anyone who wishes to read these texts themselves.

The Apocrypha or deuterocanonical books of the Christian Bible are a collection of books that never acquired the same status as holy Scripture as the rest of the books in the Bible but have been handed down with canonical Scriptures as a supplementary collection of books. Various Christian denominations have lists of books that they include in the Apocrypha but these lists do not all agree. I have used the translations that are found in the New Revised Standard Version of the Christian Bible:

- *The Holy Bible containing the Old and New Testaments with the Apocryphal / Deuterocanonical Books: New Revised Standard Version. Oxford: Oxford University Press, 1995.*

The Old Testament Pseudepigrapha are a collection of works that were in circulation in Jewish and Christian circles between the sixth century BC and the ninth century AD. They are very diverse in nature. They are not considered canonical. The translation I have used for these works is the following:

- *James H. Charlesworth. The Old Testament Pseudepigrapha. 2 vols. London: Darton, Longman and Todd, 1983–85.*

Appendix

The Dead Sea Scrolls are a collection of texts that were used by a community of Jews preparing for the establishment of a radically holy and free kingdom of Judah in the first century, probably best identified as the Essenes. Not all the texts of the Dead Sea Scrolls were written by them but their library of texts helped them to practise the kind of holiness they were seeking for the nation. I have used the following translation of their writings:

- *Florentino García Martínez and Eibert J.C. Tigchelaar. The Dead Sea Scrolls Study Edition. 2 vols. Leiden: Brill, 1997–98.*

I have used the referencing system used in this work to refer to the scrolls. In this work each scroll is given a number (occasionally a name or letters). I have used this system so as to make it easier for anyone following up my references using the above work.

Flavius Josephus (AD 37–100) was a first century Jew. Initially, he fought in the Jewish war against Rome but part way through joined the Romans. After the destruction of the temple he settled in Rome where he wrote various works defending Judaism to his Roman audience. The two works cited in this book are:

- *H. St. J. Thackeray, et al. The Jewish Antiquities. 9 vols. Loeb Classical Library. Cambridge: Harvard University Press, 1998.*

- *H. St. J. Thackeray. The Jewish War. 3 vols. Loeb Classical Library. Cambridge: Harvard University Press, 1997.*

Philo (20 BC–AD 50) was a Jewish philosopher who lived in the Egyptian city of Alexandria. He wrote many works, which comment on the Jewish Scriptures through the lens of contemporary Greek philosophy. His collected works may be found in:

- *C. D. Yonge. The Works of Philo. Peabody, MA: Hendrickson, 1997.*

The Greek Magical Papyri are papyrus texts that contain magical incantations. They readily mix aspects and ideas of different cultures and religions, although I have been most interested in the ones that use elements of Judaism or Christianity. They are generally not considered to have been written by those who practise either faith in an orthodox manner. I have used the following translation:

164

- *Hans Dieter Betz. The Greek Magical Papyri in Translation including the Demotic Spells, volume one: Texts. 2nd ed. Chicago: University of Chicago Press, 1992.*

References to these texts use the letters PGM followed by the number of the papyrus in roman numerals, and then arabic numerals to denote the lines within the papyrus.

I have referred to but not cited works of ancient Near Eastern literature and also the Babylonian Talmud (a Jewish rabbinic work). Should anybody wish to follow up these texts, the versions that I have used to check my references are:

- *William W. Hallo. The Context of Scripture, volume I: Canonical Compositions from the Biblical World. Leiden: Brill, 1997.*

- *Isidore Epstein. The Babylonian Talmud. London: Soncino, 1935–52.*

Should anyone decide to follow up any of the references I give above, then I wish you the very best as you explore the fascinating world of ancient Near Eastern, ancient Jewish, and early Christians texts.

Bibliography

Adler, Mortimer J. *The Angels and Us.* New York: MacMillan, 1982.

Alexander, Philip S. "The Demonology of the Dead Sea Scrolls." In *The Dead Sea Scrolls after Fifty Years: A Comprehensive Assessment,* edited by Peter W. Flint and James C. VanderKam, 331–53. 2 vols. Leiden: Brill, 1998–99.

Anderson, Joan W. *Where Angels Walk: True Stories of Heavenly Visitors.* London: Hodder & Stoughton, 1993.

Angel, Andrew R. *Chaos and the Son of Man: The Hebrew Chaoskampf Tradition in the Period 515 BCE to 200 CE.* Library of Second Temple Studies 60. London: T. & T. Clark, 2006.

———. "The Sea in 4Q541 7.3 and in Daniel 7.2." *Vetus Testamentum* 60 (2010) 474–78.

Arnold, Clinton E. *The Colossian Syncretism: The Interface Between Christianity and Folk Belief at Colossae.* Wissenschaftliche Untersuchungen zum Neuen Testament 77. Tübingen: Mohr, 1995.

———. *Ephesians: Power and Magic.* Society for New Testament Studies Monograph Series 63. Cambridge: Cambridge University Press, 1989.

———. *Powers of Darkness: A Thoughtful, Biblical Look at an Urgent Challenge Facing the Church.* Leicester, UK: Inter-Varsity, 1992.

Attridge, Harold W. *A Commentary on the Epistle to the Hebrews.* Hermeneia. Philadelphia: Fortress, 1989.

Aune, David E. *Revelation.* Word Biblical Commentary 52A. Dallas, TX: Word, 1997.

Ayer, Alfred J. *Language, Truth and Logic.* Rev. ed. London: Gollancz, 1946.

Baker, David, W. "Kittim." In *Anchor Bible Dictionary,* vol. 4, edited by David Noel Freedman et al., 93. New York: Doubleday, 1992.

Baldwin, Joyce G. *Daniel: An Introduction and Commentary.* Tyndale Old Testament Commentary. Leicester, UK: InterVarsity, 1978.

Bandstra, Andrew J. "The Law and Angels: *Antiquities* 15.136 and Galatians 3:19." *Calvin Theological Journal* 24 (1989) 223–40.

———. *The Law and the Elements of the World: An Exegetical Study in Aspects of Paul's Theology.* Kampen: Kok, 1964.

Barbour, Ian G. *Issues in Science and Religion.* London: SCM, 1966.

Barker, Margaret. *The Great Angel: A Study of Israel's Second God.* London: SPCK, 1992.

Bibliography

Bauckham, Richard J. *Jude, 2 Peter*. Word Biblical Commentary 50. Waco, TX: Word, 1983.

———. "The Worship of Jesus in Apocalyptic Christianity." In *The Climax of Prophecy: Studies on the Book of Revelation*, 118–49. Edinburgh: T. & T. Clark, 1993.

Beale, Gregory K. *The Book of Revelation*. New International Greek Testament Commentary. Grand Rapids: Eerdmans, 1999.

BeDuhn, Jason D. "'Because of the Angels': Unveiling Paul's Anthropology in 1 Corinthians 11." *Journal of Biblical Literature* 118 (1999) 295–320.

Begg, Christopher. "Angels in the Work of Flavius Josephus." In *Angels, The Concept of Celestial Beings—Origins, Development and Reception*, edited by Friedrich V. Reiterer et al., 525–36. Deuterocanonical and Cognate Literature Yearbook 2007. Berlin: de Gruyter, 2007.

Bentjes, Pancratius C. "Satan, God and the Angel(s) in 1 Chronicles 21." In *Angels, The Concept of Celestial Beings—Origins, Development and Reception*, edited by Friedrich V. Reiterer et al., 139–54. Deuterocanonical and Cognate Literature Yearbook 2007. Berlin: de Gruyter, 2007.

Berkhof, Hendrik. *Christ and the Powers*. Translated by John H. Yoder. Scottdale, PA: Herald, 1962.

Bernstein, Moshe J. "Angels at the Aqedah: A Study in the Development of a Midrashic Motif." *Dead Sea Discoveries* 7 (2000) 264–91.

Best, Ernest. *A Critical and Exegetical Commentary on Ephesians*. International Critical Commentary. London: T. & T. Clark, 1998.

Betz, Hans D. *The Greek Magical Papyri in Translation, Including the Demotic Spells: Volume 1, Texts*. 2nd ed. Chicago: University of Chicago Press, 1992.

Blackmore, Susan J. *Beyond the Body: An Investigation of Out of Body Experiences*. London: Granada, 1983.

Blenkinsopp, Joseph. *Isaiah 40–55: A New Translation with Introduction and Commentary*. Anchor Bible 19A. New York: Doubleday, 2002.

Bloncourt, Nelson, and Karen Engelmann. *Visions of Angels*. New York: Studio, 1998.

Bock, Darrell L. *Acts*. Baker Exegetical Commentary on the New Testament. Grand Rapids: Baker, 2007.

———. *Luke, volume 2: 9:51—24:53*. Baker Exegetical Commentary on the New Testament. Grand Rapids: Baker, 1996.

Boyd, Gregory A. *God at War: The Bible and Spiritual Conflict*. Downers Grove, IL: InterVarsity, 1997.

Braun, Roddy. *1 Chronicles*. Word Biblical Commentary 14. Waco, TX: Word, 1986.

Brother Yun and Paul Hattaway. *The Heavenly Man: The Remarkable True Story of Chinese Christian Brother Yun*. Oxford: Monarch, 2002.

Bruce, Frederick F. *The Epistle to the Galatians*. New International Greek Testament Commentary. Grand Rapids: Eerdmans, 1982.

Burnham, Sophy. *A Book of Angels: Reflections on Angels Past and Present and True Stories of How They Touch Our Lives*. New York: Ballantine, 1990.

Bultmann, Rudolph. "New Testament and Mythology: The Problem of Demythologizing the New Testament Proclamation." In *New Testament and Mythology and Other Basic Writings*, edited by Schubert M. Ogden, 1–43. Philadelphia: Fortress, 1984.

Butler, Trent. *Judges*. Word Biblical Commentary 8. Nashville: Thomas Nelson, 2009.

Caird, George B. *Principalities and Powers: A Study in Pauline Theology*. Oxford: Clarendon, 1956.

Calvin, John. *Commentary on a Harmony of the Evangelists, Matthew, Mark and Luke, Vol. 1*. Translated by William Pringle. Grand Rapids: Baker, 2009.

Carr, Wesley. *Angels and Principalities: The Background, Meaning and Development of the Pauline Phrase HAI ARCHAI KAI HAI EXOUSIAI*. Society for New Testament Studies Monograph Series 42. Cambridge: Cambridge University Press, 1981.

Carrell, Peter R. *Jesus and the Angels: Angelology and the Christology of the Apocalypse of John*. Society for New Testament Studies Monograph Series 95. Cambridge: Cambridge University Press, 1997.

Casey, P. Maurice. *From Jewish Prophet to Gentile God: The Origins and Development of New Testament Christology*. London: Clarke, 1991.

———. *The Son of Man: The Interpretation and Influence of Daniel 7*. London: SPCK, 1979.

Charles, J. Daryl. "The Angels under Reserve in 2 Peter and Jude." *Bulletin of Biblical Research* 15 (2005) 39–48.

Charlesworth, James H. "The Portrayal of the Righteous as an Angel." In *Ideal Figures in Ancient Judaism: Profiles and Paradigms*, edited by John J. Collins and George W. E. Nickelsburg, 135–51. Society of Biblical Literature Septuagint and Cognate Studies 12. Chico, CA: Scholars, 1980.

Chazon, Esther G. "Liturgical Communion with the Angels at Qumran." In *Sapiential, Liturgical and Poetical Texts from Qumran: Proceedings of the Third Meeting of the International Organization for Qumran Studies, Oslo 1998*, edited by Daniel K Falk et al., 95–105. Leiden: Brill, 2000.

Clebsch, W. and C. Jaekle. *Pastoral Care in Historical Perspective*. New York: Aaronson, 1964.

Clines, David J. A. *Job 1–20*. Word Biblical Commentary 17. Dallas, TX: Word, 1989.

Cogan, Mordechai, and Hayim Tadmor. *II Kings: A New Translation with Introduction and Commentary*. Anchor Bible 11. Garden City, NY: Doubleday, 1988.

Collins, Adela Y. *The Combat Myth in the Book of Revelation*. Harvard Dissertations in Religion 9. Missoula, MT: Scholars, 1976.

———. "The 'Son of Man' Tradition and the Book of Revelation." In *The Messiah*, edited by James H. Charlesworth, 536–68. Minneapolis: Fortress, 1992.

Collins, John J. *Apocalypse: The Morphology of a Genre*. Semeia 14. Missoula, MT: Scholars, 1979.

———. *The Apocalyptic Imagination: An Introduction to Jewish Apocalyptic*. 2nd ed. Grand Rapids: Eerdmans, 1998.

———. *Daniel: A Commentary on the Book of Daniel*. Hermeneia. Minneapolis: Fortress, 1993.

Bibliography

———. "In the Likeness of the Holy Ones: The Creation of Humankind in a Wisdom Text from Qumran." In *The Provo International Conference on the Dead Sea Scrolls: Technological Innovations, New Texts, and Reformulated Issues*, edited by Donald W. Parry and Eugene Ulrich, 609–18. Studies on the Texts of the Desert of Judah 30. Leiden: Brill, 1999.

———. "Powers in Heaven: God, Gods, and Angels in the Dead Sea Scrolls." In *Religion in the Dead Sea Scrolls*, edited by John J. Collins and Robert A. Kugler, 9–28. Studies in the Dead Sea Scrolls and Related Literature. Grand Rapids: Eerdmans, 2000.

Collins, Raymond F. *First Corinthians*. Sacra Pagina 7. Collegeville, MN: Liturgical, 1999.

Craigie, Peter C. *Psalms 1–50*. Word Biblical Commentary 19. Waco, TX: Word, 1983.

Cross, Frank M. *Canaanite Myth and Hebrew Epic: Essays in the History of the Religion of Israel*. Cambridge, MA: Harvard University Press, 1973.

Daube, David. "On Acts 23: Sadducees and Angels." *Journal of Biblical Literature* 109 (1990) 493–97.

Davidson, Maxwell J. *Angels at Qumran: A Comparative Study of 1 Enoch 1–36, 72–108 and Sectarian Writings from Qumran*. Journal for the Study of the Pseudepigrapha: Supplement Series 11. Sheffield, UK: JSOT Press, 1992.

Davies, W. D. "A Note on Josephus, Antiquities 15.136." *Harvard Theological Review* 47 (1954) 135–40.

Davies, W. D., and Dale C. Allison, *A Critical and Exegetical Commentary on the Gospel according to Saint Matthew*. 3 vols. International Critical Commentary. London: T. & T. Clark, 1988–2004.

Davila, James R. *Liturgical Works*. Eerdmans Commentaries on the Dead Sea Scrolls 6. Grand Rapids: Eerdmans, 2000.

———. "Melchizedek, Michael, and the War in Heaven." In *Society of Biblical Literature 1996 Seminar Papers*, 259–72. Society of Biblical Literature Seminar Papers 35. Atlanta, GA: Scholars, 1996.

Davis, Philip G. "Divine Agents, Mediators, and New Testament Christology." *Journal of Theological Studies* 45 (1994) 479–503.

Day, John. *God's Conflict with the Dragon and the Sea: Echoes of a Canaanite Myth in the Old Testament*. University of Cambridge Oriental Publications 35. Cambridge: Cambridge University Press, 1985.

———. *Yahweh and the Gods and Goddesses of Canaan*. JSOTSupp 265. 2000. Reprint. London: Continuum, 2002.

Day, Peggy L. *An Adversary in Heaven: Satan in the Hebrew Bible*. Harvard Semitic Monographs 43. Atlanta, GA: Scholars, 1988.

Dean-Otting, Mary. *Heavenly Journeys: A Study of the Motif in Hellenistic Jewish Literature*. Judentum und Umwelt 8. Frankfurt: Lang, 1984.

Descartes, René. *Discourse on the Method of Rightly Conducting the Reason and Seeking Truth in the Sciences*. Translated by John Veitch. London: Dent, 1912.

de Jonge, Marinus. *The Testaments of the Twelve Patriarchs: A Critical Edition of the Greek Text*. Pseudepigrapha Veteris Testamenti Graece. Leiden: Brill, 1978.

Dietrich, M., et al. *Die keilalphabetischen Texte aus Ugarit. Teil I. Transkription. Alter Orient und Altes Testament* 24. Neukirchen-Vluyn: Neukirchener, 1976.

Dillon, John. "Philo's Doctrine of Angels." In *Two Treatises of Philo of Alexandria: A Commentary on De Gigantibus and Quod Deus Sit Immutabilis*, edited by David Winston and John Dillon, 197–205. Brown Judaic Studies 25. Chico, CA: Scholars, 1983.

Dimant, Devorah. "Men as Angels: The Self-Image of the Qumran Community." In *Religion and Politics in the Ancient Near East*, edited by Adele Berlin, 93–103. Studies and Texts in Jewish History and Culture. Bethesda, MD: University of Maryland, 1996.

du Toit Laubscher, F. "God's Angel of Truth and Melchizedek: A Note on 11QMelch ₃b." *Journal for the Study of Judaism in the Persian, Hellenistic, and Roman Periods* 3 (1972) 46–51.

Dunn, James D. G. *The Epistles to the Colossians and Philemon*. New International Greek Testament Commentary. Grand Rapids: Eerdmans, 1996.

Evans, Craig A. "Inaugurating the Kingdom of God and Defeating the Kingdom of Satan." *Bulletin of Biblical Research* 15 (2005) 49–75.

Fee, Gordon D. *The First Epistle to the Corinthians*. New International Commentary on the New Testament; Grand Rapids: Eerdmans, 1987.

Fernando, Keith. "On Being Heavenly Minded." In *The Unseen World: Christian Reflections on Angels, Demons and the Heavenly Realm*, edited by Anthony N. S. Lane, 103–32. Grand Rapids: Baker, 1996.

Fiore, Benjamin. *The Pastoral Epistles: First Timothy, Second Timothy, Titus*. Sacra Pagina 12. Collegeville, MN: Liturgical, 2007.

Fitzmyer, Joseph A. *The Acts of the Apostles: A New Translation with Introduction and Commentary*. Anchor Bible 31. London: Doubleday, 1998.

———. "A Feature of Qumran Angelology and the Angels of 1 Cor 11.10." In *Essays on the Semitic Background of the New Testament*, 187–204. London: Chapman, 1971.

———. *First Corinthians: A New Translation with Introduction and Commentary*. Anchor Yale Bible 32. New Haven, CT: Yale University Press, 2008.

———. *The Gospel according to Luke X–XXIV*. Anchor Bible 28A. New York: Doubleday, 1985.

———. *Romans: A New Translation with Introduction and Commentary*. Anchor Bible 33. New York: Doubleday, 1993.

Fletcher-Louis, Crispin H. T. *Luke-Acts: Angels, Christology and Soteriology*. Wissenschaftliche Untersuchungen zum Neuen Testament 94. Tübingen: Mohr Siebeck, 1997.

Flew, Antony. *There is ̶n̶o̶ a God, How the World's Most Notorious Atheist Changed His Mind*. New York: HarperCollins, 2008.

Flew, Antony G. N., and Alexander C. MacIntyre. *New Essays in Philosophical Theology*. London: SCM, 1955.

Flusser, David. "Resurrection and Angels in Rabbinic Judaism, Early Christianity, and Qumran." In *The Dead Sea Scrolls Fifty Years After Their Discovery: Proceedings of the Jerusalem Congress, July 20–25, 1997*, edited by Lawrence H. Schiffman et al., 568–72. Israel Exploration Society: Jerusalem, 2000.

Bibliography

Forbes, Chris. "Pauline Demonology and/or Cosmology? Principalities, Powers and the Elements of the World in their Hellenistic Context." *Journal for the Study of the New Testament* 23 (2002) 51–73.

———. "Paul's Principalities and Powers: Demythologizing Apocalyptic." *Journal for the Study of the New Testament* 82 (2001) 61–88.

Forsyth, Neil. *The Old Enemy: Satan and the Combat Myth.* Princeton, NJ: Princeton University Press, 1987.

Fossum, Jarl E. *The Name of God and the Angel of the Lord: Samaritan and Jewish Concepts of Intermediation and the Origin of Gnosticism.* Wissenschaftliche Untersuchungen zum Neuen Testament 36. Tübingen: Mohr, 1985.

Foster, Benjamin R. "Epic of Creation." In *The Context of Scripture, vol. 1: Canonical Compositions from the Biblical World,* edited by William W. Hallo and K. Lawson Younger, 390–402. Leiden: Brill, 1997.

———. *From Distant Days: Myths, Tales and Poetry of Ancient Mesopotamia.* Bethesda, MD: CDL, 1995.

France, R. T. *The Gospel of Mark.* New International Greek Testament Commentary. Grand Rapids: Eerdmans, 2002.

———. *The Gospel of Matthew.* New International Commentary on the Old Testament. Grand Rapids: Eerdmans, 2007.

Francis, Fred O. "Humility and Angelic Worship in Col 2:18." In *Conflict at Colossae: A Problem in the Interpretation of Early Christianity Illustrated by Selected Modern Studies,* edited by Fred. O. Francis and Wayne A. Meeks, 163–95. Rev. ed. Sources for Biblical Study 4. Missoula, MT: Scholars, 1975.

Gammie, John G. "The Angelology and Demonology in the Septuagint of the Book of Job." *Hebrew Union College Annual* 56 (1985) 1–19.

Ganssle, Gregory E. *Reasonable God: Engaging the New Face of Atheism.* Waco, TX: Baylor University Press, 2009.

Garrett, Susan R. *No Ordinary Angel: Celestial Spirits and Christian Claims about Jesus.* Anchor Yale Bible Reference Library. New Haven, CT: Yale University Press, 2008.

Gaston, Lloyd. "Angels and Gentiles in Early Judaism and in Paul." *Studies in Religion* 11 (1982) 65–75.

Gerhardssohn, Birger. *The Reliability of the Gospel Tradition.* Peabody, MA: Hendrickson, 2001.

Gieschen, Charles A. *Angelomorphic Christology: Antecedents and Early Evidence.* Arbeiten zur Geschichte des Antiken Judentums und des Urchristentums 42. Leiden: Brill, 1998.

Gleason, Randall C. "Angels and the Eschatology of Heb 1–2." *New Testament Studies* 49 (2003) 90–107.

Goldingay, John E. *Daniel.* Word Biblical Commentary 30. Dallas, TX: Word, 1989.

Goldstein, Jonathan. *2 Maccabees: A New Translation with Introduction and Commentary.* Anchor Bible 41A. Garden City, NY: Doubleday, 1983.

Gooder, Paula R. *Only the Third Heaven: 2 Corinthians 12.1-10 and Heavenly Ascent.* Library of New Testament Studies 313. London: Clark, 2006

Goodman, David. "Do Angels Eat?" *Journal of Jewish Studies* 37 (1986) 160–75.

Graham, Billy. *Angels: God's Secret Agents.* London: Hodder & Stoughton, 1976.

Green, Alberto R. W. *The Storm-God in the Ancient Near East.* Biblical and Judaic Studies 8. Winona Lake, IN: Eisenbrauns, 2003.

Gruenwald, Ithamar. *Apocalyptic and Merkavah Mysticism.* Arbeiten zur Geschichte des antiken Judentums und des Urchristentums 14. Leiden: Brill, 1980.

Gunkel, Hermann. *Creation and Chaos in the Primeval Era and the Eschaton: A Religio-Historical Study of Genesis 1 and Revelation 12.* Translated by K. William Whitney. Grand Rapids: Eerdmans, 2006.

Hallo, William W. *Context of Scripture.* 3 vols. Leiden: Brill, 1997–2002.

Hamilton, Victor P. *The Book of Genesis, Chapters 18–50.* New International Commentary on the Old Testament. Grand Rapids: Eerdmans, 1995.

Handy, Lowell K. "Dissenting Deities or Obedient Angels: Divine Hierarchies in Ugarit and the Bible." *Biblical Research* 35 (1990) 18–35.

Hannah, Darrell D. "Guardian Angels and Angelic National Patrons in Second Temple Judaism and Early Christianity." In *Angels, the Concept of Celestial Beings— Origins, Development and Reception,* edited by Friedrich V. Reiterer et al., 414–35. Deuterocanonical and Cognate Literature Yearbook 2007. Berlin: de Gruyter, 2007.

———. *Michael and Christ: Michael Traditions and Angel Christology in Early Christianity.* Wissenschaftliche Untersuchungen zum Neuen Testament 109. Tübingen: Mohr Siebeck, 1999.

Hanson, Paul D. *The Dawn of Apocalyptic: The Historical and Sociological Roots of Jewish Apocalyptic Eschatology.* Rev. ed. Philadelphia: Fortress, 1979.

———. "Rebellion in Heaven, Azazel and Euhemeristic Heroes in 1 Enoch 6–11." *Journal of Biblical Literature* 96 (1977) 195–233.

Harrington, Daniel J. "Pseudo-Philo." In *The Old Testament Pseudepigrapha,* edited by James H. Charlesworth, 297–377. 2 vols. London: Darton, Longman and Todd, 1985.

Hartenstein, Freidhelm. "Cherubim and Seraphim in the Bible and in the Light of Ancient Near Eastern Sources." In *Angels, The Concept of Celestial Beings— Origins, Development and Reception,* edited by Friedrich V. Reiterer et al., 155–88. Deuterocanonical and Cognate Literature Yearbook 2007. Berlin: de Gruyter, 2007.

Hay, David. *Exploring Inner Space: Is God Still Possible in the Twentieth Century?* Rev. ed. London: Mowbray, 1987.

———. *Religious Experience Today: Studying the Facts.* London: Mowbray, 1990.

Heathcote-James, Emma. *After-Death Communication.* London: Metro, 2004.

———. *Seeing Angels.* London: Blake, 2001.

Heidt, William G. *Angelology of the Old Testament: A Study in Biblical Theology.* Catholic University of America Studies in Sacred Theology, Second Series no. 24. Washington, DC: Catholic University of America Press, 1949.

Hickey, Marilyn. *Angels All Around: The Present-day Ministry of Angels.* Denver, CO: Marilyn Hickey Ministries, 1991.

Himmelfarb, Martha. *Ascent to Heaven in Jewish and Christian Apocalypses.* Oxford: Oxford University Press, 1993.

Bibliography

————. *Tours of Hell: An Apocalyptic Form in Jewish and Christian Literature.* Philadelphia: University of Pennsylvania Press, 1983.

Hoehner, Harold W. *Ephesians: An Exegetical Commentary.* Grand Rapids: Baker Academic, 2002.

Hoeller, Stephan A. "Angels Holy and Unholy: The Gnostic Alternative to Mainstream Angelology." In *Angels and Mortals: Their Co-Creative Power*, edited by Maria Parisen, 97–105. Wheaton IL: Quest, 1990.

Hossfeld, Frank-Lothar, and Erich Zenger. *Psalms 2.* Hermeneia. Minneapolis: Fortress, 2005.

Hurtado, Larry W. *At the Origins of Christian Worship: The Context and Character of Earliest Christian Devotion.* Carlisle, UK: Paternoster, 1999.

————. "First Century Jewish Monotheism." *Journal for the Study of the New Testament* 71 (1998) 3–26.

————. *Lord Jesus Christ: Devotion to Jesus in Earliest Christianity.* Grand Rapids: Eerdmans, 2003.

————. *One God, One Lord: Early Christian Devotion and Ancient Jewish Monotheism.* 2nd ed. Edinburgh: T. & T. Clark, 1998.

Instone-Brewer, David. "Jesus and the Psychiatrists." In *The Unseen World: Christian Reflections on Angels, Demons and the Heavenly Realm*, edited by Anthony N. S. Lane, 133–48. Grand Rapids: Baker, 1996.

Jacobson, Howard. *A Commentary on Pseudo-Philo's Liber Antiquitatum Biblicarum* Arbeiten zur Geschichte des antiken Judentums und des Urchristentums 31. Leiden: Brill, 1996.

Jacobsen, Thorkild. *Treasures of Darkness: A History of Mesopotamian Religion.* New Haven, CT: Yale University Press, 1976.

Jewett, Robert. *Romans.* Hermeneia. Fortress: Minneapolis, 2007.

Johnson, Luke T. *The Acts of the Apostles.* Sacra Pagina 5. Collegeville, MN: Liturgical, 1992.

————. *Religious Experience in Earliest Christianity: A Missing Dimension in New Testament Studies.* Minneapolis: Fortress, 1998.

Jung, Leo. *Fallen Angels in Jewish, Christian and Mohammedan Literature.* Dropsie College for Hebrew and Cognate Learning. 1926. Reprint. New York: Ktav, 1974.

Kasher, Rimmon. "Angelology and the Supernal Worlds in the Aramaic Targums to the Prophets." *Journal for the Study of Judaism in the Persian, Hellenistic, and Roman Periods* 27 (1996) 168–91.

Kelly, Henry A. *Satan: A Biography.* Cambridge: Cambridge University Press, 2006.

Knoppers, Gary N. *1 Chronicles 10–29: A New Translation with Introduction and Commentary.* Anchor Bible 12A. New York: Doubleday, 2004.

Kobelski, Paul J. *Melchizedek and Melchiresa.* Catholic Biblical Quarterly Monograph Series 10. Washington, DC: The Catholic Biblical Association of America, 1981.

Koester, Craig R. *Hebrews: A New Translation with Introduction and Commentary.* Anchor Yale Bible 36. New York: Doubleday, 2001.

Kraus, Thomas J. "Angels in the Magical Papyri: The Classic Example of Michael, the Archangel." In *Angels, The Concept of Celestial Beings—Origins, Development and*

Reception, edited by Friedrich V. Reiterer et al., 611–27. Deuterocanonical and Cognate Literature Yearbook 2007. Berlin: de Gruyter, 2007.

Kreeft, Peter. *Angels (and Demons): What Do We Really Know about Them?* San Francisco: Ignatius, 1995.

Kuhn, Harold B. "The Angelology of the Non-Canonical Jewish Apocalypses." *Journal of Biblical Literature* 67 (1948) 217–32.

Kuhn, Thomas S. *The Structure of Scientific Revolutions.* Chicago: University of Chicago Press, 1962.

Kulik, Alexander. *3 Baruch: Greek-Slavonic Apocalypse of Baruch.* Commentaries on Early Jewish Literature. Berlin: de Gruyter, 2010.

Langton, Edward. *The Angel Teaching of the New Testament.* London: Clarke, 1937.

———. *Satan, A Portrait: A Study of the Character of Satan through all the Ages.* London: Skeffington & Son, 1945.

Law, Terry. *The Truth about Angels.* Orlando, FL: Creation House, 1994.

Lieberman, Saul. "Appendix 1. Metatron, the Meaning of his Name and his Functions." In *Apocalyptic and Merkavah Mysticism*, by Ithamar Gruenwald, 235–41. Arbeiten zur Geschichte des antiken Judentums und des Urchristentums 14; Leiden: Brill, 1980.

Lietaert Peerbolte, L. J. "Man, Woman, and the Angels in 1 Cor 11.2–16." In *The Creation of Man and Woman: Interpretations of the Biblical Narratives in Jewish and Christian Traditions*, edited by Gerard P. Luttikhuizen, 76–92. Themes in Biblical Narrative Jewish and Christian Traditions 3; Leiden: Brill, 2000.

Locke, John. *An Essay Concerning Human Understanding.* Edited by Raymond Wilburn. London: Dent, 1947.

Longman III, Tremper, and Daniel G. Reid. *God is a Warrior.* Studies in Old Testament Biblical Theology. Grand Rapids: Zondervan, 1995.

Lucas, Ernest C. *Daniel.* Apollos Old Testament Commentary 20; Nottingham: Apollos, 2002.

Luz, Ulrich. *Matthew 8–20.* Hermeneia. Minneapolis, MN: Fortress, 2001.

MacDonald, Margaret Y. *Colossians and Ephesians.* Sacra Pagina 17. Collegeville, MN: Liturgical, 2000.

MacGregor, G. H. C. "Principalities and Powers: the Cosmic Background of St Paul's Thought." *New Testament Studies* 1 (1954) 17–28.

Macy, Jonathan. *In the Shadow of His Wings: The Pastoral Ministry of Angels Yesterday, Today and for Heaven.* Eugene, OR: Cascade, 2011.

Malherbe, Abraham J. *The Letters to the Thessalonians.* Anchor Yale Bible 32B. New Haven, CT. Yale University Press, 2000.

Malina, Bruce, and John J. Pilch. *Social Scientific Commentary on the Book of Revelation.* Minneapolis: Fortress, 2000.

Marcus, Joel. *Mark 8–16.* Anchor Yale Bible 27A. New Haven, CT: Yale University Press, 2009.

Martone, Corrado. "Evil or Devil? Belial between the Bible and Qumran." *Henoch* 26 (2004) 117–27.

Martyn, J. Louis. *Galatians: A New Translation with Introduction and Commentary.* Anchor Yale Bible 33A. New Haven, CT: Yale University Press, 1997.

Bibliography

McCown, Chester C. *The Testament of Solomon*. Leipzig: J.C. Hinrich, 1922.

Meier, John P. *A Marginal Jew, Rethinking the Historical Jesus, volume IV: Law and Love*. Anchor Yale Bible Reference Library. New Haven, CT: Yale University Press, 2009.

Meister, Chad. *Introducing Philosophy of Religion*. London: Routledge, 2009.

Meyers, Carol L., and Meyers, Eric M. *Haggai, Zechariah 1–8*. Anchor Bible 25B. New York: Doubleday, 1987.

Moo, Douglas J. *The Epistle to the Romans*. New International Commentary on the New Testament. Grand Rapids: Eerdmans, 1996.

Mounce, Robert H. *The Book of Revelation*. New International Commentary on the New Testament. Grand Rapids, MI: Eerdmans, 1997.

Mullen, E. Theodore. *The Divine Council in Canaanite and Early Hebrew Literature*. Harvard Semitic Monographs 24. Chico, CA: Scholars, 1980.

Najman, Hindy. "Angels at Sinai: Exegesis, Theology and Interpretive Authority." *Dead Sea Discoveries* 7 (2000) 313–33.

Nickelsburg, George W. E. "Apocalyptic and Myth in 1 Enoch 6–11." *Journal of Biblical Literature* 96 (1977) 383–405.

———. *1 Enoch 1: A Commentary on the Book of 1 Enoch, Chapters 1–36; 81–108*. Hermeneia. Minneapolis: Fortress, 2001.

Nickelsburg, George W. E., and James C. VanderKam. *1 Enoch: A New Translation*. Minneapolis: Fortress, 2004.

Nielsen, Kirsten. *Satan: The Prodigal Son? A Family Problem in the Bible*. The Biblical Seminar 50. Sheffield, UK: Sheffield Academic, 1998.

Noll, Stephen F. *Angels of Light, Powers of Darkness: Thinking Biblically About Angels, Satan and Principalities*. Downers Grove, IL: InterVarsity, 1998.

Nowell, Irene. "The 'Work' of Archangel Raphael." In *Angels, the Concept of Celestial Beings—Origins, Development and Reception*, edited by Friedrich V. Reiterer et al., 228–38. Deuterocanonical and Cognate Literature Yearbook 2007. Berlin: de Gruyter, 2007.

O'Brien, Peter T. *Colossians, Philemon*. Word Biblical Commentary 44. Waco, TX: Word, 1982.

Olyan, Saul M. *A Thousand Thousands Served Him: Exegesis and the Naming of Angels in Ancient Judaism*. Texte und Studien zum Antiken Judentum 36. Mohr: Tübingen: Mohr, 1993.

Osborne, Grant R. *Revelation*. Baker Exegetical Commentary on the New Testament. Grand Rapids: Baker Academic, 2006.

Osiek, Carolyn. *Shepherd of Hermas: A Commentary*. Hermeneia. Minneapolis: Fortress, 1999.

Page, Sydney H. T. *Powers of Evil: A Biblical Study of Satan and Demons*. Grand Rapids: Baker, 1995.

Pagels, Elaine. *The Origin of Satan*. Harmondsworth, UK: Penguin, 1996.

Paley, William. *Natural Theology: or, Evidences of the Existence and Attributes of the Deity*. 12th ed. London: Faulder, 1809.

Peerbolte, Lietaert L.J. "Man, Woman, and the Angels in 1 Cor 11.2-16." In *The Creation of Man and Woman: Interpretations of the Biblical Narratives in Jewish and Christian*

Traditions, edited by Gerard P. Luttikhuizen, 76–92. Themes in Biblical Narrative Jewish and Christian Traditions III. Leiden: Brill, 2000.

Perry, John. *A Time to Heal: A Contribution towards the Ministry of Healing.* London: Church House, 1980.

Pervo, Richard I. *Acts: A Commentary.* Hermeneia. Minneapolis: Fortress, 2009.

Popper, Karl R. *The Logic of Scientific Discovery.* London: Hutchinson, 1956.

Ratzinger, Joseph. "Foreword." In *Renewal and the Powers of Darkness*, edited by Léon-Joseph Suenens, ix–xi. London: DLT, 1983.

Reed, Annette Y. *Fallen Angels and the History of Judaism and Christianity: The Reception of Enochic Literature.* Cambridge: Cambridge University Press, 2005.

Reimer, Andy M. "Rescuing the Fallen Angels: The Case of the Disappearing Angels at Qumran." *Dead Sea Discoveries* 7 (2000) 334–53.

Reiterer, Friedrich V. et al. *Angels, the Concept of Celestial Beings—Origins, Development and Reception.* Deuterocanonical and Cognate Literature Yearbook 2007. Berlin: de Gruyter, 2007.

Rowland, Christopher C. *The Open Heaven: A Study of Apocalyptic in Judaism and Early Christianity.* New York: Crossroad, 1982.

———. "The Vision of the Risen Christ in Rev. i. 13 ff.: The Debt of an Early Christology to an Aspect of Jewish Angelology." *Journal of Theological Studies* 31 (1980) 1–11.

Rubinkiewicz, Ryzard. *L'Apocalypse D'Abraham en Vieux Slave: Introduction, Texte Critique, Traduction et Commentaire.* Towarzysto Naukowe Katolickiego Uniwesytetu Lubelskiego 129. Lublin: Société des Lettres et des Sciences de l'Université Catholique de Lublin, 1987.

Ryle, Gilbert. *The Concept of Mind.* London: Hutchinson, 1949.

Schlier, Heinrich. *Principalities and Powers in the New Testament.* Quaestiones Disputatae 3. London: Nelson, 1961.

Sanders, E. P. *Jesus and Judaism.* London: SCM, 1985.

Schöpflin, Karin. "God's Interpreter—The Interpreting Angel in Post-Exilic Prophetic Visions of the Old Testament." In *Angels, The Concept of Celestial Beings—Origins, Development and Reception*, edited by Friedrich V. Reiterer et al., 189–203. Deuterocanonical and Cognate Literature Yearbook 2007. Berlin: de Gruyter, 2007.

Segal, Alan F. *Two Powers in Heaven: Early Rabbinic Reports about Christianity and Gnosticism.* Studies in Judaism in Late Antiquity 25. Leiden: Brill, 1977.

Sheppard, A. R. R. "Pagan Cults of Angels in Roman Asia Minor." In *Talanta: Proceedings of the Dutch Archaeological and Historical Society* vols. 12–13 (1980–1981), edited by J. G. P. Best and H. W. Pleket, 77–101. Amsterdam: Gieben, 1982.

Silberman, Lou H. "Prophets/Angels: LXX and Qumran Psalm 151 and the Epistle to the Hebrews." In *Standing Before God: Studies on Prayer in Scriptures and in Tradition with Essays*, edited by Asher Finkel and Lawrence Frizzell, 91–101. New York: Ktav, 1981.

Skehan, Patrick W., and Alexander A. Di Lella. *The Wisdom of Ben Sira: A New Translation with Notes by Patrick W. Skehan and Commentary by Alexander A. Di Lella.* Anchor Bible 39. New York: Doubleday, 1987.

Bibliography

Smith, Mark S. *The Ugaritic Baal Cycle, vol. 1: Introduction with Text, Translation and Commentary of KTU 1.1—1.2.* Supplements to Vetus Testamentum 55. Leiden: Brill, 1994.

Sollamo, Raija. "The Creation of Angels and Natural Phenomena Intertwined in the Book of Jubilees (4QJuba)." In *Biblical Traditions in Transmission: Essays in Honour of Michael A. Knibb,* edited by Charlotte Hempel and Judith M. Lieu, 273–90. Supplements to the Journal for the Study of Judaism 3. Leiden: Brill, 2006.

Spurgeon, Charles H. *Spurgeon's Sermons on Angels.* Grand Rapids: Kregel, 1996.

Steudel, Annette. "God and Belial." In *The Dead Sea Scrolls Fifty Years After Their Discovery: Proceedings of the Jerusalem Congress, July 20–25, 1997,* edited by Lawrence H. Schiffman at al., 332–40. Israel Exploration Society: Jerusalem, 2000.

Stone, Michael E. *Fourth Ezra: A Commentary on the Book of Fourth Ezra.* Hermeneia. Minneapolis: Fortress, 1990.

Stuckenbruck, Loren T. "The 'Angels' and 'Giants' of Genesis 6.4 in Second and Third Century BCE Jewish Interpretation: Reflections on the Posture of Early Apocalyptic Traditions." *Dead Sea Discoveries* 7 (2000) 354–77.

———. "'Angels' and 'God': Exploring the Limits of Early Jewish Monotheism." In *Early Jewish and Christian Monotheism,* edited by Loren T. Stuckenbruck and Wendy North, 45–70. Early Christianity in Context. JSNTSup 263. London: T. & T. Clark, 2004.

———. *Angel Veneration and Christology: A Study in Early Judaism and in the Christology of the Apocalypse of John.* Wissenschaftliche Untersuchungen zum Neuen Testament 70. Tübingen: Mohr, 1995.

Suenens, Léon-Joseph. *Renewal and the Powers of Darkness.* London: DLT, 1983.

Sullivan, Kevin P. "Sexuality and the Gender of Angels." In *Paradise Now: Essays on Early Jewish and Christian Mysticism,* edited by April DeConick, 211–28. Society of Biblical Literature Symposium Series 11. Atlanta: Society of Biblical Literature, 2006.

———. *Wrestling with Angels: A Study of the Relationship between Angels and Humans in Ancient Jewish Literature and the New Testament.* Arbeiten zur Geschichte des Antiken Judentums und des Urchristentums/Ancient Judaism and Early Christianity 55. Leiden: Brill, 2004.

Suter, David. "Fallen Angel, Fallen Priest: The Problem of Family Purity in 1 Enoch." *Hebrew Union College Annual* 50 (1979) 115–35.

Thiselton, Anthony C. *The First Epistle to the Corinthians.* New International Greek Testament Commentary. Grand Rapids: Eerdmans, 2000.

Thrall, Margaret E. *A Critical and Exegetical Commentary on the Second Epistle to the Corinthians.* 2 vols. Rev. ed. International Critical Commentary. London: T. & T. Clark, 2004.

Twelftree, Graham H. *Jesus the Exorcist: A Contribution to the Study of the Historical Jesus.* Wissenschaftliche Untersuchungen zum Neuen Testament 54. Tübingen: Mohr, 1993.

VanderKam, James C. "The Angel of the Presence in the Book of Jubilees." *Dead Sea Discoveries* 7 (2000) 378–93.

Viviano, Benedict T., and Justin Taylor. "Sadducees, Angels and Resurrection (Acts 23.8–9)." *Journal of Biblical Literature* 111 (1992) 496–98.

Wassen, Cecilia. "Angels in the Dead Sea Scrolls." In *Angels, the Concept of Celestial Beings—Origins, Development and Reception*, edited by Friedrich V. Reiterer et al., 499–523. Deuterocanonical and Cognate Literature Yearbook 2007. Berlin: de Gruyter, 2007.

———. "What do the Angels Have against the Blind and the Deaf? Rules of Exclusion in the Dead Sea Scrolls." In *Common Judaism: Explorations in Second-Temple Judaism*, edited by Wayne O. McCready and Adele Reinhartz, 115–29. Minneapolis: Fortress, 2008.

Wenham, Gordon J. *Genesis 1–15*. Word Biblical Commentary 1. Waco, TX: Word, 1987.

Wilkinson, Belinda. *Angels in Art*. London: Studio, 1994.

Williams, Jane. *Angels*. Oxford: Lion, 2006.

Williams, Jay G. "On Reimagining Angels." In *Angels and Mortals: Their Co-Creative Power*, edited by Maria Parisen, 18–31. Wheaton IL: Quest, 1990.

Williams, Peter S. *The Case for Angels*. Carlisle, UK: Paternoster, 2002.

Wilson, Robert McL. *A Critical and Exegetical Commentary on Colossians and Philemon*. International Critical Commentary. London: T. & T. Clark, 2005.

Wink, Walter. *Engaging the Powers: Discernment and Resistance in a World of Domination*. Philadelphia: Fortress, 1992.

———. *Naming the Powers: The Language of Power in the New Testament*. Philadelphia: Fortress, 1984.

———. *Unmasking the Powers: The Invisible Forces That Determine Human Existence*. Philadelphia: Fortress, 1986.

Winston, David. *The Wisdom of Solomon*. Anchor Bible 43. New York: Doubleday, 1979.

Witherington III, Ben. *The Jesus Quest: The Third Search for the Jew of Nazareth*. Rev. ed. Downers Grove, IL: InterVarsity, 1997.

Wold, Benjamin G. *Women, Men and Angels: The Qumran Wisdom Document Musar leMevin and its Allusions to Genesis Creation Traditions*. Wissenschaftliche Untersuchungen zum Neuen Testament 201. Tübingen: Mohr Siebeck, 2005.

Wright, N. T. *The Resurrection of the Son of God*. London: SPCK, 2003.

Wyatt, Nicholas. *Religious Texts from Ugarit: The Words of Ilimilku and his Colleagues*. The Biblical Seminar 53. Sheffield, UK: Sheffield Academic, 1998.

Yamauchi, Edwin M. *Pre-Christian Gnosticism: A Survey of the Proposed Evidence*. London: Tyndale, 1973.

Yates, Roy. "Angels in the Old Testament." *Irish Theological Quarterly* 38 (1971) 164–67.

———. "The Worship of Angels (Col 2.18)." *Expository Times* 97 (1985) 12–15.

Yoder Neufeld, Thomas R. *Put on the Armour of God: The Divine Warrior from Isaiah to Ephesians*. JSNTSup 140. Sheffield, UK: Sheffield Academic, 1997.

Index of Ancient Sources

Index of Ancient Sources

Index of Modern Authors

195

Meier, John P., 107
Meister, Chad, 13
Meyers, Carol L., 104
Meyers, Eric, 104
Moo, Douglas J., 112
Mounce Robert H., 111
Mullen, E., Theodore, 24
Najman, Hindy, 46
Nickelsburg, George W. E., 24, 25, 59, 60, 77, 80, 123
Nielsen, Kirsten, 105–6, 116
Noll, Stephen F., 88
Nowell, Irene, 41
O'Brien, Peter T., 118
Olyan, Saul M., 151
Osborne, Grant R., 111
Osiek, Carolyn, 78
Page, Sydney H. T., 113
Pagels, Elaine, 114–16
Paley, William, 13–14
Peerbolte, Lietaerte, 62
Perry, John, 145
Pervo, Richard I., 72
Pilch, John J., 56
Popper, Karl R., 3
Ratzinger, Joseph, 148
Reed, Annette Y., 63
Reid, Daniel G., 85
Reimer, Andy M., 61
Reiterer, Friedrich V., 150
Rowland, Christopher C., 17, 27, 55
Rubinkiewicz, Ryzard, 26
Ryle, Gilbert, 11
Schlier, Heinrich, 126
Sanders, E. P., 115
Schöpflin, Karin, 20
Segal, Alan F., 31
Sheppard, A. R. R., 143
Silberman, Lou H., 45

Skehan, Patrick W., 80
Smith, Mark S., 85
Sollamo, Raija, 49
Spurgeon, Charles H., 154
Steudel, Annette, 109
Stone, Michael E., 18, 20, 49, 73
Stuckenbruck, Loren T., 59–60, 67
Suenens, Léon-Joseph, 145
Sullivan, Kevin P., 50, 67–70
Suter, David, 60
Tadmor, Hayim, 76, 88
Taylor, Justin, 73
Thackeray, H. St. J., 164
Thiselton, Anthony C., 118
Thrall, Margaret E., 28, 109
Tigchelaar, Eibert J. C., 164
Twelftree, Graham H., 110
VanderKam, James C., 24, 25, 32
Viviano, Benedict T., 73
Wassen, Cecilia, 31, 33, 92
Wenham, Gordon J., 48, 49, 59
Wilkinson, Belinda, 48
Williams, Jane, 81
Williams, Peter S., 3, 10, 12, 15, 81, 131–32
Wilson, Robert McL., 118, 121, 124
Wink, Walter, 104, 118–19, 124, 127–36, 148, 159
Winston, David, 112
Witherington, Ben, 59
Wold, Benjamin G., 67
Wright, N. T., 71, 73, 98, 115
Wyatt, Nicholas, 24, 85
Yamauchi, Edwin M., 151
Yates, Roy, 36
Yoder Neufeld, Thomas R., 124
Yonge, C. D., 165
Zenger, Erich, 52, 122